The Civil War

THE
CIVIL WAR
BRUCE CATTON

AMERICAN HERITAGE PRESS
NEW YORK

Front endpaper: Lincoln reviews a regiment of Union volunteers at the White House shortly after the fall of Fort Sumter.

Title page: A wash drawing by Alfred R. Waud shows Kearny leading his division against the Confederate rear guard at Williamsburg.

Back endpaper: Still the proud, erect soldier, Robert E. Lee leaves the McLean House at Appomattox after surrendering to Grant.

Library of Congress Catalog Card Number: 77-119671
07-010266-x (hard-cover)
07-010265-1 (paperback)
    6789   VBVB   798765

TABLE OF CONTENTS

A HOUSE DIVIDED

The American people in 1860 believed that they were the happiest and luckiest people in all the world, and in a way they were right. Most of them lived on farms or in very small towns, they lived better than their fathers had lived, and they knew that their children would do still better. The landscape was predominantly rural, with unending sandy roads winding leisurely across a country which was both drowsy with enjoyment of the present and vibrant with eagerness to get into the future. The average American then was in fact what he has been since only in legend, an independent small farmer, and in 1860—for the last time in American history—the products of the nation's farms were worth more than the output of its factories.

This may or may not have been the end of America's golden age, but it was at least the final, haunted moment of its age of innocence. Most Americans then, difficult as the future might appear, supposed that this or something like it

When Abraham Lincoln was inaugurated in Washington on March 4, 1861, the Capitol dome was a gaping, half-completed shell.

The Currier lithograph at top reveals the subtle transition from rural independence to a market economy. The Giroux painting of a plantation at bottom is a stereotype; small farms far outnumbered slave-worked land.

would go on and on, perhaps forever. Yet infinite change was beginning, and problems left unsolved too long would presently make the change explosive, so that the old landscape would be blown to bits forever, with a bewildered people left to salvage what they could. Six hundred thousand young Americans, alive when 1860 ended, would die of this explosion in the next four years.

At bottom the coming change simply meant that the infinite ferment of the industrial revolution was about to work its way with a tremendously energetic and restless people who had a virgin continent to exploit. One difficulty was

2

that two very different societies had developed in America, one in the North and the other in the South, which would adjust themselves to the industrial age in very different ways. Another difficulty was that the differences between these two societies were most infernally complicated by the existence in the South of the institution of chattel slavery. Without slavery, the problems between the sections could probably have been worked out by the ordinary give-and-take of politics; with slavery, they became insoluble. So in 1861 the North and the South went to war, destroying one America and beginning the building of another which is not even yet complete.

In the beginning slavery was no great problem. It had existed all across colonial America, it died out in the North simply because it did not pay, and at the turn of the century most Americans, North and South alike, considered that eventually it would go out of existence everywhere. But in 1793 Yankee Eli Whitney had invented the cotton gin—a simple device which made it possible for textile mills to use the short-staple cotton which the Southern states could grow so abundantly—and in a very short time the whole picture changed. The world just then was developing an almost limitless appetite for cotton, and in the deep South enormous quantities of cotton could be raised cheaply with slave labor. Export figures show what happened. In 1800 the United States had exported $5,000,000 worth of cotton—7 per cent of the nation's total exports. By 1810 this figure had tripled, by 1840 it had risen to $63,000,000, and by 1860 cotton exports were worth $191,000,000—57 per cent of the value of all American exports. The South had become a cotton empire, nearly four million slaves were employed, and slavery looked like an absolutely essential element in Southern prosperity.

But if slavery paid, it left men with uneasy consciences. This unease became most obvious in the North, where a man who demanded the abolition of slavery could comfort himself with the reflection that the financial loss which abolition would entail would, after all, be borne by somebody

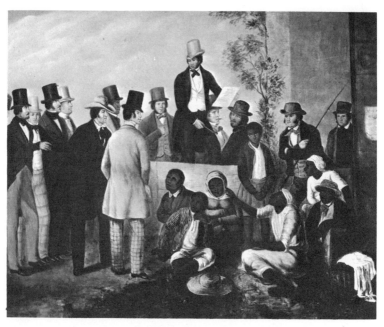

When the slave auction scene above was painted in 1852, slaves accounted for 40 per cent of the South's population. The defensive Southern image of slavery is shown in the idyllic Currier and Ives lithograph below.

else—his neighbor to the south. In New England the fanatic William Lloyd Garrison opened a crusade, denouncing slavery as a sin and slaveowners as sinners. More effective work to organize antislavery sentiment was probably done by such Westerners as James G. Birney and Theodore Weld, but Garrison made the most noise—and, making it, helped to arouse most intense resentment in the South. Southerners liked being called sinners no better than anyone else. Also, they undeniably had a bear by the tail. By 1860 slave property was worth at least two billion dollars, and the abolitionists who insisted that this property be outlawed were not especially helpful in showing how this could be done without collapsing the whole Southern economy. In a natural reaction to all of this, Southerners closed ranks. It became first unhealthy and then impossible for anyone in the South to argue for the end of slavery; instead, the institution was increasingly justified as a positive good. Partly from economic pressure and partly in response to the shrill outcries of men like Garrison, the South bound itself to slavery.

Yet slavery (to repeat) was not the only source of discord. The two sections were very different, and they wanted different things from their national government.

In the North society was passing more rapidly than most men realized to an industrial base. Immigrants were arriving by the tens of thousands, there were vast areas in the West to be opened, men who were developing new industries demanded protection from cheap European imports, systems of transportation and finance were mushrooming in a fantastic manner—and, in short, this dynamic society was beginning to clamor for all sorts of aid and protection from the Federal government at Washington.

In the South, by contrast, society was much more static. There was little immigration, there were not many cities, the factory system showed few signs of growth, and this cotton empire which sold in the world market wanted as many cheap European imports as it could get. To please the South, the national government must keep its hands off as many things as possible; for many years Southerners had feared that if the North ever won control in Washington it would pass legislation ruinous to Southern interests.

John C. Calhoun of South Carolina had seen this first and most clearly. Opposing secession, he argued that any state could protect its interests by nullifying, within its own borders, any act by the Federal government which it considered unconstitutional and oppressive. Always aware that the North was the faster-growing section, the South foresaw the day when the North would control the government. Then, Southerners believed, there would be legislation—a stiff high-tariff law, for instance—that would ruin the South. More and more, they developed the theory of states' rights as a matter of self-protection.

Although there were serious differences between the sections, all of them except slavery could have been settled through the democratic process. Slavery poisoned the whole situation. It was the issue that could not be compromised, the issue that made men so angry they did not want to compromise. It put a cutting edge on all arguments. It was not the only cause of the Civil War, but it was unquestionably the one cause without which the war would not have taken place. The antagonism between the sections came finally, and tragically, to express itself through the slavery issue.

Many attempts to compromise this issue had been made. All of them worked for a while; none of them lasted. Perhaps the most that can be said is that they postponed the conflict until the nation was strong enough—just barely so —to survive the shock of civil war.

There had been the Missouri Compromise, in 1820, when North and South argued whether slavery should be permitted in the land acquired by the Louisiana Purchase. Missouri was admitted as a slave state, but it was decreed that thereafter there should be no new slave states north of the parallel that marked Missouri's southern boundary. Men hoped that this would end the whole argument, although dour John Quincy Adams wrote that he considered the debate over the compromise nothing less than "a title-page to a great, tragic volume."

Then there was the Compromise of 1850, which followed the war with Mexico. Immense new territory had been acquired, and Congressman David Wilmot of Pennsylvania introduced legislation stipulating that slavery would never be permitted in any of these lands. The Wilmot Proviso failed to pass, but it was argued furiously, in Congress and out of it, for years, and immense heat was generated. In the end the aging Henry Clay engineered a new compromise. California was to be admitted as a free state, the territories of New Mexico and Utah were created without reference to the Wilmot Proviso, the slave trade in the District of Columbia was abolished, and a much stiffer act to govern the return of fugitive slaves was adopted. Neither North nor South was entirely happy with this program, but both sections accepted it in the hope that the slavery issue was now settled for good.

This hope promptly exploded. Probably nothing did more to create anti-Southern, antislavery sentiment in the North than the Fugitive Slave Act. It had an effect precisely

Abolitionist attacks on slavery eventually turned to propaganda against the entire South. Here, violence of all kinds is shown as commonplace.

opposite to the intent of its backers: it aroused Northern sentiment in favor of the runaway slave, and probably caused a vast expansion in the activities of the Underground Railroad, the informal and all but unorganized system whereby Northern citizens helped Negro fugitives escape across the Canadian border. With this excitement at a high pitch, Harriet Beecher Stowe in 1852 brought out her novel *Uncle Tom's Cabin,* which sold three hundred thousand copies in its first year, won many converts to the antislavery position in the North, and, by contrast, aroused intense new resentment in the South.

On the heels of all of this, in 1854 Senator Stephen A. Douglas of Illinois introduced the fateful Kansas-Nebraska Act, which helped to put the whole controversy beyond hope of settlement.

Douglas was a Democrat, friendly to the South and well liked there. He cared little about slavery, one way or the other; what he wanted was to see the long argument settled so that the country could go about its business, which, as he saw it, included the development of the new Western country between the Missouri River and California. Specifically, Douglas wanted a transcontinental railroad, and he wanted its eastern terminus to be Chicago. Out of this desire came the Kansas-Nebraska Act.

Building the road would involve grants of public land. If the northerly route were adopted the country west of Iowa and Missouri must be surveyed and platted, and for this a proper territorial organization of the area was needed. But the South wanted the road to go to the Pacific coast by way of Texas and New Mexico. To get Southern support for his plan, the Illinois Senator had to find powerful bait.

He found it. When he brought in a bill to create the territories of Kansas and Nebraska he put in two special provisions. One embodied the idea of "popular sovereignty"—the concept that the people of each territory would decide for themselves, when time for statehood came, whether to permit or exclude slavery—and the other specifically repealed the Missouri Compromise. The South took the bait, the bill was passed—and the country moved a long stride nearer to war.

For the Kansas-Nebraska Act raised the argument over slavery to a desperate new intensity. The moderates could no longer be heard; the stage was set for the extremists, the fire-eaters, the men who invited violence with violent words. Many Northerners, previously friendly to the South, now came to feel that the "slave power" was dangerously aggressive, trying not merely to defend slavery where it already existed but to extend it all across the national domain. Worse yet, Kansas was thrown open for settlement under conditions which practically guaranteed bloodshed.

Settlers from the North were grimly determined to make Kansas free soil; Southern settlers were equally determined to win Kansas for slavery. Missouri sent over its Border Ruffians—hardfisted drifters who crossed the line to cast illegal votes, to intimidate free-soil settlers, now and then to raid an abolitionist town. New England shipped in boxes of

Felix Darley drew these grimly resolute, heavily armed Border Ruffians from Missouri as they invaded Kansas bent on creating a new slave state.

rifles, known as Beecher's Bibles in derisive reference to the Reverend Henry Ward Beecher, the Brooklyn clergyman whose antislavery fervor had led him to say that there might be spots where a gun was more useful than a Bible. The North also sent down certain free-lance fanatics, among them a lantern-jawed character named John Brown.

By 1855 all of this was causing a great deal of trouble. Proslavery patrols clashed with antislavery patrols, and there were barn-burnings, horse-stealings, and sporadic shootings. The free-soil settlement of Lawrence was sacked by a pro-slavery mob; in retaliation, John Brown and his followers murdered five Southern settlers near Pottawatomie Creek. When elections were held, one side or the other would complain that the polls were unfairly rigged, would put on a boycott, and then would hold an election of its own; presently there were two territorial legislatures, of clouded legality, and when the question of a constitution arose there were more boycotts, so that no one was quite sure what the voters had done.

Far from Kansas, extremists on both sides whipped up fresh tensions. Senator Charles Sumner, the humorless, self-righteous abolitonist from Massachusetts, addressed the Sen-

Abolitionists were determined to make Kansas "the homestead of the free." Below, a Kansas Free State battery stands poised for action.

The vengeful "Bully" Brooks attacks Charles Sumner in the U.S. Senate.

ate on "the crime against Kansas," loosing such unmeasured invective on the head of Senator Andrew Butler of South Carolina that Congressman Preston Brooks, also of South Carolina, a relative of Senator Butler, caned him into insensibility on the Senate floor a few days afterward. Senator William H. Seward of New York spoke vaguely but ominously of an "irrepressible conflict" that was germinating. Senator Robert Toombs of Georgia predicted a vast extension of slavery and said that he would one day auction slaves on Boston Common itself. In Alabama the eloquent William Lowndes Yancey argued hotly that the South would never find happiness except by leaving the Union and setting up an independent nation.

Now the Supreme Court added its bit. It had before it the case of Dred Scott, a Negro slave whose master, an army surgeon, had kept him for some years in Illinois and Wisconsin, where there was no slavery. Scott sued for his freedom, and in 1857 Chief Justice Roger Taney delivered the Court's opinion. That Scott's plea for freedom was denied was no particular surprise, but the grounds on which the denial was based stirred the North afresh. A Negro of slave descent, said Taney, was an inferior sort of person who could not be a citizen of any state and hence could not sue anyone; furthermore, the act by which Congress had forbidden slavery in the Northern territories was invalid because the Constitution gave slavery ironclad protection. There was no legal way in which slavery could be excluded from any territory.

An intense political ferment was working. The old Whig Party had collapsed utterly, and the Democratic Party was showing signs of breaking into sectional wings. In the North there had risen the new Republican Party, an amalgamation of former Whigs, free-soilers, business leaders who wanted a central government that would protect industry, and ordinary folk who wanted a homestead act that would provide free farms in the West. The party had already polled an impressive number of votes in the Presidential campaign of 1856, and it was likely to do better in 1860. Seward of New York hoped to be its next Presidential nominee; so did Salmon P. Chase, prominent antislavery leader from Ohio; and so, also, did a lawyer and former congressman who was not nearly so well known as these two, Abraham Lincoln of Illinois.

In 1858 Lincoln ran for the Senate against Douglas. In a series of famous debates which drew national attention, the two argued the Kansas-Nebraska Act and the slavery issue up and down the state of Illinois. In the end Douglas won re-election, but he won on terms that may have cost him the Presidency two years later. Lincoln had pinned him down: Was there any lawful way in which the people of a territory could exclude slavery? (In other words, could Douglas' "popular sovereignty" be made to jibe with the Supreme Court's finding in the Dred Scott case?) Douglas replied that the thing was easy. Slavery could not live a day unless it were supported by protective local legislation. In fact, if a territorial legislature simply refused to enact such legislation, slavery would not exist regardless of what the Supreme Court had said. The answer helped Douglas win re-election, but it mortally offended the South. The threatened split in the Democratic Party came measurably nearer, and such a split could mean nothing except victory for the Republicans.

The 1850's were the tormented decade in American history. Always the tension mounted, and no one seemed able to provide an easement. The Panic of 1857 left a severe business depression, and Northern pressure for higher tariff rates and a homestead act became stronger than ever. The depression had hardly touched the South, since world demand for cotton was unabated, and Southern leaders became more than ever convinced that their society and their economy were sounder and stronger than anything the North could show. There would be no tariff revision, and although Congress did pass a homestead act President James Buchanan, a Pennsylvanian but a strong friend of the South, promptly vetoed it. The administration, indeed, seemed unable to do anything. It could not even make a state out of Kansas, in which territory it was clear, by now, that a strong majority opposed slavery. The rising antagonism between the sections had almost brought paralysis to the Federal government.

And then old John Brown came out of the shadows to add the final touch.

With a mere handful of followers, Brown undertook, on the night of October 16, 1859, to seize the Federal arsenal at Harpers Ferry and with the weapons thus obtained to start a

Marines under Lieutenant J. E. B. Stuart storm the building where Brown holds eleven hostages. Brown is shown in the inset at left.

slave insurrection in the South. He managed to get possession of an enginehouse, which he held until the morning of the eighteenth; then a detachment of U.S. marines—temporarily led by Colonel Robert E. Lee of the U.S Army—overpowered him and snuffed out his crack-brained conspiracy with bayonets and clubbed muskets. Brown was quickly tried, was convicted of treason, and early in December he was hanged. But what he had done had a most disastrous effect on men's minds. To people in the South, it seemed that Brown confirmed their worst fears: this was what the Yankee abolitionists really wanted—a servile insurrection, with unlimited bloodshed and pillage, from one end of the South to the other! The fact that some vocal persons in the North persisted in regarding Brown as a martyr simply made matters worse. After the John Brown raid the chance that the bitter sectional argument could be harmonized faded close to the vanishing point.

It was in this atmosphere that the 1860 election was held. The Republicans nominated Lincoln, partly because he was

Lincoln conducted a front-porch campaign in Springfield, where he was said to be "not too proud to sit down upon his doorstep . . . and chat with his neighbors." At this August rally he is standing to the right of the door.

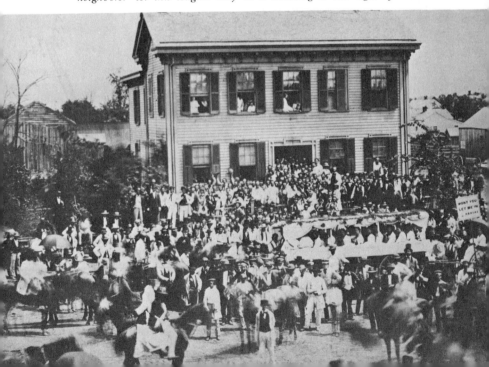

considered less of an extremist than either Seward or Chase; he was moderate on the slavery question, and agreed that the Federal government lacked power to interfere with the peculiar institution in the states. The Republican platform, however, did represent a threat to Southern interests. It embodied the political and economic program of the North —upward revision of the tariff, free farms in the West, railroad subsidies, and all the rest.

But by now a singular fatalism gripped the nation. The campaign could not be fought on the basis of these issues; men could talk only about slavery, and on that subject they could neither talk nor, for the most part, even think, with moderation. Although it faced a purely sectional opposition, the Democratic Party promptly split into halves. The Northern wing nominated Douglas, but the Southern wing flatly refused to accept the man because of his heresy in regard to slavery in the territories; it named John C. Breckinridge of Kentucky, while a fourth party, hoping desperately for compromise and conciliation, put forward John Bell of Tennessee.

The road led steadily downhill after this. The Republicans won the election, as they were bound to do under the circumstances. Lincoln got less than a majority of the popular votes, but a solid majority in the electoral college, and on March 4, 1861, he would become President of the United States . . . but not, it quickly developed, of all of the states. Fearing the worst, the legislature of South Carolina had remained in session until after the election had been held. Once it saw the returns it summoned a state convention, and this convention, in Charleston on December 20, voted unanimously that South Carolina should secede from the Union.

This was the final catalytic agent. It was obvious that one small state could not maintain its independence; equally obvious that if South Carolina should now be forced back into the Union no one in the South ever need talk again about secession. The cotton states, accordingly, followed suit. By February, South Carolina had been joined by Mississippi, Alabama, Georgia, Florida, Louisiana, and Texas, and on

February 8 delegates from the seceding states met at Montgomery, Alabama, and set up a new nation, the Confederate States of America. A provisional constitution was adopted (to be replaced in due time by a permanent document, very much like the Constitution of the United States), and Jefferson Davis of Mississippi was elected President, with Alexander Stephens of Georgia as Vice-President.

Perhaps it still was not too late for an adjustment. A new nation had come into being, but its creation might simply be a means of forcing concessions from the Northern majority; no blood had been shed, and states which voluntarily left the old Union might voluntarily return if their terms were met. Leaders in Congress worked hard, that winter of 1861, to perfect a last-minute compromise, and a committee led by Senator John J. Crittenden of Kentucky worked one out. In effect, it would re-establish the old line of the Missouri Compromise, banning slavery in territories north of the line and protecting it south; it would let future states enter the Union on a popular sovereignty basis; it called for enforcement of the fugitive slave law, with Federal funds to compensate slaveowners whose slaves got away; and it provided that the Constitution could never be amended in such a way as to give Congress power over slavery in any of the states.

The Crittenden Compromise hung in the balance, and then collapsed when Lincoln refused to accept it. The sticking point with him was the inclusion of slavery in the territories; the rest of the program he could accept, but he wrote to a Republican associate to "entertain no proposition for a compromise in regard to the extension of slavery."

So the last chance to settle the business had gone, except for the things that might happen in the minds of two men —Abraham Lincoln and Jefferson Davis. They were strangers, very unlike each other, and yet there was an odd linkage. They were born not far apart in time or space; both came from Kentucky, near the Ohio River, and one man went south to become spokesman for the planter aristocracy, while the other went north to become representative of the best the frontier Northwest could produce. In the haunted decade that had just ended, neither man had been known as a radical. Abolitionists considered Lincoln too conservative, and Southern fire-eaters like South Carolina's Robert B. Rhett felt that Davis had been cold and unenthusiastic in regard to secession.

Now these two men faced one another, figuratively, across an ever-widening gulf, and between them they would say whether a nation already divided by mutual misunderstanding would be torn apart physically by war.

Behind an erect military bearing, Jefferson Davis (right) concealed the physical suffering caused by frequent attacks of neuralgia. The portrait of Lincoln below was made by Mathew Brady on February 23.

THE
OPENING
GUNS

There had been many woeful misunderstandings between North and South in the years that led up to the Civil War, but the most tragic misunderstanding of all was that neither side realized, until it was too late, that the other side was desperately in earnest. Not until the war had actually begun would men see that their rivals really meant to fight. By that time it was too late to do anything but go on fighting.

Southerners had been talking secession for many years, and most people in the North had come to look on such talk as a counter in the game of politics. You wanted something, and you threatened that dire things would happen if you did not get what you wanted; but you didn't necessarily mean to do what you were threatening to do, and there was no sense in taking brash words at their face value. America as a nation of poker players understood all about the business of calling bluffs. Not until the guns began to go off would the

A Confederate flag flies over Fort Sumter on April 14, 1861; a siege of three and one half months had finally forced Union surrender the day before.

North realize that when men like Jefferson Davis talked about seceding from the Union they meant every word of it.

The same was true, in reverse, in the South. It seemed incomprehensible there that the Federal Union meant so much in the North that millions of people would be ready to make war to preserve it. The North seemed to dislike both slavery and slaveowners; to the average Southerner, it stood to reason that the North would be happy to get rid of both. Furthermore, it was not supposed that the North could fight even if it wanted to do so. It was a nation of mudsills and undigested immigrants, ruled by money-mad Yankees, and any army it raised would dissolve like the morning mists once it ran into real soldiers. The Southern orator who promised to wipe up, with his handkerchief, all of the blood that would be spilled because of secession was expressing a very common viewpoint.

For a while it looked as if the doubters on both sides might be right. Lincoln was inaugurated in Washington, and in his inaugural address he gave plain warning that he would do all in his power to "hold, occupy and possess" the property and places belonging to the Federal government which lay in Confederate territory. But after this speech was made nothing much seemed to happen, and the new Lincoln administration began to look strangely like that of the departed Buchanan.

When Lincoln said that he would hold all Federal property he referred chiefly to Fort Sumter, a pentagonal brick stronghold on an island near the mouth of Charleston Harbor. The commanding officer there was Major Robert Anderson, a regular army officer from Kentucky, and Anderson had sixty-eight soldiers, enough food to last a few more weeks, and a United States flag which he was determined to keep flying until he was compelled to haul it down. The sight of that flag was an offense to South Carolinians, and through them to the entire Confederacy. An independent nation could not countenance the existence of a foreign fort in the middle of one of its most important harbors, and the Confederate authorities tried hard but unsuccessfully to in-

William Waud's wash drawing shows a Negro crew mounting a Rebel cannon on Morris Island in preparation for the attack on Fort Sumter.

duce Washington to evacuate the place. They also put some thousands of Southern troops in gun pits and encampments all around the harbor, planting batteries where they would do the most good. In the end, negotiations having failed, and Lincoln having sent word that he was going to run supplies into the beleaguered fort, a clear indication that he proposed to hold it indefinitely, Jefferson Davis gave the word to open fire and bombard the place into submission. The Confederate commander at Charleston was the flamboyant General P. G. T. Beauregard, and he obeyed orders promptly. Sumter was ringed with fire, and after a thirty-four-hour bombardment Anderson hauled down his flag, turned the fort over to the Confederacy, and embarked his men on a steamer for New York. And the war was on.

The bombardment of Fort Sumter was spectacular, momentous—and, somehow, anticlimactic. It was the visible symbol that the war had begun—the thunderous announcement, to America and to all nations, that the New World's experiment in democracy had taken a strange new turn—yet when the guns were fired they merely ratified decisions which Lincoln and Davis had already made. Both men had made up their minds to fight rather than to yield, and each man had come to see Fort Sumter as the place for the showdown. (Oddly enough, the long bombardment killed no one on either side, and the war which was to be so costly began with a bloodless battle. The only lives lost at Sumter were lost after the surrender, when Major Anderson was firing a last salute to his flag; a powder charge exploded and killed two men.)

A hysterical wave of emotion swept across the country when the news of Fort Sumter came out. War actually seemed to be welcomed, as if a tension which had grown completely unendurable had at last been broken. Whatever might happen next, at least the years of drift and indecision were over. Grim knowledge of the reality of war would come quickly enough, but right at first an unsophisticated people surged out under waving flags with glad cries and with laughter, as if the thing that had happened called for rejoicing.

The first move was up to Lincoln, and he made it without delay. He announced to the nation that "combinations too powerful to be suppressed" by the ordinary machinery of peacetime government had assumed control of various Southern states; to restore order and suppress these combinations he called on the states to place 75,000 militia at the service of the Federal government. This call to arms brought a rush of enthusiastic recruiting all across the North, but at the same time it immediately put four more states into the Southern Confederacy. Virginia, North Carolina, Tennessee, and Arkansas had not yet left the Union; their sympathies were with the states which had seceded, but they had been

Below is "Going to War," the opening scene in William Travis' 528-foot Civil War panorama celebrating the Federal Army of the Cumberland.

Gay Street Knoxville Tenn. (1862). (Drawn from Memory.)

At divided Knoxville, Tennessee, rival Union and Confederate meetings drew equal crowds in 1861. Southern forces won out: Tennessee left the Union.

clinging to the hope that the schism might yet be healed without bloodshed. Now they had to choose, and they chose promptly: all four left the Union and entered the Confederacy, and the Davis administration began to make arrangements to transfer the Confederate capital from Alabama to Richmond.

Neither North nor South was in the least ready for a war, and very few people in either section had any conception of the immense demands which the war was going to make. When the conflict began, the country's regular army consisted of no more than 16,000 men—barely enough to police the Indian country and the frontier and to man the coastal fortifications on a skeletonized basis. For whatever it might be worth, the army was at the disposal of the Federal government. It was obvious, however, that even if all of it could be massed in one spot (which was out of the question), it would not be nearly large enough for the job at hand. The load would have to be carried mainly by volunteers—which, at the beginning, meant state militia—and neither the weapons which the volunteers would use nor the uniforms they would wear, to say nothing of the officers who would lead them, as yet existed. Both sides were going to have to improvise.

The states did have their militia regiments, and these went to the colors at once. They were of uneven quality; none of them had ever had anything resembling combat training, and the best of them were drilled almost solely for parade-ground maneuvers. Even for parade, most units were poorly prepared. The average militia regiment was composed of one company from this town, another from that town, and so on, the ten companies scattered all across the state, and in many cases the individual companies had never been brought together to maneuver as a regiment. This was a serious handicap. By the military tactics of the 1860's, the ability of troops to maneuver as regiments or brigades was extremely important. To get from column into line—that is, from the formation in which they could march into the formation in which they could fight—called for a variety of highly intricate movements, for which incessant drill was required. A first-rate militia company which had never worked as part of a larger unit would be of little use on the battlefield until it had put in many hours of regimental and brigade drill.

The Sumter Light Guards of Georgia rally proudly to their bonnie new flag in April, 1861. Uniform details were largely a matter of local option.

These satirical sketches of Southern militia are by David Hunter Strother, who toured the South for Harper's *in the years before the war.*

Still, both sides were equally unready, and in both sections the work of preparation went on with excited haste if not with complete efficiency. All of these assorted military outfits went in for gaudy and impractical uniforms; most of them adopted flamboyant names, not realizing that the separate companies would quickly lose their identities as cogs in a larger machine. There were Frontier Guards, Rough-and-Ready Grays, Susquehanna Blues, and the like, and there were Game Cocks, Tigers, Invincibles, Fencibles, and Rangers beyond computation. (Some of the Blues, at this stage, were Southern, and some of the Grays were Northern; the adoption of recognizable national uniforms would come later, after a certain amount of battlefield confusion.) These separate companies were led by officers elected by the rank and file, which was also the case with most of the regiments. In most cases the officers owed their election to their talents as vote-getters, or simply to the fact that they were "leading citizens." Very few were chosen because they had any especial qualifications for military command. In time, field experience would weed out most of the misfits, but in the beginning the rival armies would consist of amateurs led by amateurs.

There were regular officers on hand, to be sure, but in the North the government did not quite know what to do with them. Lieutenant General Winfield Scott was general in chief; a fine soldier and an able strategist once, but very old now, physically all but helpless, perhaps touched with senility. He hoped to keep the regular army more or less intact, as the hard core around which the army of militiamen and volunteers would be built, and he did not want to see regular officers resign to take commissions with the amateurs. From the regulars, to be sure, would come the general officers—but not all of the general officers, at that, for the administration was going to make generals out of a certain number of political leaders, and some of these would be given very important commands. The army immediately in front of Washington, which would be known as the Army of the Potomac, was given to Brigadier General Irvin McDowell, a regular. An army which was being raised in Ohio, which presently would invade western Virginia, was led by Major General George B. McClellan, a brilliant young West Pointer who had served in the Mexican War and then had left the army to become a railroad president. In St. Louis command was held by another regular, Brigadier General William A. Harney; he would be replaced before long by Major General John Charles Frémont, who had served in the regular army and had won fame as "The Pathfinder" of Far Western exploration. He was no West Pointer, and his service had been with the topographical engineers rather than with the line. Many new brigadiers would be named, some of them West Pointers, others not. For some time to come the administration would feel its way toward its new command setup, with no fixed program.

The Confederacy was a little more systematic. Jefferson Davis was a West Pointer himself, with a good deal of field experience, and he had served as Secretary of War. He had a good understanding of the military arts, although he apparently believed that his talents in this field were a bit more extensive than was actually the case, and as far as possible he intended to use trained soldiers for his general officers. About a third of the West Pointers in the regular army had resigned to serve with the South; one of the Confederacy's assets lay in the fact that these included some of the most capable men on the army roster. There was Robert E. Lee, for instance, to whom at the outbreak of the war command of the Federals' principal field army had been offered. Lee had rejected the offer and had gone with his state, Virginia, and Davis would make him a full general. The Beauregard who had taken Fort Sumter, and who now commanded the chief Confederate army in Virginia, was a professional soldier, highly regarded. From the West was coming another West Pointer of substantial reputation, General Albert Sidney Johnston. Still another former regular who would play a prominent part was General Joseph E. Johnston, who had many talents, but who would prove utterly unable to get along with President Davis.

One oddity about the whole situation was the fact that the regular army before the war had been very small, with an officer corps whose members knew one another quite intimately. A Civil War general, as a result, was quite likely to be very well acquainted with the man who was commanding troops against him, knowing his strengths and his weaknesses. There would be times when this mutual knowledge would have a marked effect on strategic and tactical decisions.

The war aims of the two sides were very simple. The Confederacy would fight for independence, the North for re-establishment of the Union. So far, slavery itself was definitely not an issue. The North was far from unity on this point; it was vitally important for Lincoln to keep the support of Northern Democrats, most of whom had little or no objection to the continued existence of slavery in the South; and both he and the Congress itself were explicit in asserting that they wanted to restore the Union without interfering with the domestic institutions of any of the states. In addition, there were the border states, Maryland and Kentucky and Missouri, slave states where sentiment apparently was pro-Union by a rather narrow margin, but where most people had no use at all for abolitionists or the abolitionist cause. If these states should join the Confederacy, the Union cause was as good as lost; probably the most momentous single item on Lincoln's program was the determination to hold these states in the Union. If he could help it, Lincoln was not going to fight a straight Republican war.

War aims would govern war strategy. The Confederacy was a going concern: it had built a government, it was building an army, it considered itself an independent nation and it was functioning as such, and as far as Davis was concerned there would be no war at all unless the Lincoln administration forced one. The Confederacy, then, would act strictly on the defensive, and the opposite side of this coin was the fact that it was up to the North to be aggressive. Unless he could successfully take the offensive and keep at it until all of the "combinations too powerful to be suppressed" had been overthrown, Lincoln would have lost the war. In plain English, Northern armies had to invade the South and destroy the opposing government. This fact would go far to counterbalance the enormous advantages which the Federal government possessed in respect to manpower, riches, and the commercial and industrial strength that supports armies.

These advantages were impressive—so much so that Northern officers like William T. Sherman and James B. McPherson warned Southern friends at the outbreak of the war that the Confederacy was bound to fail. In the North there were over eighteen million people; the South had hardly more than nine million, of whom more than a third were Negro slaves. Nine-tenths of the country's manufacturing capacity was situated in the North, which also had two-thirds of the railway mileage, to say nothing of nearly all of the facilities for building rails, locomotives, and cars. The North contained most of the country's deposits of iron, coal, copper, and precious metals. It controlled the seas and had access to all of the factories of Europe; it was also producing a huge surplus of foodstuffs which Europe greatly needed, and these would pay for enormous quantities of munitions. Taken altogether, its latent advantages were simply overpowering.

They did not, however, mean that Northern victory would be automatic. For the North had to do the invading, and in any war the invader must have a substantial advantage in numbers. The Confederacy occupied an immense territory, and the supply lines of the invader would be long,

At left, a flamboyant "Spirit of '61" typified the delirious response to Lincoln's call for volunteers. At right, the belles of the Pennsylvania Academy of Fine Arts have gathered to sew an outsize flag for the boys.

immobilizing many troops for their protection. Although the North controlled the seas, the Confederacy's coast line was almost endless; to seal the Southland off from the outside world would require a navy far larger than anything the United States previously had dreamed of possessing. Finally, the terms on which the war would be fought meant that the average Southerner would always have a clearer, more emotionally stimulating picture of what he was fighting for than the average Northerner could hope to have. For the Southerner would see himself as fighting to protect the home place from the invader; the Northerner, on the other hand, was fighting for an abstraction, and the sacred cause of "the Union" might look very drab once real war weariness developed. To put it in its simplest terms, the North could lose the war if its people lost the desire to go on with the offensive; it could win only if it could destroy the Confederate people's *ability* to fight. In the end it would need every ounce of advantage it could get.

Old Winfield Scott had sketched in a plan. It would take

time to raise, equip, and train armies big enough to beat the South; start, therefore, by blockading the seacoast, seal off the inland borders as well, then drive down the Mississippi, constricting the vitality out of the Confederacy—and, at last, send in armies of invasion to break the Southern nation into bits. As things worked out, this was not unlike the plan that was actually followed, but when it was first proposed—news of it leaked out immediately, Washington's ability to keep things secret being very limited—the newspapers derided it, calling it the "Anaconda Plan" and intimating that it was far too slow for any use. Very few men, either in the North or in the South, were ready to admit that the war would be a long one. The militia had been called into Federal service for just ninety days, the limit under existing law; it seemed reasonable to many people to suppose that before their term of service expired they ought to win the war.

Before the war could be won, however, the border states had to be secured, and to secure them the Lincoln administration used a strange combination of tactful delicacy and hardfisted ruthlessness.

Kentucky got the delicate handling. This state had a secessionist governor and a Unionist legislature, and in sheer desperation it was trying to sit the war out, having proclaimed its neutrality. For the time being both Lincoln and Davis were willing to respect this neutrality. They knew that it could not last, but the side that infringed it was apt to be the loser thereby, and until the situation elsewhere began to jell, both leaders were willing to leave Kentucky alone. (Both sides unofficially raised troops there, and there was a home guard organization which might turn out to be either Unionist or Confederate.)

If Kentucky got delicate handling, what Maryland and Missouri got was the back of the Federal government's hand.

Not long after Fort Sumter, the 6th Massachusetts Regiment was marching through Baltimore en route to Washington. There were many ardent Southerners in Baltimore, and these surrounded the marching column, jeering and catcalling. Inevitably, people began to shove and throw things, and

Four infantrymen were killed and 36 wounded when a Baltimore mob attacked Massachusetts troops being moved through the city streets on April 19.

finally the troops opened fire and there was a bloody fight in the streets. Soldiers and civilians were killed—more civilians than soldiers, as it happened—and although the 6th Regiment finally got to Washington, railroad connection via Baltimore was temporarily broken, and Lincoln took speedy action. Federal troops occupied Baltimore. Secessionist members of the legislature were thrown in jail, as were various city officials of Baltimore, and they were kept there until the Unionists got things firmly in hand. All of this, of course, was plainly illegal, but the Federal government was not going to let the secessionists cut Washington off from the rest of the North, no matter what it had to do to prevent it; with dissident legislators in jail, the Unionist governor of Maryland had little trouble holding the state in the Union.

What happened in Missouri was somewhat similar. The state had refused to secede, sentiment apparently being almost evenly divided, but like Kentucky it had a pro-Southern governor, and he maintained a camp of state troops on the edge of St. Louis. The presence of these troops worried the Federal commander, General Harney, not at all, but it worried other Unionists a great deal, the fear being that the state troops would seize the government arsenal in St. Louis. With the weapons taken there the governor could arm enough secessionist Missourians to take the state out of the Union. So Washington temporarily replaced General Har-

A month after Lyon's raid on the militia camp, a company of loyal Germans was attacked in St. Louis. In William Streeter's painting they are firing at the second story of an engine house from which the first shot came.

ney with a fiery young regular, Captain Nathaniel S. Lyon —putting a captain in a brigadier's job was stretching things a bit, but not all of the old rules would be valid in this war —and Lyon took his soldiers out, arrested the state troops, disarmed them, and broke up their camp. As he marched his men back to barracks a street crowd collected; as in Baltimore there was jostling, shoving, name-calling, and a display of weapons; and at last the troops opened fire, killing more than a score of civilians. It may be instructive to note that the first fighting in the Civil War, after Fort Sumter, involved men in uniform shooting at men who were not in uniform—the classic pattern of a civil war.

Lyon was all flame and devotion, too impetuous by half. In an effort to keep some sort of peace in Missouri, Harney had worked out an informal truce with the governor of the state, the essence of it being that nobody would make any hostile moves until the situation had taken more definite shape. Lyon swiftly disavowed this truce, drove the governor away from the machinery of government, and marched his little army clear down into southwest Missouri in an effort to rid the state of all armed Confederates. He got into a sharp fight at Wilson's Creek and lost his life. His army had to retreat, and the Confederates continued to hold southwestern Missouri; and partly because of the bitterness growing out of Lyon's highhanded actions the unhappy state was plagued for the rest of the war by the most virulent sort of partisan warfare. But Missouri did not leave the Union, which was all that Washington cared about at the moment. Legally or otherwise, the Federal government was making the border secure.

Western Virginia also had to be dealt with, but that was easier.

The western counties of Virginia had long been antipathetic to the tidewater people, and when Virginia left the Union, the westerners began to talk about seceding from Virginia. Young General McClellan got an army over into the mountain country early in the war and without too great difficulty defeated a small Confederate force which he found there. With victorious Federal troops in their midst, the western Virginia Unionists perked up; in due course they would organize their own state of West Virginia, which the Federal government would hasten to admit to the Union; and although there might be a good deal to be said about the legal ins and outs of the business, the government had at least made certain that the Ohio River was not going to be the northern border of the Confederacy.

But if the border states had been held, the gain was negative. The South seemed unworried, and it was visibly building up its strength. Richmond now was the capital, new troops were pouring in for its defense, and cadets from the Virginia Military Institute were putting in busy days acting as drillmasters. (They had been led to Richmond by a blue-eyed, ungainly professor, a West Pointer who would soon be a Confederate general of renown, Thomas J. Jackson.) The North was never going to win the war by thwarting secessionist designs in Missouri and Maryland. It could win it only by moving south and giving battle; and as the summer of 1861 came on the time for such a move was at hand.

THE
CLASH OF
AMATEUR
ARMIES

The way General Scott had planned it, the first year of the war would be spent, mostly, in getting ready. The old general had a poor opinion of volunteer troops—like most West Pointers, he felt that they had behaved badly in the Mexican War—and he believed that it would take a long time to prepare them for field service. It would also take a long time to get the supply service organized, so that boots and pants and coats and tents and muskets and all of the other things the new armies would need could be produced in adequate quantities. It would be absurd to start offensive operations until properly trained armies, fully supplied and equipped, were ready to move.

In all of this General Scott was quite correct, by the standards of military logic. Unfortunately, however, military logic was not going to be controlling in this war. What was going on between North and South was a violent extension of a political contest, and the rules and axioms of formalized

War was still an adventure to these ardent, well-equipped Southerners, striking a truculent pose before the First Battle of Bull Run.

warfare were not going to mean much.

By those rules and axioms, for instance, Mr. Davis' Confederacy was in hopeless shape. Some of the best manpower any soldier ever saw was flocking to the colors—lean, sinewy men used to handling weapons and to outdoor life, men who could get along very well on poor rations and skimpy equipment, violent men who had a positive taste for fighting—but much of this manpower could not be used because there were no arms. At the beginning of the war the U.S. government arsenals held more than 500,000 small arms, and 135,-000 of these were in the South. These, of course, the Confederacy had promptly seized, but it needed a great many more, and anyway only 10,000 of the confiscated guns were modern rifles. The rest were old-fashioned smoothbores, many of them flintlocks little different from the Brown Bess of Revolutionary War days. Frantic state governors had tried to collect weapons from their backwoods owners—shotguns, country rifles, and whatnot—but very little could be done with these; their use would complicate the ammunition supply pattern beyond solution.

To make things worse, the Confederate government had made a miscalculation in respect to cotton which would have a permanently crippling effect.

The Northern blockade was not yet effective, and it would be many months before it would be. The markets of Europe were open, and all of the munitions which the South so desperately needed were for sale in them. Furthermore, they could very easily be paid for with cotton, of which the South had millions of bales. Energetic action in the first few months of the war could have solved all of the Confederacy's problems of equipment.

But the Southern leaders had chanted "Cotton is King" so long that they had come to believe it. If England and France, and most particularly England, could not get the cotton which their mills needed, it was believed, they would presently intervene in this war, break the Union blockade (which did not yet really exist), and underwrite the Confederacy's independence in order to insure their own supply of

Cut off from sea lanes by the blockade, Charleston's Union Wharf eventually presented this scene of stranded ships and baled cotton lying useless.

cotton. Consequently, the Confederate government in its wisdom refused to export cotton, in order to make certain that England and France would feel the pressure. In effect, it made the Federal blockade effective until such time as the Federal navy could handle the job unaided; and what it had failed to figure on was that because there had been heavy cotton crops during the years just before the war began, there was a substantial carry-over on the world market in 1861. England and France could get along nicely for months to come; so nicely that even in 1862 England was actually shipping some of its cotton back to New England.

Because of all this the Confederacy was not getting the

weapons it wanted at the time when it needed them most, and when it could unquestionably have got them without the slightest difficulty. So it could not arm all of the men who were clamoring to get into the army, and the ones who were armed were armed most imperfectly. In time, this problem of weapons would be adjusted. Meager as its industrial facilities were, the South would do wonders with what was available and would produce artillery, small arms, powder, and bullets; it would eventually import European goods in spite of the tightening blockade; and from first to last it would capture a great deal of war material from the Yankees. But in 1861 it was in dire straits, with untrained armies, inadequate in size and very poorly outfitted. By military logic it was little better than helpless.

But the North was not a great deal better off. To be sure, it had more weapons than the South had, and its means of adding to its supply were much broader. Washington by now was ringed with camps, very martial-looking, with some

Dust clouds rise over newly cut fields near Washington as raw regiments like the Pennsylvanians below learn the mysteries of close-order drill.

of the new three-year volunteer regiments mingling with the ninety-day militia units, and to Northern editors and politicians it seemed that it was high time for a little action. That the generals who would control these formless levies had never handled large bodies of troops before, that the soldiers themselves were mere civilians in arms with very little discipline and no understanding of the need for any, that what was believed to be an army was simply a collection of independent companies and regiments hopelessly unready to maneuver or fight as a coherent mass—of all of these things few people had any comprehension. The pressure for an immediate advance on the new Confederate capital at Richmond became stronger. Horace Greeley, the forceful but eccentric editor of the powerful New York *Tribune,* was sounding off with his "Forward to Richmond!" war-cry; and although General McDowell, commander of the troops around Washington, knew perfectly well that it would be a long time before his men were ready for a battle, there was nothing he could do about it. Ready or not, he was going to have to move.

Events in western Virginia in June and early July seemed to show that the time for a big offensive campaign was at hand.

General McClellan had taken some 20,000 men across the Ohio River and was moving east from Parkersburg along the line of the Baltimore and Ohio Railroad. With a portion of his army he surprised and routed a small contingent of Confederates at the town of Philippi, winning a very small victory which a jubilant press enlarged into a major achievement. With other troops he made an advance to Beverly, on the turnpike that led via Staunton to the upper end of the Shenandoah Valley, and at Rich Mountain, near Beverly, he routed a Confederate army of 4,500 men. Western Virginia apparently was safe for the Union now, and McClellan's dispatches spoke enthusiastically of the way his men had "annihilated two armies . . . intrenched in mountain fastnesses fortified at their leisure." To a country hungry for good news this was most welcome. Furthermore, McClellan's

An artist for Leslie's magazine sketched McClellan's advance on the hills near Philippi. The notations were for the editors and engravers at home.

troops were no better trained than McDowell's. If they could campaign in rough mountain country, annihilating their foes and storming lofty passes, it seemed reasonable to suppose that McDowell's men could do as well in the more open country between Washington and Richmond. Early in July, McDowell was directed to organize and launch a thrust at the principal Confederate army, which lay at and around Manassas Junction, some twenty-five miles from Washington, behind a meandering little river known as Bull Run.

The military situation in Virginia was complicated.

Federal troops under one of the newly created political generals, Ben Butler of Massachusetts, occupied Fort Monroe, at the tip of the Virginia Peninsula. Butler had essayed a mild advance up the Peninsula but had given it up when his advance guard lost a sharp little skirmish at a place known as Big Bethel. He would be inactive, his force not large enough to require more than a small Confederate contingent to watch it.

Up the Potomac River, in the vicinity of Harpers Ferry, there were 16,000 Federal troops commanded by an aged regular, Major General Robert Patterson. Patterson meant well, but he was far past his prime and would very shortly demonstrate that he was much too infirm for field command.

In a driving rain, Union troops catch up with the Confederate rear guard retreating from Rich Mountain, crossing Carrick's Ford to flank the Rebels.

Facing him were perhaps 9,000 Confederates under the canny Joe Johnston.

Behind Bull Run there were approximately 20,000 Confederates under Beauregard. Johnston outranked Beauregard, but while Johnston remained in the Shenandoah Valley, Beauregard was virtually independent. Since Beauregard had the biggest force, and since he lay squarely across the line of the Orange and Alexandria Railroad, which looked like the best way for a Federal army to approach Richmond, Beauregard's army was the chosen target.

McDowell, therefore, would march down overland to make his attack. He noted that a railway line ran from Manassas Junction to the Shenandoah Valley, within convenient range of Johnston's men; if Johnston could give Patterson the slip he could quite easily move his troops down to the Bull Run area and reinforce Beauregard. Patterson, accordingly, was instructed to keep pressure on Johnston so that he could not detach any troops. McDowell, whose army would total about 35,000 men, thus would have what ought to be a decisive numerical advantage when he made his fight. On the afternoon of July 16 his troops started out.

There is nothing in American military history quite like the story of Bull Run. It was the momentous fight of the am-

Vintage guns pulled by heavy draft animals made up this Confederate "Bull Battery," sketched by an unknown artist before the first Bull Run battle.

ateurs, the battle where everything went wrong, the great day of awakening for the whole nation, North and South together. It marked the end of the ninety-day militia, and it also ended the rosy time in which men could dream that the war would be short, glorious, and bloodless. After Bull Run the nation got down to business.

When it set out from Washington, McDowell's army was at least brilliant to look at. The militia regiments wore a variety of uniforms. Many of the contingents were dressed in gray. Others wore gaudy clothing patterned after the French Zouaves—baggy red breeches, short blue coats, yellow or scarlet sashes about the waist, turbans or fezzes for the head. There was a New York regiment which called itself the Highlanders, and it had kilts for dress parade, although on this campaign the men seem to have worn ordinary pants. Regimental flags were of varicolored silk, all new and unstained. Baggage trains, which were somewhat tardy, were immense. A regiment at that time had as many wagons as a brigade would have a little later. From McDowell on down no one knew anything about the mechanics of handling a large army on the march, and logistics were badly fouled up. The fact that most of the soldiers would break ranks as the mood took them—to wander into a field to pick blackberries, to visit a well for drinking water, or simply to take a breather in the shade—did not help matters much. No more informal, individualistic collection of men in uniform ever tried to make a cross-country march. The weather was hot, and great clouds of dust settled over the fancy uniforms.

42

Artillery batteries were usually pulled by horses. At Manassas Southern artillery distinguished itself in combat with superior Federal guns.

Beauregard, at Manassas Junction, knew that the Yankees were coming. He had a good intelligence service, with spies in Washington who kept him posted, and in any case there was nothing secret about this move; half of the country knew about it, and Beauregard had ample time to make preparations. He was an able soldier, this Beauregard, but rather on the flashy side, given to the construction of elaborate plans, and he considered that he would smite this invading host by a clever flank attack without waiting for it to assault him. His troops were in line along eight miles of Bull Run, covering the bridges and the fords, and Beauregard planned to swing his right over the stream and strike the Union left before McDowell was ready. Oddly enough, McDowell was planning a somewhat similar move himself—to demonstrate before the Confederate center, cross the bulk of his troops a few miles upstream, and come down hard on the Confederate left.

McDowell's army moved very slowly—which, considering everything, is hardly surprising—and contact with the Confederates was not made until July 18. On this day a Union division prowled forward to Blackburn's Ford, near the center of the line, to make a demonstration; it prowled too far, and was driven back with losses, and the Confederates were mightily encouraged.

Meanwhile, in the Shenandoah Valley, Joe Johnston had given Patterson the slip. He had moved forward and had made menacing gestures, which led Patterson to believe that he was about to be attacked; then, while the old Federal

43

took thought for his defenses, Johnston got most of his men away and took the cars for Manassas. His men would arrive at Bull Run just in time. Johnston himself, ranking Beauregard, would be in command of the united armies, although this was a point that Beauregard never quite seemed to understand.

In any case, the great battle finally took place on July 21, 1861. This was the day on which Beauregard was to make his flank attack, modeled, he proudly remarked, on Napoleon's battle plan at Austerlitz. (Most professional soldiers then had the Napoleon complex, and of all armies that of the French was the most respected.) Beauregard's move, however, was a complete fiasco. Like McDowell, he had no staff worthy of the name, and routine staff work in consequence never got done. Orders went astray, those that did reach their destination were not understood or followed, and the advance of the Confederate right amounted to nothing more than a series of convulsive twitches by a few brigades.

All in all, this was a lucky break for the Confederates. The Rebel army at Bull Run was in no better shape than the Federal army, but when the showdown came it was able to fight on the defensive—which, as numerous battles in this war would show, was infinitely easier for untrained troops. For McDowell's flank move was actually made, and although it was inordinately slow and confused, it did at last put a solid segment of the Union army across Bull Run at a place called Sudley Church, in position to march down and hit the Confederates' left flank. A doughty Confederate brigadier commanding troops at the Stone Bridge, where the main road to Washington crossed Bull Run, saw the Yankees coming and fought a stout delaying action which held them off until Johnston and Beauregard could form a new line, on the wooded plateau near the Henry House, to receive the attack. McDowell sent forward two excellent regular army batteries, and the battle was on.

For men who had never fought before, and who had been given no training of any real consequence, the Northerners and Southerners who collided here did a great deal better

Burnside's novice Rhode Islanders (above), sketched by W. A. Waud, led the attack against Rebel batteries at Bull Run. The Rebel defenders at right fell at Matthews Hill in the first heavy fighting.

than anyone had a right to expect. A good many men ran away, to be sure, but most of them stayed and fought, and the struggle was a hot one. For a time it seemed that the Confederate line would be broken and that the "Forward to Richmond" motif would come to a triumphant crescendo. The two regular batteries that had been doing such good work were advanced to the crest of Henry House Hill, infantry came surging along with them, and a number of the Confederate units weakened and began to drift to the rear.

Then came one of those moments of dramatic inspiration that men remember. Brigadier General Barnard Bee sought to rally some of the wavering Confederate regiments. Not far

45

At an evacuated Confederate post near Centreville, Union patrols found a "Quaker gun," a log painted black. This gag photograph resulted.

away he saw a Virginia brigade of Johnston's troops, standing fast and delivering a sharp fire: a brigade led by that former V.M.I. professor, Brigadier General T. J. Jackson.

"There is Jackson standing like a stone wall!" cried Bee, gesturing with his sword. "Rally behind the Virginians!"

So a great name was born. From that moment on the man would be Stonewall Jackson.

Bee's troops rallied. Fresh Confederate troops, just off the train from the Valley, kept coming in on their flank. The two pestiferous Union batteries, placed too far forward to get proper support from their own infantry, were taken by a sudden Confederate counterattack—the Rebels here wore blue uniforms, and the gunners held their fire until too late, supposing the attacking wave to be Unionists coming up to help—and suddenly the Union offensive, which had come so near to success, collapsed, all the heart gone out of it, and the soldiers who had been involved in it turned and headed for the rear.

There was no rout here. The Union attack had failed and the men were withdrawing, but there was no panic. One trouble apparently lay in the fact that the tactical maneuver by which troops fighting in line would form column and go to the rear was very complicated, and most of these green Union troops did not have it down pat; a withdrawal under fire was bound to become disordered and finally uncontrollable, not because the men had lost their courage but simply because they had not had enough drill. McDowell saw that nothing more could be done here and passed the word for a retreat to his advanced base at Centreville, four or five miles nearer Washington.

It was after the beaten army had crossed Bull Run that the real trouble came, and the fault lies less with the soldiers than with the reckless Washington civilians who had supposed that the edge of a battlefield would be an ideal place for a picnic.

For hundreds of Washingtonians had come out to see the show that day. They came in carriages, wagons, buggies, and on horseback, they brought hampers of food and drink with them, and they were spread all over the slanting fields east of Bull Run, listening to the clangor of the guns, watching the smoke clouds billowing up to the July sky, and in general making a holiday out of it. Now, as Union wagon trains, ambulances, reserve artillery, and knots of disorganized stragglers began to take the road back to Washington, all of these civilians decided that it was high time for them to get out of there. They got into their conveyances and went swarming out onto the highway which the army wanted to use, creating the father and mother of all traffic jams; and just as things were at their worst a stray Confederate shell came arching over and upset a wagon on a bridge over a little stream called Cub Run, blocking the road completely.

After this there was unadulterated turmoil, growing worse every moment, with disorganized troops and panicky civilians trying to force their way through a horrible tangle of wheeled vehicles, mounted men riding around and past them, bodies of troops trying in vain to march where they had been told to march; a new surge of fear rising every now and then when someone would shout that Confederate cavalry was coming on the scene. In the weeks before the battle, imaginative newspaper and magazine writers had written extensively about the "black horse cavalry" which the Confederates had developed, and what they said had stuck in men's

The Bull Run rout, shown above in a period engraving, was a great disaster in the minds of those Northerners who were intent on a one-stroke victory.

minds. In the dust and confusion of this disorganized retreat, frightened individuals began to shout that the black horse cavalry was upon them, and outright panic developed, with bewildered thousands dropping their weapons and starting to run, communicating their fears to others by the simple act of running. Before dark there was complete and unregimented chaos spilling all over the landscape, and hardly anyone who could move at all stopped moving until he had reached the Potomac River. For the time being most of McDowell's army had simply fallen apart. The bits and pieces of it might be useful later on, but right now they were nothing more than elements in a universal runaway.

The Confederates might have pursued, but did not. Jefferson Davis had reached the scene, and he conferred extensively with Johnston and Beauregard, almost ordered a pursuit, finally did not; and, as a matter of fact, the Confederate army was almost as disorganized by its victory as the Union army was by its defeat. In the end it stayed in camp, sending cavalry patrols to pick up Yankee stragglers and gleaning the field of an immense quantity of military loot, including many stands of small arms which soldiers had thrown away. Stonewall Jackson, it is said, muttered that with 5,000 men he could destroy what remained of the Yankee army, but Stonewall was not yet a man to whom everybody listened. The Confederate high command was content. It had won a

Before the reality of war struck, a Confederate soldier drew this peaceful camp scene in which everyone was contented and happily occupied.

shattering victory, and men believed that night that Confederate independence might be a reality before much longer.

It seemed at the time that the casualty lists were fearful, although by the standards of later Civil War battles they would look moderate. The Federals had lost 2,896 men in killed, wounded, and missing, and Confederate losses came to 1,982. For an unmilitary country which had been subconsciously expecting that the war would not really be very costly, these figures were shocking. People began to see that beneath the romance which had been glimpsed in the bright uniforms, the gay flags, and the lilting tunes played by the military bands, there would be a deep and lasting grimness. Holiday time was over. No one was going to play at war any longer. The militia units could go home now; it was time to get ready for the long pull.

For Bull Run was what awakened the North to reality. (It may have had an opposite effect in the South; the victory looked so overwhelming that many Southerners considered the Yankees poor fighters and expected a speedy final triumph.) Before there could be another campaign, a real army would have to be put together, and expert attention would have to be given to matters of organization, training, and discipline. To attend to this job, Lincoln plucked George B. McClellan out of the western Virginia mountains and put him in command of the Army of the Potomac.

REAL
WARFARE
BEGINS

For the time being there was an uneasy breathing space. The victory at Bull Run left the Confederate command feeling that the next move was pretty largely up to the Yankees, and the Yankees would not be ready to make another move for months to come. The Confederate army around Manassas built extensive lines of entrenchments, and in many redoubts General Johnston mounted wooden guns, which looked like the real thing from a distance but which would never kill any Yankees if a fight developed. He also edged patrols forward to the hills on the south bank of the Potomac and erected batteries downstream so that during the summer and fall the water approach to Washington was fairly effectively blockaded. To the Shenandoah Valley, Johnston sent Stonewall Jackson with a division of infantry and a handful of undisciplined but highly effective partisan cavalry led by a minor genius named Turner Ashby.

In Washington glamorous young General McClellan ap-

These rows of mortars and cannon were a part of the Federal ordnance build-up at Yorktown, Virginia, for McClellan's campaign against Richmond.

plied himself to the creation of a new army. It would be a national army—the ninety-day militia regiments were sent home and demobilized—and except for a small contingent of regular troops this army would be composed of volunteer regiments enlisted for a three-year term. Yet although these were Federal troops, the states' rights tradition was still powerful, and the new volunteer regiments were recruited and officered by the governors of the separate states. In effect, each governor was a separate and largely independent war department. Washington told him how many regiments he was to provide, but the raising and organizing of these troops were entirely up to him. Only after a regiment was fully up to strength, with its proper complement of officers, was it transferred from state to Federal control. The system was cumbersome, and because the appointment of officers provided a governor with a handy form of political patronage, it made impossible the creation of any effective system of replacements for battle-worn regiments. When new men were needed, it was politically profitable for a governor to raise whole new regiments rather than to recruit men to strengthen outfits that already existed. However, in the summer of 1861 the system worked well enough, and scores of new units came down to the chain of camps around Washington.

McClellan was an exceptionally able organizer. Camps were laid out in formal military pattern, the service of supply was reorganized so that food, munitions, and equipment were properly distributed, and there was an unending program of drill. At frequent intervals there would be reviews, with McClellan himself riding the lines to inspect the newly organized brigades and divisions, and the men were taught to cheer lustily whenever the general appeared. They needed very little urging. McClellan made them feel like soldiers, and they responded by giving him their complete confidence and a deep, undying affection. As summer drew on into fall the Washington scene was completely transformed. The army was beginning to be an army, and the slapdash informality of the militia days was gone. The capital took heart. But it was clear that there would be no major campaign in the Virginia area for some time to come. McClellan was going to do what the luckless McDowell had not been allowed to do—get everything ready before he moved—and in addition he was excessively cautious—cautious, his detractors finally would complain, to the point of outright timidity. He had put Allan Pinkerton, already famous as a detective, in charge of military intelligence, and Pinkerton was sadly out of his depth: through a series of fantastic miscalculations he consistently estimated Confederate numbers at double or treble their actual strength, and McClellan trusted him implicitly. On top of all this, the disaster at Ball's Bluff served as a powerful deterrent to hasty action.

Ball's Bluff was a wooded hill on the south bank of the Potomac, thirty-odd miles upstream from Washington. Confederate infantry was camped in the area, and in October McClellan ordered a subordinate to make a reconnaissance in force and see what the Rebels were doing. Several regiments crossed the river, inexpertly led, blundered into a more expertly handled force of Confederates, and were routed with substantial losses. The whole affair had little military significance, but Congress made an issue of it—Colonel Edward D. Baker, a prominent member of the Senate, was among the killed—and the subsequently notorious Joint Committee on the Conduct of the War was set up to look into the doings of the generals. All in all, enough fuss was raised to make it clear that any general who stumbled into defeat might be in for a rough time in Washington.

Still, for the time being McClellan's star was rising. In November Winfield Scott resigned, age and physical infirmities making it impossible for him to continue in active command, and Lincoln made McClellan general in chief of all the armies. McClellan had boundless self-confidence, this fall, and when Lincoln feared that the load of command might be too heavy, McClellan replied jauntily: "I can do it all." He would control military operations all across the board, but he would remain with the Army of the Potomac and would make it his first concern.

Yet the war really began to get into high gear a long way from Virginia. Then and now, what happened in Virginia took the eye. The two capitals were only a hundred miles apart, the armies which defended and attacked them got the biggest headlines, but the war actually took shape in the West. Before McClellan got the Army of the Potomac into action, battles of lasting consequence had been fought in the Mississippi Valley.

To begin with, early in September Kentucky ceased to be neutral and reluctantly but effectively cast its lot with the North. The Federals had a concentration of troops at Cairo, Illinois, where the Ohio River joins the Mississippi, and these troops obviously would invade the Southland sooner or later, either via the Mississippi or up the channels of the Tennessee and the Cumberland. General Frémont, commanding for the Federals in the western area, lacked competence and would presently be replaced, but he had done two things of prime importance: he had started construction of a fleet of gunboats, and he had put a remarkably capable, although then little known, brigadier general named U.S. Grant in command at Cairo.

Top man for the Confederacy in western Tennessee was Major General Leonidas Polk, a classmate of Jefferson Davis at West Point, who had resigned from the army years ago to take holy orders and had become a bishop in the Episcopal Church. When the war began, he returned to military service, and this fall he rightly concluded that the Yankees would soon be occupying Kentucky. He beat them to it, moving troops up to seize and fortify the bluffs at the town of Columbus, on the Mississippi, northern terminus of the Mobile and Ohio Railroad. Grant countered by seizing Paducah, which controlled the mouths of the Tennessee and Cumberland rivers, and Kentucky was squarely in the war.

Davis sent out a new man to take over-all command in the West: a highly regarded regular army officer, General Albert Sidney Johnston, who was thought to be perhaps the ablest

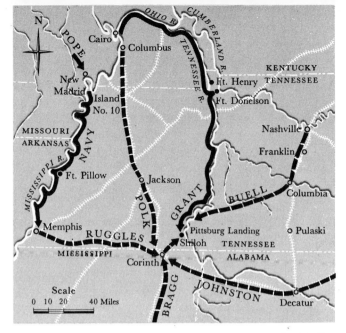

The first Federal thrusts in 1862, aimed at seizing the Mississippi Valley, are shown by solid lines; the South's moves by dotted lines. Included are the capture of Forts Henry and Donelson, the Battle of Shiloh, and the opening of the Mississippi as far south as Memphis.

of all the professional soldiers who had joined the Confederacy. Johnston was woefully handicapped by a shortage of manpower and equipment, but he did his best with the materials at hand. He made a strong point out of Columbus, mounting heavy guns to control the river and establishing a garrison of some 20,000 troops there. The rest of his line extended eastward through Kentucky, with 25,000 men or more in and around Bowling Green, and with a smaller contingent anchoring the eastern end of the line in the mountainous country along the Tennessee border near the upper reaches of the Cumberland River. Rising in the Kentucky mountains, the Cumberland makes a long loop into Tennessee, passing the state capital, Nashville, and then turning north to flow into the Ohio. Just below the Kentucky-Tennessee line it flows more or less parallel with the Tennessee, twelve miles to the west.

These two rivers offered a military highway of prime importance. The Cumberland led to Nashville, and the Tennessee led all the way to northern Mississippi and Alabama.

With the powerful works at Columbus blocking the way down the Mississippi, a Federal invasion was almost certain to follow the line of these two rivers, and just below the Kentucky line the Confederates had built two forts to bar the way—Fort Henry on the Tennessee and Fort Donelson on the Cumberland. These forts drew Federal attention as the year 1862 began.

Federal command in the West was divided. Frémont had been replaced by Major General Henry Wager Halleck, a professional soldier who possessed vast book knowledge of war, had certain talents as an administrator, and was known, somewhat irreverently, in the old army as Old Brains. Halleck's control, however, extended only to the Cumberland. East of that, Federal forces in Kentucky were commanded by Brigadier General Don Carlos Buell, a close friend of McClellan and a cautious type who shared McClellan's reluctance to move until every preparation had been made. Between them, Halleck and Buell commanded many more men than Johnston could bring to oppose them, but neither man had real driving force, and it seemed to be very hard for them to co-operate effectively. McClellan, who could give orders to both of them, was too far away to enforce real co-ordination, and most of his attention was centered on Virginia.

In any case, as the new year began these armies started to move. The first action came at the eastern end of the line,

Gunboats and armored transports shell Fort Henry at point-blank range.

where Johnston's right wing, under Major General George B. Crittenden, crossed the Cumberland and began an advance toward central Kentucky. Buell's left was led by Virginia-born Brigadier General George H. Thomas, and Thomas fell on Crittenden's little force near the hamlet of Mill Springs and completely routed it. The eastern anchor of Johnston's defensive line was to all intents and purposes annihilated.

Shortly afterward, Halleck ordered Grant to move on Fort Henry. Grant took 15,000 men and a squadron of new iron-clad gunboats commanded by Flag Officer Andrew Foote, and by February 6 he got boats and men up to this bastion. Fort Henry proved unexpectedly weak: built on low ground, it was partly under water, the Tennessee being almost at flood stage then, and Foote's gunboats pounded it into surrender before the infantry could get into position to make the attack. Grant promptly turned east, marching his troops cross-country to attack Fort Donelson, on the Cumberland, and sending Foote around to join him by water, and a week after Fort Henry had fallen, the Federals opened their attack.

Donelson was a tougher nut to crack. The fall of Fort Henry made Johnston see that the whole center of his line was in peril, and he evacuated Bowling Green, sending 15,-000 men to defend Fort Donelson and taking the rest back

Federals storm the line of Confederates trying to fight their way out of Fort Donelson. The effort failed when they turned to meet the assault.

to Nashville. Donelson held out for three days, but Grant got strong reinforcements and shelled the place into submission. It surrendered on February 16, and Grant suddenly found himself famous—not only had he captured 15,000 Confederates, but his note demanding capitulation had struck a chord that stirred Northern emotions powerfully: "No terms except an immediate and unconditional surrender can be accepted."

Now the Confederates were in serious trouble. Johnston could do nothing but retreat, posthaste, and this he did without delay. Nashville could not be held, and it was evacuated, with substantial military stores falling into Union hands. Even the fortress at Columbus had to be given up. Beauregard, so unhappy in Virginia, had been sent west to be second in command to Johnston, and he led the Columbus garrison south: he and Johnston, if the Federals let them, would reunite their forces at Corinth, Mississippi, just below the Tennessee line. Here the vital railway line which led east from Memphis, connecting the western part of the Confederacy with Virginia, crossed the north-south line of the Mobile and Ohio. Richmond was scraping the seacoast garrisons to provide reinforcements, and if Johnston could reassemble his forces he would have perhaps 50,000 men. Halleck and Buell, between them, could send 70,000 against him if they managed things properly.

Really effective management was not forthcoming. As a reward for victory, Halleck had been given top command in the West and Grant had been made a major general, and under Halleck's orders Grant was moving up the Tennessee with approximately 45,000 men while Buell was marching down from Nashville with 25,000 more. But Halleck had his columns moving slowly; both Grant and Foote wanted to press the beaten foe with vigor, but one delay succeeded another, and Johnston and Beauregard were given just time to regroup and reorganize their troops at Corinth. There Johnston realized that the Federals would before long bring overpowering numbers against him. Grant had put his army on the western bank of the Tennessee at Pittsburg Landing,

On April 7, the second day of the Battle of Shiloh, the 14th Wisconsin Volunteers charge and take a New Orleans battery.

with most of the men in camp near a country meetinghouse known as Shiloh Church, a little more than twenty miles from Corinth. Johnston concluded that his only hope was to strike Grant before Buell could arrive, and in the first days of April the Confederate army marched up from Corinth to give battle.

The result was the bewildering and bloody Battle of Shiloh, fought on April 6 and 7, 1862. Grant was caught off guard, and in the first day's fight his army was almost pushed into the Tennessee River. It rallied just in time, Johnston was killed in action, and at dark Buell's troops began to arrive and one of Grant's divisions which had been delayed in reaching the field got to the scene. On the second day the Federals reversed the tide, and by midafternoon Beauregard had to admit defeat. He drew his badly battered army back toward Corinth, and the Federals, equally battered, made no more than a gesture at pursuit. The greatest battle ever fought on the American continent, up to that date, was over. The Federals had lost 13,000 men, the Confederates, 10,000. The troops had fought with impressive valor, but they had been poorly handled, especially on the Union side.

But although the terrible casualty list and the fact that Grant had let himself be taken unawares stirred violent criticism in the North, the battle nevertheless had been of decisive importance. At Shiloh the Confederacy made its supreme bid to regain western Tennessee. It failed, and after that the Confederate path in the West went downhill all the way. Nor was Shiloh the only disaster, that spring. At Pea Ridge, Arkansas, a Union army under Brigadier General Samuel Curtis defeated a Confederate army led by Major General Earl Van Dorn. Other Union forces came down the Mississippi itself, taking New Madrid, Missouri, and capturing a powerful fort at Island Number Ten. Union gunboats came down and destroyed a Confederate river fleet at Memphis, and two months after Shiloh, Memphis itself had to be abandoned. Halleck assembled an army of substantially more than 100,000 men near Pittsburg Landing and moved slowly down to take Corinth—moved with excessive caution, for Beauregard had not half of Halleck's numbers and dared not stay to give battle, but Halleck was the most deliberate of generals. In the end Beauregard left Corinth and retreated toward central Mississippi, the Federals held all of western Tennessee and were in a fair way to reclaim the entire Mississippi Valley, and in the West the Southern cause was well on the way to defeat.

But in Virginia everything was very different.

Like Halleck, McClellan moved with deliberation. He also suffered from a handicap which never afflicted Halleck: he had aroused the active distrust and hostility of the radical Republican leaders in Washington, including the Secretary of War, Edwin M. Stanton. These men had come to distrust McClellan's will to fight. Some of them even believed he was pro-Confederate at heart, and they suggested openly that he was potentially a traitor, willing to let the enemy win the war. What McClellan did in the spring of 1862 cannot be appraised fairly unless this bitter hostility and suspicion are taken into account. If McClellan moved later than he said he would move (which was usually the case), he was certain to be accused of sabotaging the war effort; if a battle went against him, there were sure to be grandstand critics in Washington who would proclaim that he might easily have won if he had really wanted to win.

The first result of all of this was that in the middle of

Above is Confederate artillerist Hunt Wilson's painting of Rebel forces assembled at Pea Ridge near Pratt's store. Below is Alexander Simplot's painting of the brief, savage battle at Memphis. Of the eight lightly armed and armored Confederate craft, only one, the **Van Dorn,** *escaped.*

March McClellan lost his job as general in chief of all the armies and was limited to command of the Army of the Potomac. The second result was that when he finally made his move he made it under great difficulties, some of them self-inflicted.

McClellan had given up the idea of moving on Richmond via Manassas. Instead he wanted to go down to Fort Monroe by steamboat and then advance up the Virginia Peninsula, with rivers to protect his flanks and a secure line of communications. President Lincoln and Secretary Stanton agreed to this very reluctantly. A Union army moving overland toward Richmond would always stand between Washington and the main Confederate army; but it seemed to these men that under McClellan's plan the capital would be dangerously open to capture by a sudden Confederate thrust. As a soldier, McClellan considered this highly unlikely; as politicians, Lincoln and Stanton were bound to realize that if Washington should be captured the Union cause was irretrievably lost, and they refused to take chances. They let McClellan make his move, therefore, on condition that he

Federal troops, jaunty and eager for action, stream onto the Peninsula from their transports in Hampton Roads, near Fort Monroe, Virginia.

leave enough troops in Washington (which by now was strongly fortified) to make it safe beyond question. McClellan agreed to this, but apparently he did not take the business very seriously. After he and the army had taken off for the Peninsula, the President and the Secretary of War began counting heads and discovered that the numbers McClellan had promised to leave behind just were not there. Accordingly, they removed an entire army corps from his command —it was commanded by the General McDowell who had had such bad luck at Bull Run—and ordered it to cover the area between Washington and Fredericksburg. Simultaneously, they created a separate command in the Shenandoah Valley, entrusting it to a political major general from Massachusetts,

McClellan had 44 of these huge mortar batteries in place near Yorktown, Virginia, but the Rebels withdrew before they had a chance to fire a shot.

the distinguished, if unmilitary, Nathaniel P. Banks. As a final step they called General Frémont back from retirement and put him in command in western Virginia, with instructions to begin moving east.

So McClellan started up the Peninsula with only 90,000 men instead of the 130,000 he had expected to have. His troubles immediately began to multiply.

Joe Johnston had long since evacuated Manassas, but he had not yet got all of his men down to the Peninsula. At Yorktown he had a chain of earthworks and some 15,000 soldiers under Major General John Bankhead Magruder. In the old army Magruder had been famous as an amateur actor, and he used all of his talents now to bemuse McClellan. As the Yankees approached the Yorktown lines Magruder marched his troops up hill and down dale, safely out of range but plainly visible, and he did it so well that the Unionists concluded that he had a very substantial army. McClellan took alarm, erected works facing the Yorktown lines, and prepared to lay siege. He could certainly have overwhelmed Magruder with one push, and even after Johnston got the rest of his army to the scene the Confederate works could probably have been stormed; but McClellan played it safe, and as a result he lost an entire month. Johnston evacuated Yorktown on May 4—McClellan had his big guns in position, and was going to open a crushing bombardment next day—and the long move up the Peninsula began. The Confederates fought a brisk delaying action at Williamsburg the next day, but they did not try to make a real stand until they had reached the very outskirts of Richmond.

Meanwhile, other things had been happening which would have a marked effect on McClellan's campaign. The canny Confederates quickly discovered the extreme sensitivity of Lincoln and Stanton about the safety of Washington and made cruel use of it. In the Shenandoah Valley, Stonewall Jackson with 8,000 men faced Banks, who had nearly twice that number; and Frémont was beginning to edge in through the western mountains with as many more. Jackson was given reinforcements, nearly doubling his numbers;

This Federal camp was at Cumberland Landing on the Pamunkey River.

then he set out on one of the war's most dazzling campaigns. A quick march west of Staunton knocked back Frémont's advance; then Jackson swept down the Valley, completely deceiving Banks as to his whereabouts, breaking his supply line and forcing him to retreat, and then striking him viciously while he was retreating and turning his withdrawal into a rout. Banks had to go clear north of the Potomac River, and Jackson's quick movements convinced Secretary Stanton that a major invasion of the North was beginning. McDowell had been under orders to march down and join McClellan, who had drawn his lines astride of the Chickahominy River no more than half a dozen miles from Richmond: these orders were canceled, and McDowell had to send troops posthaste to the Shenandoah to break up Jackson's game. Jackson coolly waited until the Federal panic was at its height, then withdrew up the Valley, bloodied the noses of two pursuing Federal columns—and then slipped swiftly down to Richmond to take a hand in the coming fight with McClellan's Army of the Potomac.

All in all, the Federal government had been utterly bamboozled. By skillful use of his 17,000 men Jackson had immobilized more than 50,000 Yankee troops. When the Con-

At left is the Federal observation balloon Intrepid *being inflated; at right it is ascending to reconnoiter the battlefield at Fair Oaks.*

federacy fought to defend its capital, it would not have to face nearly as many men as might easily have been sent against it.

Joe Johnston would not be in command in this fight. At the end of May his troops had fought a hard two-day battle with McClellan's left wing at Fair Oaks—an indecisive struggle that left both sides about where they had been before—and Johnston had been seriously wounded. To replace him, Davis called on Robert E. Lee, who would command the most famous of all Confederate levies, the Army of Northern Virginia, until the end of the war.

Lee's part in the war thus far had been onerous and not particularly happy. He had tried to direct Confederate operations in western Virginia, but the situation there had been hopeless and the area had been lost. He had helped fortify the Southern seacoast, and then he had served Davis as military adviser, in a post which carried heavy responsibility but no genuine authority. (If Jackson had executed the Valley Campaign, the underlying idea was largely Lee's.) Now he was taking an active field command, and within a few weeks he would prove that he was the ideal man for the job.

Because of the success of the Valley Campaign, McClellan's army lay on both sides of the Chickahominy River with substantially less strength than McClellan had expected to have when he took that position. It contained, as June drew to a close, more than 100,000 soldiers, of whom 25,000 were north of the Chickahominy. Lee, his army reinforced to a strength of nearly 85,000, left a few divisions to hold the lines immediately in front of Richmond, marched some 65,-000 men to the north bank of the Chickahominy, and struck savagely at the exposed Federal flank.

There followed the famous Seven Days' battles—Mechanicsville, Gaines' Mill, Savage's Station, Frayser's Farm, Malvern Hill, and a host of lesser fights and skirmishes in between—and at the end of all of this McClellan's army had been roundly beaten and compelled to retreat to Harrison's Landing on the James River, badly shattered and greatly in need of a refit. McClellan's stock at the War Department was lower than ever, his army was effectively out of action as an offensive unit for some time to come, and the way was open for Lee to take the offensive and give some substance to President Lincoln's fears for the safety of Washington. This General Lee would very quickly do; and as he did it the Southern cause would reach its brief, tragic high-water mark for the war.

McClellan's withdrawal was so hasty that 2,500 sick and wounded Federals in the field hospital at Savage's Station had to be abandoned to the Rebels.

THE NAVIES

While the rival armies swayed back and forth over the landscape, wreathing the countryside in smoke and visiting the dread and sorrow of long casualty lists on people of the North and the South, a profound intangible was slowly beginning to tilt the balance against the Confederacy. On the ocean, in the coastal sounds, and up and down the inland rivers the great force of sea power was making itself felt. By itself it could never decide the issue of the war; taken in conjunction with the work of the Federal armies, it would ultimately be decisive. In no single area of the war was the overwhelming advantage possessed by the Federal government so ruinous to Southern hopes.

The Civil War came while one revolution in naval affairs was under way, and it hastened the commencement of another. The world's navies were in the act of adjusting themselves to the transition from sail to steam when the war began; by the time it ended, the transition from wooden

As Farragut's fleet passes forts on the Mississippi in April, 1862, the U.S. frigate Mississippi (lower left) destroys the Rebel ram Manassas.

The crew of the U.S. gunboat Hunchbeick *poses for a portrait while stationed on the James River, Virginia.*

ships to ironclads was well along. Taken together, the two revolutions were far-reaching. The era of what is now thought of as "modern" warfare was foreshadowed by what happened on land; it actually began on the water, and by 1865 naval warfare would resemble the twentieth century much more than it resembled anything Lord Nelson or John Paul Jones had known.

At the start of the war the South had no navy at all, and the North had one which, although it was good enough for an ordinary combat with an overseas enemy, was almost wholly unadapted for the job which it had to do now. Both sides had to improvise, and in the improvisation the South displayed fully as much ingenuity and resourcefulness as the North. The great difference was that the North had so much more to improvise with. The South was compelled to enter a contest which it had no chance to win.

When the flag came down on Fort Sumter in April, 1861, the Federal government possessed some ninety warships. More than half of these were sailing vessels—models of their class a generation earlier, obsolete now. About forty ships were steam-driven, and a great number of these were tied up at various navy-yard docks, out of commission—"in ordinary," as the expression then went. Some of them were badly in need of repair. Of the steamers that were in commission, many were scattered on foreign stations, and it would take time to get them back into home waters.

Pride of the navy was its set of five steam frigates. They were powerful wooden vessels, ship-rigged, with adequate power plants and exceptionally heavy armament—forty 9-inch rifles on the gun decks, and a few larger weapons mounted on the spar decks. They were probably as powerful as any ships then afloat. All of these were out of commission.

Then there were five first-class screw sloops, smaller and less formidable than the steam frigates but sturdy fighting craft all the same. There were four side-wheelers, dating back to the navy's first experiments with steam power: they were practically obsolete, because machinery and boilers were largely above the water line, but they could still be used. There were eight lighter screw sloops and half a dozen of third-class rating, along with a handful of tugs and assorted harbor craft. That was about the lot.

With this navy the United States had to blockade more than 3,500 miles of Confederate coast line. It had, also, to control such rivers as the Mississippi and the Tennessee, to say nothing of the extensive sounds along the Atlantic coast. Furthermore, it had to be prepared to strike at Southern seaports, most of them substantially fortified, and to join with the army in amphibious offensives all the way from Cape Hatteras to the Rio Grande. To do all of these things it did not have nearly enough ships, and most of the ones it did have were of the wrong kind. The powerful frigates and sloops were designed for combat on the high seas or for commerce raiding, not for blockade duty. They drew too much water to operate in shallow sounds and rivers. For war with a European power they would have been excellent, once they were all repaired and commissioned; for war with the Confederacy they were not quite what the navy needed.

At the very beginning of the war Lincoln proclaimed a

blockade of all Southern ports. This, as he soon discovered, was a serious tactical error. A nation "blockaded" the ports of a foreign power; when it dealt with an internal insurrection or rebellion it simply closed its ports. The proclamation of blockade almost amounted to recognition of the Confederacy's independent existence, and European powers promptly recognized the Southland's belligerent rights. On top of this, foreign nations were not obliged to respect a blockade unless it were genuinely effective. A paper blockade would do no good: unless the navy could make it really dangerous for merchant ships to trade with Confederate ports, the blockade would have no standing in international law. So the navy's first problem was to find, somewhere and somehow, at any expense but in a great hurry, enough ships to make the paper blockade a real one.

The job was done, but it cost a great deal of money and resulted in the creation of one of the most heterogeneous fleets ever seen on the waters of the globe. Anything that would float and carry a gun or two would serve, for most of these blockaders would never have to fight; they were simply

The Confederate gunboat General Bragg *was sunk by the Union navy in 1862. Later it was raised and outfitted with this 32-pound pivot gun and converted into a Federal gunboat, still impudently bearing the Rebel name.*

cops on the beat, creating most of their effect just by being on the scene. Vessels of every conceivable variety were brought into service, armed, after a fashion, and sent steaming down to take station off Southern harbors: ferryboats, excursion steamers, whalers, tugs, fishing schooners, superannuated clippers—a weird and wonderful collection of maritime oddities, which in the end gave more useful service than anyone had a right to expect. They made the blockade legally effective, and their work was aided by the Confederate government's folly in withholding cotton from the overseas market. At the very least they gave the navy time to build some new vessels specially designed for the job.

These included two dozen 500-ton gunboats, steam powered, of shallow draft and moderate armament— "ninety-day gunboats," they were called, because it took just three months from keel-laying to final commissioning. Deep-sea cruisers to run down Confederate commerce destroyers were built, along with forty-seven double-enders—unique, canoe-shaped side-wheelers, with rudders and pilothouses at each end, for use in the narrow rivers that fed into the coastal sounds where there was no room to turn around. The double-enders could change course by reversing their engines.

In the end the blockade was made highly effective, and by the final year of the war its effect was fatally constrictive. It was never airtight, and as long as a Southern port remained open, daring merchant skippers would slip in and out with priceless cargoes of contraband; but the measure of its effectiveness was not the percentage of blockade-runners which got through the net, but the increasing quantity of goods which the Confederacy had to do without. Under the blockade the Confederacy was doomed to slow strangulation.

For offensive operations the Federal navy was in much better shape, and the war was not very old before offensive operations got under way. Late in August, 1861, a squadron of warships commanded by Flag Officer Silas Stringham, accompanied by transports bearing infantry under Ben Butler, dropped down the coast for an assault on the Confederate forts which guarded Hatteras Inlet, North Carolina, princi-

The map above illustrates the slow, strangling effect of the Northern blockade
in closing Confederate ports. Dates indicate Union seizure of various points
along the coast.

pal entrance to the vast reaches of Pamlico Sound.
Stringham had two of the huge steam frigates with him, and
his bombardment pounded the unprepared forts into submission. The government apparently had not done its advance planning very carefully, and for the time being neither the army nor the navy was prepared to do anything but
hold the captured position. However, the operation did set a
pattern, and important results would grow from it.

In November a much stronger expedition, the naval part
of it commanded by Flag Officer Samuel F. Du Pont, broke
into the waters of South Carolina, shelling Forts Walker and
Beauregard into surrender and occupying Port Royal, which
became a secure base for the blockading fleet. Early in 1862
Flag Officer Louis M. Goldsborough and Brigadier General
Ambrose E. Burnside led an amphibious foray into the
North Carolina sounds from Hatteras Inlet. Roanoke Island

was seized, Elizabeth City and New Bern were captured, and powerful Fort Macon, commanding the approach to Beaufort, was taken. In effect, this action gave the Unionists control of nearly all of the North Carolina coast line and made the task of the blockading fleet much easier; it also added appreciably to Jefferson Davis' problems by posing the constant threat of an invasion between Richmond and Charleston. Simultaneously, another army-navy expedition took Fort Pulaski, at the mouth of the Savannah River.

Most important of all was the blow at New Orleans, largest city in the Confederacy. This was entrusted to an elderly but still spry officer named David Glasgow Farragut, who had a strong fleet of fighting craft and a flotilla of mortar vessels converted schooners, each mounting a tub-shaped mortar that could lob a 13-inch shell high into the air and drop it inside a fort with surprising accuracy. Farragut got his vessels into the mouth of the Mississippi and in mid-April opened a prolonged bombardment of Forts Jackson and St. Philip, which guarded the approach to New Orleans. The mortar boats, commanded by Captain David Dixon Porter, tossed shells into the forts for a week; then, in the blackness of two in the morning on April 24, Farragut's ships went steaming up the river to run past the forts.

The Confederates sent fire rafts downstream, but these were dodged. A collection of armed river vessels put up as much of a fight as they could, and the big guns in the forts flailed away in the darkness, Farragut's broadsides replying, the river all covered with heavy smoke lit by the red flares from the burning rafts and the sharp flashes of the guns— and suddenly most of Farragut's ships were past the forts with only moderate damage, the Confederate vessels were sunk or driven ashore, and Farragut went plowing on to occupy New Orleans. Hopelessly cut off, the forts presently surrendered, Ben Butler came in with troops to take possession of the forts and the city, and the mouth of the great river was in Federal hands.

The capture of New Orleans strikingly illustrated the immense value of unchallenged sea power. The Federals could strike when and where they pleased, and all the Southern coast was vulnerable. The Confederates had known that New Orleans was in danger, but they had supposed that the real peril lay upriver, where Shiloh had just been lost and where the Federal gunboats were hammering their way down to Memphis: coming up through the mouth of the river, Farragut had, so to speak, entered by the back door. The loss of New Orleans was one of the genuine disasters to the Southern cause, and it proved irretrievable.

Yet if the Lincoln government had the enormous advan-

This lithograph gives a bird's-eye view of Du Pont's Port Royal battle plan. Moving in circles, the vessels shell Forts Beauregard and Walker.

Eight men propelled the Rebel submarine Hunley at a speed of four miles an hour. The Union artist has overpopulated the vessel and has failed to link the drive shaft to the propeller.

tage that goes with control of the sea, the Confederacy made valiant attempts to redress the balance. The South lacked a merchant marine and a seafaring population, and it had very little in the way of shipyards and the industrial plant that could build machinery and armament for warships, but it had vast ingenuity and much energy, and its naval authorities, working with very little, accomplished much more than anyone had a right to expect. Not even the Yankees were any more inventive: the chief difference was that it was easier for the Yankees to turn an invention into a working reality.

The case of the *Merrimac* offers an interesting example.

Merrimac was one of the Federal navy's great steam frigates. Her engines were in bad order, and when the war began she was laid up in the Norfolk navy yard, out of commission. Situated in an ardently pro-Confederate community, the navy yard was quickly lost; and by seizing it on April 20, 1861, the Confederates acquired not only the physical plant but more than a thousand powerful cannon, which served to arm Confederate forts all along the seacoast.

When the Federals were driven from the yard they set fire to *Merrimac* and scuttled her, but Confederate engineers had little trouble raising the hulk, and on inspection it was found sound, only the upper works having been destroyed by fire. The imaginative Southerners thereupon proceeded to construct a fighting ship the likes of which no one had ever seen.

Merrimac's hull was cut down to the berth deck, and a citadel with slanting sides was built on the midships section, with ports for ten guns. The walls of this citadel were made of pitch pine and oak two feet thick, and on this was laid an iron sheathing four inches thick. An open grating covered the top of this citadel, admitting light and air to the gun deck. An armored pilothouse was forward, and a four-foot iron beak was fastened to the bow. When she left the dry dock, *Merrimac*, rechristened *Virginia*, looked like nothing so much as a barn gone adrift and submerged to the eaves.

The decks forward and aft of the citadel were just awash. *Merrimac*'s engines, defective to begin with, had not been improved by the fact that they had spent weeks under water, but somehow the engineers got them into running order, and the ship could move. She could not move very fast, and she was one of the unhandiest brutes to steer that was ever put afloat; but in all the navies of the world there were not more than two ships that could have given her a fight. (The French had one ironclad frigate, and the British had another; all the rest of the world's warships were of wood.)

It should be pointed out that since warships had never worn armor, no one had ever bothered to create an armor-piercing shell, and *Merrimac*'s iron sides—very thinly armored, by later standards—were impervious to anything the ordinary warship would fire at her. It developed, as the war wore along, that the only way to deal with an ironclad was to fire solid shot from the largest smoothbore cannon available —15-inch, if possible—at the closest possible range. These would not exactly pierce good iron sheathing, but repeated blows might crack it so that other projectiles could pierce it. This worked sometimes, and sometimes it did not; but when *Merrimac* left the Elizabeth River, on March 8, 1862, and chugged laboriously out into the open waters of Hampton Roads, none of the Federal warships in sight mounted guns that could do her any particular damage.

On her first day in action *Merrimac* created a sensation and put the Lincoln administration—especially Secretary of War Stanton—into something like a panic. She destroyed two of the navy's wooden warships, *Congress* and *Cumberland*, drove the big steam frigate *Minnesota* aground, and was herself so little damaged by the shot which the Union warships threw at her that it almost looked as if she could whip the entire Federal navy. When evening came *Merrimac* went back into her harbor, planning to return in the morning, destroy *Minnesota,* and sink any other ships that cared to stick around and fight.

The next day, March 9, brought what was certainly the most dramatic naval battle of the war—the famous engagement between *Merrimac* and *Monitor*.

It had taken the Confederates many months to design and construct their pioneer ironclad, and word of what they were doing quickly got North—very few military secrets were really kept, in that war—and the Federal Navy Department had to get an ironclad of its own. It went to the redoubtable Swedish-American inventor John Ericsson for a design, getting a craft which in its own way was every bit as odd-looking as the rebuilt *Merrimac*. Ericsson built a long, flat hull with no more than a foot or two of freeboard, putting amidships a revolving iron turret mounting two 11-inch guns. A smoke pipe came up aft of this, and forward there was a stubby iron pilothouse; people who saw *Monitor* afloat said she looked like a tin can on a shingle. This craft was finished just in the nick of time, came down to the Chesapeake from New York in tow of a tug, almost foundering en route—neither of these great ironclads was very seaworthy—and steamed in past the Virginia capes late in the afternoon of March 8, just as *Merrimac* was completing her day's chores. Next day the two ships met in open combat.

The fight was singularly indecisive. Each ship took a sound hammering, but neither one was badly damaged. Although *Merrimac*, in the end, retired to a safe spot in the

The two ironclads, Monitor *and* Merrimac, *according to a report, "fought part of the time touching each other, from 8 A.M. to noon."*

The Cairo, *one of the Union ironclads designed by James B. Eads, was the first victim of yet another Civil War innovation, the torpedo.*

Elizabeth River, *Monitor* did not try to follow her, nor did the Federal craft ever attempt to force a finish fight. *Merrimac* destroyed no more Union warships, but she remained afloat until May 10, effectively keeping the Federals out of the James River; indeed, her continued existence was one of the reasons why McClellan was so very slow in moving up the Virginia Peninsula. She was lost, finally, when the Federals occupied Norfolk, which left her without a home port. She drew too much water to go up the James to Richmond, and she was far too unseaworthy to go out into the open ocean, and her crew had no recourse but to scuttle her. But by any standard she had been a success, she had helped to create a revolution in naval warfare, and her design and construction proved that Southern engineers were quite as ready as Yankees to move into the new mechanical age.

If the South had had Northern industrial facilities, the story of the war at sea might have been very different. A number of ironclads on the *Merrimac* pattern were built, and most of them were highly serviceable. There was *Arkansas,* built in Memphis, Tennessee, which ran straight through a fleet of Yankee gunboats above Vicksburg, outfought the best the Yankees could send against her, and was destroyed by her own crew when her engines failed and sent her hopelessly aground near Baton Rouge. There was *Albemarle,* which shook Federal control of the North Carolina sounds until young Lieutenant William Cushing sank her with a torpedo; and there was *Tennessee,* which single-handed fought Farragut's entire fleet at Mobile Bay in the summer of 1864, surrendering only after having survived one of the most one-sided contests in naval history. As a matter of fact, a Confederate ironclad almost saved the day at New Orleans. A very heavily armored vessel named *Louisiana* was built to hold the lower river, but Farragut came along before she was quite ready: her engines were not serviceable, and her gun ports needed to be enlarged so that her guns could train properly, and she was tied to the bank, virtually useless, when the Federal fleet steamed by. When the forts surrendered, *Louisiana* was blown up.

The marvel in all of this is not that the Confederacy did so poorly with its navy, but that it did so well. Almost uniformly, her ironclads gave the Federal navy much trouble, and it is worth recording that most of them finally failed not because they were poorly designed, but because the industrial facilities that could put them into first-class shape and keep them there did not exist. The South was painfully short of mechanics, short of metal, short of fabricating plants; there was never any chance that she could create a fleet solid enough to go out and challenge the Federal navy, and what was done had to be done on a bits-and-pieces basis. All things considered, the Confederate Navy Department acquitted itself very well.

Confederate commerce raiders drew a great deal of attention during the war and in the generations that followed, but although they were a most expensive nuisance to the North, they could never have had a decisive effect on the course of the war. The best of them, like *Alabama* and *Shenandoah,* were built in England: ably commanded, they roamed the seven seas almost at will, helping to drive the American merchant fleet out from under the American flag but ultimately having only a minor bearing on the war itself. Toward the close of the war English yards did undertake the construction of a number of ironclad rams for the Confederacy, ships meant for close combat rather than for commerce destroying, and if these had been delivered they might have changed everything. But their construction and intended destination became known, the United States government plainly meant to go to war with Great Britain if they were actually delivered, and in the end the British government saw to it that they were kept at home.

Far more important to the Southern cause than the commerce destroyers were the blockade-runners. Most of these were built abroad for private account—long, lean, shallow-draft side-wheelers, for the most part, capable of high speeds, painted slate gray to decrease their visibility, and burning anthracite coal so that smoke from their funnels would not betray them to the blockading fleets. In the usual course of things, goods meant for the Confederacy were shipped from England (or from a port on the Continent) to Nassau, in the

In June, 1865, the famous raider Shenandoah *was still destroying Yankee whalers in the Bering Sea, unaware that the war had ended in April.*

Many blockade-runners also served as commissioned commerce raiders, one step above privateers. Here, the Nashville *burns a captured merchant ship.*

Bahamas—a little port that enjoyed a regular Klondike boom while the war lasted. There the cargoes were transferred to the blockade-runners, which would make a dash for it through the Federal cruisers to some such Southern seaport as Wilmington, North Carolina. Many of these were caught, to be sure, but many of them got through, and profits were so remarkable that if a ship made one or two successful voyages her owners were money ahead, even if thereafter she were captured. On the return trip, of course, the blockade-runners took out cotton.

Not all of the material imported via these vessels was for military use. It paid to bring in luxuries, and so luxuries were brought in, to be sold at fantastic prices; and eventually the Confederate government took a hand, outlawing the importation of some luxuries entirely and stipulating that one-half of the space on every ship must be reserved for government goods. Tightly as the Federal squadrons might draw their patrols, they were never able to stop blockade-running entirely; it ceased, at last, only when the last of the Confederate ports was occupied. But if the traffic could not be entirely stopped, it was increasingly restricted, and the very fact that the blockade-runners could make such outlandish profits testified to the Southland's desperate shortage of goods from the outside world.

CONFEDERATE HIGH-WATER MARK

Toward the end of the summer of 1862 the mirage of final Southern independence looked briefly and dazzlingly like an imminent reality. In April the Confederacy had been on the defensive everywhere—New Orleans lost, McClellan approaching the gates of Richmond, Halleck coming in on Corinth as slowly and as irresistibly as a glacier, Missouri gone and the whole Mississippi Valley apparently about to follow it. But by August the Southern nation had gone on the offensive, and for a few weeks it looked as if the gates were about to open. Never before or afterward was the Confederacy so near to victory as it was in the middle of September, 1862.

There was a tremendous vitality to the Southern cause, and it was aided this summer by fumbling military leadership on the part of the North. For a time the Federals had no over-all military commander except for the President and the Secretary of War, who were men who knew exactly what

Dead Rebel gunners lie amid the debris of their battery at the Dunker Church after the bloody Battle of Antietam, in which more than 20,000 died.

they wanted but who did not quite know how to get it. Then, in July, Lincoln called General Halleck to Washington and made him general in chief of the Union armies.

On form, the choice looked good. The great successes had been won in Halleck's territory, the West, and as far as anyone in Washington could tell, he was fully entitled to take the credit. Except for continuing guerrilla activity, Kentucky and Missouri had been swept clear of armed Confederates, western Tennessee had been reclaimed, there was a Yankee army in Cumberland Gap, another one was approaching Chattanooga, and a third was sprawled out from Memphis to Corinth, preparing to slice down through Mississippi and touch hands with the Union occupation forces in Baton Rouge and New Orleans. If any Northern general was entitled to promotion, that general certainly appeared to be Halleck.

Halleck was a bookish sort of soldier, a headquarters operator who could handle all of the routine chores of military housekeeping with competence, but who somehow lacked the vital quality which such Confederates as Lee and Jackson possessed in abundance—the driving, restless spirit of war. The impulse to crowd a failing foe into a corner and compel submission simply was not in him, nor did he have the knack of evoking that spirit in his subordinates. His grasp of the theories of strategy was excellent, but at heart he was a shuffler of papers.

He came east to repair disaster. McClellan had been beaten in front of Richmond, and his army was in camp on the bank of the James River—still close enough to the Confederate capital, and still strong enough to resume the offensive on short notice, yet temporarily out of circulation for all that. (Like Halleck, McClellan was not especially aggressive.) In northern Virginia the Federal government had put together a new army, 50,000 men or thereabouts, troops who might have gone down to help McClellan in the spring, but who had been held back because of Jackson's game in the Shenandoah Valley. This army had been entrusted to one of Halleck's old subordinates, John Pope, who had taken Island Number Ten and New Madrid, and who seemed to have a good deal of energy and a desire to fight. Pope was moving down toward Richmond along the line of the Orange and Alexandria Railroad, and the general notion was that Robert E. Lee could not possibly fend off both Pope and McClellan.

The general notion was good enough, but Lee had accurately appraised the generals he was fighting. He suspected that McClellan would be inactive for some time to come, so while he held the bulk of his own army in the defensive lines around Richmond, he detached Stonewall Jackson with 25,000 men and sent him north to deal with Pope. (Pope was given to bluster and loud talk, and Lee held him in contempt: he told Jackson he wanted Pope "suppressed," as if the man were a brawling disturber of the peace rather than a general commanding an army of invasion.)

Arriving in Washington, Halleck could see that the Union military situation in Virginia was potentially dangerous. Pope and McClellan together outnumbered Lee substantially, but they were far apart, and communication between them was slow and imperfect. Lee was squarely between them, and unless both armies advanced resolutely he might easily concentrate on one, put it out of action, and then deal with the other at his leisure. Halleck went down to the James to see McClellan and find out if he could immediately move on Richmond.

This McClellan could not quite do. He needed reinforcements, material, time, and he had no confidence that Pope was going to do anything important anyway. Convinced that the Army of the Potomac would not advance, Halleck ordered it to leave the Peninsula and come back to Washington. It seemed to him that the sensible thing was to unite both armies and then resume the drive on the Confederate capital. Protesting bitterly, McClellan prepared to obey. But it would take a long time to get all of his troops back to the Washington area, and the move presented Lee with a free gift of time to attend to General Pope. Of this gift Lee took immediate advantage.

Union troops under Banks hit Jackson's left flank at Cedar Mountain.

It began on August 9, when Jackson advanced, met a detachment of Pope's army at Cedar Mountain, not far from Culpeper, and drove it in retreat after a sharp battle. This Confederate victory gained very little, since Pope's main body was not far away and Jackson soon had to withdraw, but it was a forecast of things to come. Concentrating his troops in front of Pope, and leaving only detachments to see McClellan off, Lee began a series of maneuvers which caused Pope to retreat to the north side of the upper Rappahannock River. Pope held the river crossings and, for the time at least, seemed quite secure. McClellan's troops were coming north, some of them marching west from Fredericksburg and others going by boat to Alexandria, across the Potomac from Washington; with Halleck's blessing, Pope proposed to stay where he was until these troops joined him. Then the Federal offensive could begin in earnest.

Lee could see as clearly as anyone that time was on the side of the Federals. If McClellan and Pope finally got together, their strength would be overwhelming; Lee's only hope was to beat Pope before this happened. With consummate skill he set about this task, although he was compelled to take some hair-raising risks in the process.

According to the military textbooks, no general should ever divide his forces in the presence of the enemy. This is a very sound rule in most cases, but it is a rule that was made

Later the Stonewall Brigade routed Banks with casualties of 30 per cent.

to be broken now and then, and Lee was the man to break it. He was in the immediate presence of John Pope's army, with the shallow Rappahannock River between; and now he divided his army, sending half of it, under Stonewall Jackson, on a long hike to the northwest, and holding the remainder, with Major General James Longstreet in immediate command, to keep Pope occupied. Jackson swung off behind the Bull Run Mountains, came swiftly east through Throughfare Gap, and pounced suddenly on the Federal army's base of supplies at Manassas Junction, twenty miles or more in Pope's rear. Pope turned to attend to Jackson, and Lee and Longstreet then followed Jackson's route, to join him somewhere east of the Bull Run Mountains.

Seldom has a general been more completely confused than Pope was now. He had vast energy, and he set his troops to marching back and forth to surround and destroy Jackson, but he could not quite find where Jackson was. With his 25,000 men, Stonewall had left Manassas Junction before the Federals got there—destroying such Federal supplies as could not be carried away—and took position, concealed by woods and hills, on the old battlefield of Bull Run. Pope wore out his infantry and his cavalry looking for him, blundered into him at last, and gathered his men for a headlong assault. There was a hard, wearing fight on August 29, in which Jackson's men held their ground with great difficulty;

As Pope withdrew after the Cedar Mountain repulse, his army was followed across the Rappahannock by Virginia Negroes escaping from slavery.

on the morning of August 30 Pope believed he had won a great victory, and he sent word to Washington that the enemy was in retreat and that he was about to pursue.

No general ever tripped over his own words more ingloriously than Pope did. Unknown to him, Lee and Longstreet had regained contact with Jackson on the afternoon of August 29, and on August 30, when Pope was beginning what he considered his victorious pursuit, they struck him furiously in the flank while Jackson kept him busy in front. Pope's army was crushed, driven north of Bull Run in disorder, and by twilight of August 30 the Confederates had won a sensational victory. Pope had lost the field, his reputation, and about 15,000 men. The Confederate casualty list had been heavy, but in every other respect they had won decisively.

Lee had acted just in time. Some of McClellan's divisions had joined Pope and had taken part in the battle, and the rest of McClellan's army was not far off. Two or three days more would have made the Union force safe: the big point about Lee was that he was always mindful of the difference that two or three days might make.

By any standard, Lee's achievements this summer had been remarkable. He had taken command of the Army of Northern Virginia in June, almost in the suburbs of Richmond, badly outnumbered by an enemy which had thousands upon thousands of additional troops not far away. By the end of August he had whipped the army that faced him, had whipped the army that came to its relief, and had transferred the war from the neighborhood of Richmond to the neighborhood of Washington. (After the Bull Run defeat the Federals withdrew to the fortifications of Washington, leaving practically all of Virginia to the Confederates.) Now Lee was about to invade the North.

In the spring the Federal War Department had been so confident that it had closed the recruiting stations. Now Secretary Stanton was frantically appealing to the Northern governors for more troops, and President Lincoln—to the great joy of the soldiers—was reinstating McClellan in command of the Army of the Potomac, with which Pope's troops were incorporated.

Technically, McClellan had never actually been removed from that command. His army had simply been taken away from him, division by division, and when the Second Battle of Bull Run was fought, McClellan was in Alexandria, forwarding his men to Manassas but unable to go with them. After the battle, speedy reorganization was imperative, and Lincoln could see what Stanton and the Republican radicals could not see—that the only man who could do the job was McClellan. Such men as Stanton, Secretary of the Treasury Salmon P. Chase, and Senators Ben Wade and Zachariah Chandler believed that McClellan had sent his men forward slowly, hoping that Pope would be beaten; Lincoln had his own doubts, but he knew that the dispirited soldiers had full confidence in McClellan and that it was above all things necessary to get those soldiers back into a fighting mood. So Pope was relieved and sent off to Minnesota to fight the Indians, a task which was well within his capacities; and McClellan sorted out the broken fragments of what had been two separate armies, reconstituted the Army of the Potomac, manned the Washington fortifications, and early in September marched northwest from Washington with 95,000 men to find General Lee, who had taken the Army of Northern Virginia across the Potomac into western Maryland on September 5.

Lee seemed bent on getting into Pennsylvania. He had gone to Frederick, Maryland, forty miles from Washington, and then he went off on the old National Road in the direction of Hagerstown, vanishing from sight behind the long barrier of South Mountain, whose gaps he held with Jeb Stuart's cavalry. Following him, McClellan did not know where Lee was or what he was up to, and until he found out, he was in trouble: to lunge straight through the gaps with his massed force would be to risk letting Lee slip past him on either flank and seize Washington itself. A real advance was impossible until he had better information, the news that was coming out of western Maryland was confused, contradictory, and of no value to anyone . . . and if Lee was not quickly caught, fought, and driven below the Potomac, the Northern cause was lost forever.

It was not only in Maryland that the Federals were in trouble. In the western area, where everything had looked so prosperous, there had been a similar reversal of fortune. At the beginning of the summer a sweeping Federal triumph west of the Alleghenies looked inevitable; by mid-September the situation there looked almost as bad as it did in the East, one measure of the crisis being the fact that Cincinnati had called out the home guard lest the city be seized by invading Rebels.

Several things had gone wrong in the West, but the root of the trouble was General Halleck's fondness for making war by the book. The book said that in a war it was advisable to occupy enemy territory, and after the capture of Corinth, Halleck had set out to do that. He had had, in front of Corinth, well over 100,000 men, and with that army he could have gone anywhere in the South and beaten anything the Davis government could have sent against him. But instead of continuing with the offensive under circumstances which guaranteed victory, Halleck had split his army into detachments. Grant was given the task of holding Memphis and western Tennessee. Buell was sent eastward to occupy Chattanooga, rebuilding and protecting railway lines as he moved—a task that took so much of his time and energy that he never did get to Chattanooga. Other troops were sent to other duties, and by August the war had come to a standstill.

Halleck was in Washington by now, and Grant and Buell were independent commanders.

The principal Confederate army in the West, the Army of Tennessee, was commanded now by General Braxton Bragg —a dour, pessimistic martinet of a man, who had an excellent grasp of strategy and a seemingly incurable habit of losing his grip on things in the moment of climax. (Beauregard, this army's former commander, had been relieved, the victim of ill-health and inability to get along with President Davis.) Bragg had his men, 30,000 strong, in Chattanooga; Major General Edmund Kirby Smith was in Knoxville with 20,000 more; and in August these generals moved northward in a campaign that anticipated nothing less than the reoccupation of western Tennessee and the conquest—or liberation, depending on the point of view—of all of Kentucky.

The small Union force at Cumberland Gap beat a hasty retreat all the way to the Ohio River. Buell, outmaneuvered, gave up railroad-building and turned to follow Bragg, who had slipped clear past him. Grant was obliged to send all the troops he could spare to join Buell; and to keep him additionally occupied, the Confederates brought troops from across the Mississippi and formed an army of between 20,000 and 25,000 men in northern Mississippi under Earl Van Dorn. By late September, Bragg had swept aside the hastily assembled levies with which the Federals tried to bar his path and was heading straight for the Ohio River, Buell marching desperately to overtake him, Kirby Smith near at hand. It looked very much as if Bragg's ambitious plan might succeed, and if Van Dorn could defeat or evade Grant and reach Kentucky too the Union situation in the West would be almost hopeless.

Never had military events better illustrated the folly of surrendering the initiative in war. In both the East and West the Federals had a strong advantage in numbers; but in each area an inability to make use of that advantage in a vigorous, unceasing offensive, and a desire to protect territory rather than to compel the enemy's army to fight, had caused the Federals to lose control of the situation. Now, in

Maryland, in Kentucky, and in Tennessee, the North was fighting a defensive war, and the Confederates were calling the tune. (To use an analogy from football, the North had lost the ball and was deep in its own territory.)

This was the authentic high-water mark of the Confederacy. Never again was the South so near victory; never again did the South hold the initiative in every major theater of war. Overseas, the British were on the verge of granting outright recognition—which, as things stood then, would almost automatically have meant Southern independence. Cautious British statesmen would wait just a little longer, to see how this General Lee made out with his invasion of the North. If he made out well, recognition would come, and there would be a new member in the world's family of nations.

Then, within weeks, the tide began to ebb.

Preparing to move into Pennsylvania, Lee wanted to maintain some sort of line of communications with Virginia. At Harpers Ferry the Federals had a garrison of 12,000 men, and these soldiers were almost on Lee's communications. It seemed to the Confederate commander that it would be well to capture Harpers Ferry and its garrison before he went on into the Northern heartland. He knew that McClellan was very cautious and deliberate, and he believed the man would be even more so now because he had to reorganize his army. So it looked as if the Army of Northern Virginia could safely pause to sweep up Harpers Ferry: with the South Mountain gaps held, McClellan could be kept in the dark until it was too late for him to do anything about it.

So Lee once more divided his army. The advance, under Longstreet, was at Hagerstown, Maryland, not far from the Pennsylvania border. One division, under Major General D. H. Hill, was sent back to Turner's Gap in South Mountain, to make certain that no inquisitive Federals got through. The rest, split into three wings but all under the general control of Jackson, went down to surround and capture Harpers Ferry.

Now sheer, unadulterated chance took a hand, and

Jackson's spoils from Harpers Ferry included 13,000 small arms and 73 cannon. In 1861 the Confederates had blown the railroad bridge seen in the foreground and removed the machinery from the arsenal.

Federal gunnery at Antietam was particularly effective, due in part to artillery spotters. This tower on Elk Mountain overlooked Rebel positions.

changed the course of American history.

Some Confederate officer lost a copy of the orders which prescribed all of these movements. Two Union enlisted men found the order, and it got to McClellan's headquarters, where there was an officer who could identify the handwriting of Lee's assistant adjutant general and so convince McClellan that the thing was genuine. Now McClellan had the game in his hands: Lee's army was split into separate fragments, and McClellan was closer to the fragments than they were to each other. If he moved fast, McClellan could destroy the Army of Northern Virginia.

McClellan moved, although not quite fast enough. He broke through the gap in South Mountain, compelling Lee to concentrate his scattered forces. Lee ordered his troops to assemble at Sharpsburg, on Antietam Creek, near the Potomac. At that point Jackson, who had had just time to capture Harpers Ferry, rejoined him; and there, on September

17, McClellan and Lee fought the great Battle of Antietam.

Tactically, the battle was a draw. The Federals attacked savagely all day long, forcing the Confederates to give ground but never quite compelling the army to retreat, and when Lee's battered army held its position next day, McClellan did not renew the attack. But on the night of September 18 Lee took his worn-out army back to Virginia. Strategically, the battle had been a Northern victory of surpassing importance. The Southern campaign of invasion had failed. The Federals had regained the initiative. Europe's statesmen, watching, relaxed: the time to extend recognition had not arrived, after all.

Antietam was not only strategically decisive: it has the melancholy distinction of having seen the bloodiest single day's fighting in the entire Civil War. The Union army lost over 12,000 men, and the Confederate loss was nearly as great. Never before or after in all the war were so many men shot on one day.

In the West, too, the Confederate offensive collapsed.

In the lithograph below, two Ohio regiments capture a post-and-rail fence at Turner's Gap on South Mountain. Lieutenant Colonel Rutherford B. Hayes (left, above the wagons) was a Union casualty.

Lincoln inspects the headquarters of the Army of the Potomac on October 1.
General McClellan (sixth from left) was removed from command a month later.

Until he actually arrived in Kentucky, Bragg had handled his campaign with vast skill. Now, however, he became irresolute, and his grasp of strategic principles weakened. It had been supposed that the people of Kentucky, crushed under the heel of Northern despots, would rise in welcome once they were liberated by Confederate armies, and whole wagonloads of weapons were carried along by the Confederates to arm the new recruits. The anticipated welcome did not develop, however, recruits were very few in number, and Bragg's swift drive became slower. He lost time by going to Frankfort to see that a secessionist state government was formally installed—it would fall apart, once his troops left— and Buell was just able to get his own army between Bragg's Confederates and the Ohio River.

Buell managed to bring Bragg to battle at Perryville, Kentucky, on October 8. Only parts of the two armies were engaged, and the fight was pretty much a standoff; but afterward the mercurial Bragg concluded, for some reason, that his whole campaign had been a failure, and he and Kirby Smith drew off into eastern Tennessee. Buell pursued with such lack of spirit that the administration removed him and put William S. Rosecrans in his place, and Rosecrans got his army into camp just below Nashville, Tennessee, and awaited further developments. Meanwhile, in northern Mississippi, a part of Grant's army, then led by Rosecrans, had beaten a detachment from Van Dorn's at Iuka on September 19 and 20, and early in October defeated the entire force in

These two paintings from the William Travis Civil War panorama show the Battle of Perryville. At top the Federals attack to regain a farm lot on the Union left. Below, a Yankee officer rallies his men.

a hard-fought engagement at Corinth. Van Dorn retreated toward central Mississippi, and Grant began to make plans for a campaign against Vicksburg.

So by the middle of October the situation had changed once more. The one great, co-ordinated counteroffensive which the Confederacy was ever able to mount had been beaten back. In the East the Federals would begin a new campaign aimed at Richmond; in the West they would resume the advance on Chattanooga and would continue with the drive to open the whole Mississippi Valley. They would have many troubles with all of these campaigns, but they had at least got away from the defensive. The danger of immediate and final Northern defeat was gone.

A SEARCH
FOR
ALLIES

In spite of all of its material handicaps, the South during the first eighteen months of the war did have one great advantage which probably would have proved decisive if it had continued. Its war aims were perfectly clear and definite, and every Southerner could understand them both with his mind and with his heart. The South wanted its independence: its people, struggling for their freedom, were fighting off invaders. The ordinary Confederate soldier might understand little and care less about the intricacies of the states' rights argument, but he did feel that he was protecting the home place against people who wanted to despoil it, and that was enough for him.

By contrast, the Federal government seemed to be fighting for an abstraction. The call to make war for the Union did indeed arouse deep feelings of patriotism, but as the hard months passed and the casualty lists grew longer and longer this rallying call did not seem quite adequate. Much blood

Distinguished, highly respected Charles Francis Adams faithfully served the Union from 1861 to 1868 as Minister to Great Britain.

was being shed for it, but by itself it seemed bloodless. The deep principle that was involved in it became hard to see through the thick layers of battle smoke. Simply to defend the *status quo* against a revolutionary upheaval offers little nourishment for the blood and muscles and spirit when war weariness sets in. In plain terms, the Union cause was not quite broad enough to support a war of this magnitude.

All of this had a direct bearing on the United States' foreign relations.

The relations that were most important were those with the two dominant powers of Europe, England and France. Each country was a monarchy, and a monarchy does not ordinarily like to see a rebellion succeed in any land. (The example may prove contagious.) Yet the war had not progressed very far before it was clear that the ruling classes in each of these two countries sympathized strongly with the Confederacy—so strongly that with just a little prodding they might be moved to intervene and bring about Southern independence by force of arms. The South was, after all, an aristocracy, and the fact that it had a broad democratic base was easily overlooked at a distance of three thousand miles. Europe's aristocracies had never been happy about the prodigious success of the Yankee democracy. If the nation now broke into halves, proving that democracy did not contain the stuff of survival, European rulers would be well pleased.

To be sure, the Southern nation was based on the institution of chattel slavery—a completely repugnant anachronism by the middle of the nineteenth century. Neither the British nor the French people would go along with any policy that involved fighting to preserve slavery. But up to the fall of 1862 slavery was not an issue in the war. The Federal government had explicitly declared that it was fighting solely to save the Union. If a Southern emissary wanted to convince Europeans that they could aid the South without thereby aiding slavery, he could prove his case by citing the words of the Federal President and Congress. As far as Europe was concerned, no moral issue was involved; the game of power politics could be played with a clear conscience.

So it *was* played, and the threat of European intervention was real and immediate. Outright war with England nearly took place in the fall of 1861, when a hot-headed U.S. naval officer, Captain Charles Wilkes, undertook to twist the lion's tail and got more of a reaction than anyone was prepared for.

Jefferson Davis had named two distinguished Southerners, James M. Mason of Virginia and John Slidell of Louisiana, as commissioners to represent Confederate interests abroad, Mason in England and Slidell in France. They got out of Charleston, South Carolina, on a blockade-runner at the beginning of October and went via Nassau to Havana, where they took passage for England on the British mail steamer *Trent.*

Precisely at this time U.S.S. *San Jacinto* was returning to the United States from a long tour of duty along the African coast. She put in at a Cuban port, looking for news of Confederate commerce raiders which were reported to be active in that vicinity, and there her commander, Captain Wilkes, heard about Mason and Slidell. He now worked out a novel interpretation of international law. A nation at war (it was generally agreed) had a right to stop and search a neutral merchant ship if it suspected that ship of carrying the enemy's dispatches. Mason and Slidell, Wilkes reasoned, were in effect Confederate dispatches, and he had a right to remove them. So on November 8, 1861, he steamed out into the Bahama Channel, fired twice across *Trent*'s bows, sent a boat's crew aboard, collared the Confederate commissioners, and bore them off in triumph to the United States, where they were lodged in Fort Warren, in Boston Harbor. Wilkes was hailed as a national hero. Congress voted him its thanks, and Secretary of the Navy Gideon Welles, ordinarily a most cautious mortal, warmly commended him.

But in England there was an uproar which almost brought on a war. The mere notion that Americans could halt a British ship on the high seas and remove lawful passengers was intolerable. Eleven thousand regular troops were sent to Canada, the British fleet was put on a war footing, and a

This Punch *cartoon by John Tenniel appeared during the* Trent *affair. Lincoln, as a timorous raccoon, has been treed by a stalwart John Bull.*

sharp note was dispatched to the United States, demanding surrender of the prisoners and a prompt apology.

If the general tempo of things had not been so feverish just then, experts on international law might have amused themselves by pointing out that the American and British governments had precisely reversed their traditional policies. In the Napoleonic wars British warships had exercised the right of search and seizure without restraint, stopping American merchant ships on the high seas to remove persons whom they suspected of being British subjects—doing, in fact, exactly what Wilkes had done with a slightly different object. The United States government had protested that this was improper and illegal, and the whole business had helped bring on the War of 1812. Now an American naval officer had done what British naval officers had done half a century earlier, and the British government was protesting in the same way the earlier American government had done. If anyone cared to make anything of it, the situation was somewhat ironic.

It was touch and go for a while, because a good many brash Yankees were quite willing to fight the British, and the seizure of the Confederate commissioners had somehow seemed like a great victory. But Lincoln stuck to the policy of one war at a time, and after due deliberation the apology was made and the prisoners were released. The *Trent* incident was forgotten, and the final note was strangely anticlimactic. The transports bearing the British troops to Canada arrived off the American coast just after the release and apology. Secretary of State Seward offered, a little too graciously, to let the soldiers disembark on American soil for rapid transportation across Maine, but the British coldly rejected this unnecessary courtesy.

The *Trent* affair had been symptomatic. The war had put a heavy strain on relations between the United States and Great Britain, and there would always be danger that some unexpected occurrence would bring on a war. Yet the two countries were fortunate in the character of their diplomats. The American Minister in London was Charles Francis Adams, and the British Minister in Washington was Lord Lyons, and these two had done all they could, in the absence of instructions from their governments, to keep the *Trent* business from getting out of hand. Even Secretary of State Seward, who earlier had shown a politician's weakness for making votes in America by defying the British, proved supple enough to retreat with good grace from an untenable position; and Earl Russell, the British Foreign Secretary, who had sent a very stiff note, nevertheless phrased it carefully so that Seward could make his retreat without too great difficulty.

Much more serious was the situation that developed late in the summer of 1862. At that time, as far as any European could see, the Confederacy was beginning to look very much like a winner—a point which James Mason insistently pressed home with British officialdom. The Northern attempt to capture the Confederate capital had failed, Virginia's soil had been cleared of invaders, and in the East and West alike the Confederates were on the offensive. Minister

Adams warned Seward that the British government might very soon offer to mediate the difficulty between North and South, which would be a polite but effective way of intimating that in the opinion of Great Britain the quarrel had gone on long enough and ought to be ended—by giving the South what it wanted. Adams knew what he was talking about. Earl Russell had given Mason no encouragement whatever, but after news of the Second Battle of Bull Run reached London, he and Lord Palmerston, the Prime Minister, agreed that along in late September or thereabouts there should be a cabinet meeting at which Prime Minister and Foreign Secretary would ask approval of the mediation proposal. (Implicit in all of this was the idea that if the Northern government should refuse to accept mediation, Britain would go ahead and recognize the Confederacy.) With a saving note of caution, Russell and Palmerston concluded not to bring the plan before the cabinet until they got further word about Lee's invasion of the North. If the Federals were beaten, then the proposal would go through; if Lee failed, then it might be well to wait a little longer before acting.

On October 7 the Chancellor of the Exchequer, William E. Gladstone, made a notable speech at Newcastle in which he remarked that no matter what one's opinion of slavery might be, facts had to be faced: "There is no doubt that Jefferson Davis and other leaders of the South have made an army; they are making, it appears, a navy; and they have made what is more than either—they have made a nation." He added, "We may anticipate with certainty the success of the Southern States so far as regards their separation from the North."

Naturally enough, this raised a sensation. Gladstone explained that he had simply been expressing his own opinion rather than that of the government, and when Earl Russell saw the speech, he wrote Gladstone that he "went beyond the latitude which all speakers must be allowed." His lordship went on to say that he did not think the cabinet was prepared for recognition, but that it would meet very soon to discuss the project.

Another Tenniel cartoon is typical of Punch's *attitude toward the Union cause. Lord Palmerston, reminded that he has ignored Jeff Davis, says that he may have to recognize him "some of these days."*

In all of this there was less of actual hostility toward the North than is usually supposed. Palmerston and Russell were prepared to accept an accomplished fact, when and if such a fact became visible; if the Confederacy was definitely going to win, the fact ought to be admitted and the war ought to be ended. But they were not prepared to go further than that. Gladstone might commit his calculated indiscretion, the upper class might continue to hold the Confederates as sentimental favorites, and the London *Times* might thunder at intervals against the Northern government; but the British government itself tried to be scrupulously correct, and long before the war ended, ardent Southerners were complaining that the government's attitude had been consistently hostile to the Confederacy. Even the business of the British-built cruisers and ironclad rams did not alter this situation. Legally, vessels like the *Alabama* were simply fast merchant ships, given arms and a warlike character only after they had left English waters, and the government had no legal ground to prevent their construction and delivery. The famous rams themselves were technically built for French purchasers, and even though it was an open secret that they would ultimately go into the Confederate navy, there was never anything solid for the British authorities to put their teeth into. When the British government finally halted the deal and forced the builders to sell the rams to

Several blockade-runners were outfitted at British ports. The American Consul at Bristol had this one photographed to aid in its interception.

the British navy, it actually stretched the law very substantially. That it did this under a plain threat of war from the United States did not alter the fact that in the end the Confederacy could not get what it desperately wanted from Great Britain.

Nor was the United States without active friends in England. Such reformers as John Bright and Richard Cobden spoke up vigorously in support of the Lincoln government, and even when the cotton shortage threw thousands of textile workers out of employment, the British working class remained consistently opposed to the Confederacy. But the decisive factor, in the fall of 1862 and increasingly thereafter, was the Battle of Antietam and what grew out of it.

Antietam by itself showed that Lee's invasion was not going to bring that final, conclusive Confederate triumph which had been anticipated. The swift recession of the high Confederate tide was as visible in England as in America, and as the autumn wore away Palmerston and Russell concluded that it would not be advisable to bring the mediation-recognition program before the cabinet.

Far more significant than Antietam, however, was the Emancipation Proclamation, which turned out to be one of the strangest and most important state papers ever issued by an American President.

During the late spring and early summer of 1862 Lincoln

had come to see that he must broaden the base of the war. Union itself was not enough; the undying vitality and drive of Northern antislavery men must be brought into full, vigorous support of the war effort, and to bring this about the Northern government must officially declare itself against slavery. Lincoln was preparing such a declaration even before McClellan's army left the Virginia Peninsula, but he could not issue it until the North had won a victory. (Seward pointed out that to issue it on the heels of a string of Northern defeats would make it look as if the government were despairingly crying for help rather than making a statement of principle.) Antietam gave Lincoln the victory he had to have, and on September 22 he issued the famous proclamation, the gist of which was that on January 1, 1863, all slaves held in a state or a part of a state which was in rebellion should be "then, thenceforward and forever free."

Technically, the proclamation was almost absurd. It proclaimed freedom for all slaves in precisely those areas where the United States could not make its authority effective, and allowed slavery to continue in slave states which remained under Federal control. It was a statement of intent rather than a valid statute, and it was of doubtful legality; Lincoln had issued it as a war measure, basing it on his belief that the President's undefined "war powers" permitted him to do just about anything he chose to do in order to win the war, but the courts might not agree with him. Abolitionists felt that it did not go nearly far enough, and border-state people and many Northern Democrats felt that it went altogether too far. But in the end it changed the whole character of the war and, more than any other single thing, doomed the Confederacy to defeat.

The Northern government now was committed to a broader cause, with deep, mystic overtones; it was fighting for union and for human freedom as well, and the very nature of the Union for which it was fighting would be permanently deepened and enriched. A new meaning was given to Daniel Webster's famous "Liberty *and* Union, now and forever, one and inseparable"; the great Battle Hymn now rang

Confederate caricaturist Adalbert Volck, hinting darkly at slave uprisings, showed a satanical Lincoln, surrounded by symbols of evil, composing the Emancipation Proclamation with a foot on the Constitution.

out as an American Marseillaise, and Northerners who had wondered whether the war was quite worth its terrible cost heard, at last, the notes of the bugle that would never call retreat. A war goal with emotional power as direct and enduring as the Confederacy's own had at last been erected for all men to see.

And in Europe the American Civil War had become something in which no western government dared to intervene. The government of Britain, France, or any other nation could play power politics as it chose, as long as the war meant nothing more than a government's attempt to put

A. A. Lamb viewed emancipation from an entirely different point of view.

down a rebellion; but no government that had to pay the least attention to the sentiment of its own people could take sides against a government which was trying to destroy slavery. The British cabinet was never asked to consider the proposition which Palmerston and Russell had been talking about, and after 1862 the chance that Great Britain would decide in favor of the Confederacy became smaller and smaller and presently vanished entirely. The Emancipation Proclamation had locked the Confederates in an anachronism which could not survive in the modern world.

Along with this there went a much more prosaic material factor. Europe had had several years of short grain crops, and during the Civil War the North exported thousands of tons of grain—grain which could be produced in increasing quantities, despite the wartime manpower shortage, because the new reapers and binders were boosting farm productivity so sharply. Much as Great Britain needed American cotton, just now she needed American wheat even more. In a showdown she was not likely to do anything that would cut off that source of food.

All of this did not mean that Secretary Seward had no more problems in his dealings with the world abroad. The recurring headache growing out of the British habit of building ships for the Confederate navy has already been noted. There was also Napoleon III, Emperor of the French, who was a problem all by himself.

Napoleon's government in many ways was quite cordial to the Confederates, and in the fall of 1862 Napoleon talked with Slidell and then proposed that France, England, and Russia join in trying to bring about a six-month armistice. To Slidell the Emperor remarked that if the Northern government rejected this proposal, that might give good reason for recognition and perhaps even for active intervention. Neither Britain nor Russia would go along with him, but early in 1863 Napoleon had the French Minister at Washington suggest to Seward that there ought to be a meeting of Northern and Southern representatives to see whether the war might not be brought to a close. Seward politely but firmly rejected this suggestion, and the Congress, much less politely, formally resolved that any foreign government which made such proposals was thereby committing an unfriendly act. Whether Napoleon really expected anything to come of his suggestion is a question; probably he strongly wanted a Southern victory but was afraid to do anything definite without British support. His real interest was in Mexico, where he took advantage of the war to create a French puppet state, installing the Hapsburg Maximilian as Emperor of Mexico in direct violation of the Monroe Doctrine. Propped up by French troops, Maximilian managed to hang on to his shaky throne for several years, and if his control over the country had been firmer, Napoleon would probably have given the Confederacy, from that base, more active support. Shortly after Appomattox the Federal government sent Phil Sheridan and 50,000 veterans to the Mexican border in blunt warning, Seward filed a formal protest against the occupation, and Napoleon withdrew his soldiers. When the French troops left, the Mexicans regained control, and Maximilian was deposed and executed.

Singularly enough the one European country which showed a definite friendship for the Northern government was Czarist Russia. In the fall of 1863 two Russian fleets entered American waters, one in the Atlantic and one in the Pacific. They put into New York and San Francisco harbors and spent the winter there, and the average Northerner expressed both surprise and delight over the visit, assuming that the Russian Czar was taking this means of warning England and France that if they made war in support of the South, he would help the North. Since pure altruism is seldom or never visible in any country's foreign relations, the business was not quite that simple. Russia at the time was in some danger of getting into a war with England and France, for reasons totally unconnected with the Civil War in America; to avoid the risk of having his fleets ice-bound in Russian ports, the Czar simply had them winter in American harbors. If war should come, they would be admirably placed to raid British and French commerce. For many years

The crew of the Russian ship Osliaba *posed for this picture at Alexandria, Virginia. It was not learned until 50 years later that the Russian fleet visited American ports to protect itself rather than to support the Union.*

most Americans believed that for some inexplicable reason of his own the Czar had sent the fleets simply to show his friendship for America.

Considering the course of the war as a whole, it must be said that Northern diplomacy was highly successful and that Southern diplomacy was a flat failure. At the time, most Northerners bitterly resented what they considered the unfriendly attitude of Britain and France, but neither country did much that would give the South any real nourishment. The British commerce raiders were indeed expensive nuisances to the North, and the famous *"Alabama* claims" after the war were prosecuted with vigor; but cruisers like the *Alabama* might have ranged the seas for a generation without ever compelling the North to give up the struggle. The open recognition, the active aid, the material and financial support which the South needed so greatly were never forthcoming. Europe refused to take a hand in America's quarrel. North and South were left to fight it out between themselves.

STALEMATE, EAST AND WEST

After the failure of the great Southern counteroffensive in the fall of 1862, the North tried to pick up the lost threads afresh. Its problem, then as always, was deceptively simple: to use its immense preponderance of physical strength in a sustained, increasing pressure that would collapse the Confederate defenses and destroy the Confederate armies and the government which they supported. In the spring it had seemed that success was very near; by autumn the vast difficulties that lay across the path were much more clearly visible. Momentum, so important to military success, had been lost, and in the East and in the West a new start would have to be made.

In this effort three armies would be chiefly involved—the Army of the Potomac in Virginia, the Army of the Cumberland in central Tennessee, and the Army of the Tennessee along the Mississippi River. The Army of the Potomac was led now by Major General Ambrose E. Burnside, a hand-

Andrew Humphreys leads his untried Pennsylvanians against a Rebel "sheet of flame" in an attack on Fredericksburg, where the Union lost 20,000 men.

some, likable, unassuming West Pointer with a legendary growth of side whiskers, a man whose sincere desire to do the right thing was a good deal stronger than his ability to discern what that right thing might be. McClellan had at last been removed. He had let six weeks pass after Antietam before he crossed the Potomac and began a new offensive, and then he moved, as always, with much deliberation; Lincoln had lost patience, McClellan was in retirement, and Burnside now had the army.

It lay in the neighborhood of Warrenton, Virginia, east of the Blue Ridge. Burnside did not like the advance down the Orange and Alexandria Railroad which McClellan seemed to have projected, and he devised a new plan: go east to Fredericksburg, cross the Rappahannock there and force Lee to give battle somewhere between Fredericksburg and Richmond, and then drive on toward the Confederate capital. By the middle of November, Burnside had the army on the move.

The Army of the Cumberland was just below Nashville, Tennessee. Like the Army of the Potomac, this army had a new commander: bluff, red-faced William S. Rosecrans, who had taken Buell's place when that officer proved unable to overtake Bragg on the retreat from Kentucky. Rosecrans was well-liked by his troops, and he was a stout fighter. He had commanded the portion of Grant's force which won the bloody battle at Corinth, and although Grant had been critical of the way he pursued Van Dorn's beaten army after the battle (it seemed to Grant that that army should have been destroyed outright), Rosecrans' general record of performance was good. He devoted some weeks now to refitting and reorganization, and late in December he began to move south from Nashville with 45,000 men. The Confederate army under Braxton Bragg lay in camp at Murfreesboro, behind Stones River, thirty miles away. At the moment it numbered some 37,000 soldiers.

The third army, Grant's, held western Tennessee, and it had two principal functions: to occupy the western third of the state, holding Memphis and the important network of railroads that ran east and northeast from that city and north from the Mississippi border to the upper Mississippi River; and to move down the great river, capture the Confederate stronghold at Vicksburg, join hands with the Union forces which held New Orleans and Baton Rouge, and so open the river from headwaters to gulf. Grant had 80,000 men in his department, but half of them were needed for occupation duties. When he moved against Vicksburg he would be able to put fewer than 40,000 in his field army. He would follow the north-and-south railroad that ran to the Mississippi capital, Jackson, forty miles east of Vicksburg, and then he would swing west. Opposing him was an undetermined number of Confederates led by Lieutenant General John C. Pemberton, a Pennsylvania-born West Pointer who had cast his lot with the South.

These three Federal armies, then, would move more or less in concert, and if all went well, the Confederacy would be pressed beyond endurance. If all did not go well, the Lincoln administration might be in serious trouble. The Emancipation Proclamation was meeting with a mixed reception in the North, and the fall elections had gone badly. The Democrats had sharply reduced the Republican majority in Congress and had elected Horatio Seymour governor of New York; and to the Republican radicals, Seymour, lukewarm about the war at best, looked no better than an arrant Copperhead. In the Northwest war weariness was clearly visible, and Lincoln was being warned that if the Mississippi were not soon opened, there would be an increasing demand for a negotiated peace with the South. For political reasons he needed new military successes.

For the immediate present he did not get them. Instead he got one disaster and a series of checks which looked almost as bad.

First there was Burnside. He got his army to the Rappahannock, opposite Fredericksburg, and if he could have crossed the river at once, he might have made serious trouble for Lee, who did not have all of his men on hand just yet. But the pontoon trains which Burnside needed to

Fredericksburg residents fled the artillery bombardment that covered the Union crossing of the river. A Union officer, horrified at the sack of the town, noted that his men "seemed to delight in destroying everything."

bridge the river had gone astray somewhere, and Burnside could think of nothing better to do than wait quietly where he was until they arrived. They reached him, eventually, but a fortnight had been lost, and by the end of it Lee had both Jackson and Longstreet in position on the opposite shore— 75,000 veteran fighters of high morale, ably led, ready for the kind of defensive battle in which they were all but unbeatable.

Burnside lacked the mental agility to change his plan, and he tried to go through with it even though the conditions essential for success had gone. He built his bridges, crossed the Rappahannock, and on December 13 assailed Lee's army in its prepared positions. As made, the attack had no chance to succeed. Solidly established on high ground with a clear field of fire, the Confederates beat off a succession of doomed assaults in which the Federals displayed great valor but an almost total lack of military acumen. At the end of the day the Army of the Potomac had lost more than 12,000 men, most of them in front of a stone wall and a sunken road that ran along the base of Marye's Heights. The Confederates had lost fewer than half that many men, and at no time had they been in any serious danger of being dislodged. Burnside called for new assaults the next day—he proposed to lead them in person, there being nothing wrong with his personal courage—but his subordinates managed to talk him out of it, and the Army of the Potomac sullenly withdrew to the north side of the river, its morale all but ruined. The two armies glowered at each other from opposite banks of the river for several weeks; then Burnside tried to move upstream, to cross beyond Lee's left flank and fight a new battle, but three days of steady, icy rain turned the unpaved roads into bottomless mud and left his army completely bogged down. In the end the soldiers managed to pull themselves, their wagons, and their artillery out of the mire and came slogging back to camp, utterly dispirited. This fiasco was too much for everybody, and Burnside was removed from command. To all intents and purposes the Army of the Potomac was out of action for the winter.

In central Tennessee things went better, although what was gained cost a good deal more than it was worth. Rosecrans moved down to Murfreesboro, and Bragg waited for him, and on December 31 their armies fought a desperate, inconclusive battle on a desolate frozen field. Tactically, the fight presented an interesting oddity; each general prepared

A. R. Waud's drawing of Burnside's famous "Mud March" up the Rappahannock indicates the cause for an officer's humorous request for "50 men, 25 feet high, to work in mud 18 feet deep."

to hold with his right and attack with his left, and if the two plans had been carried out simultaneously the armies would have swung around like a huge revolving door. As it happened, however, Bragg's men struck first, crushing the Federal right wing and compelling Rosecrans to abandon all thought of an advance with his left. For a time it appeared that the Union army would be completely routed, but Rosecrans' center was commanded by George Thomas, and that stolid Virginian was very hard to dislodge. His corps hung on while the shattered right was re-formed far to the rear, and the sound of musket fire rose to such a deafening pitch that Confederates charging across a weedy cotton field stopped and plucked raw cotton from the open bolls and stuffed it in their ears before going on with the advance.

When night came, Rosecrans' line, which had been more or less straight at dawn, was doubled back like a jackknife with a partly opened blade, but it had not been driven from the field. Bragg notified Richmond that he had won a signal victory—and then, unaccountably, failed to renew the attack the next day. Through all of January 1 the armies faced each other, inactive; late in the afternoon of January 2 Bragg finally assailed the Union left, but his columns were broken up by Federal artillery, and at nightfall the armies were right where they had been at dawn. On January 3, again, they remained in contact, with sporadic firing along the picket lines

A panel from the Travis panorama shows Federal troops retreating before a Rebel charge at Murfreesboro on December 31.

In the above scene from the Travis panorama Union troops are cheered by the sight of General Rosecrans (right) and rally near the railroad (left).

but no real activity. Then, after dark, the unpredictable Bragg drew off in retreat, marching thirty-six miles south to Tullahoma. Rosecrans moved on into Murfreesboro, but his army was too badly mangled to go any farther. Six months would pass before it could resume the offensive.

No one quite knew who had won this battle, or what its military significance was, if indeed it had any. The Federals did occupy the field, and the Confederates had retreated, so the North accepted it as a victory; but nothing of any consequence had been gained, Bragg's army was still in position squarely across the road to Chattanooga, the key city which the Federals wanted to possess, and the only concrete result seemed to be that both armies had been immobilized for some time to come. Since the North could not possibly win the war if armies were immobilized, this victory was not quite worth the price.

The casualties had been shocking. The Federals had lost 13,000 men and the Confederates 10,000 or more—in each case, more than a fourth of the army's total strength. Few Civil War battles ever cost more or meant less.

If the Federals were to get anything at all out of the winter's operations, they would have to get it from Grant, and for a long time it did not seem that his luck was going to be any better than anybody else's.

He started out brightly enough, beginning in November

John Richards' painting, based on an engraving that appeared shortly after the Battle of Fredericksburg, shows a field hospital at which amputations are being performed directly in front of nervous reserves waiting to march.

to advance down the line of the railroad. He established a base of supplies at the town of Holly Springs, two dozen miles south of the Tennessee-Mississippi border, and went on with a methodical advance toward the town of Grenada. His progress, however, was first delayed and then brought to a complete halt by two unexpected developments—a strange case of military-political maneuvering among the Federals, and a display of highly effective aggressiveness by Confederate cavalry led by Van Dorn and Forrest.

Grant had hardly begun his advance before he began to realize that something odd was going on in the rear. He was moving so as to approach Vicksburg from the east—the only point from which that riverside stronghold could really be attacked with much hope of success. But as he moved he got persistent reports that there was also going to be an expedition straight down the river, some sort of combined army-navy operation apparently intended to break the river defenses by direct assault. He had planned no such operation, but it was going to take place in his department, and although he could get no clear information about it from Halleck, it seemed that the business would be more or less under his command if he played his cards carefully. It took him a long time to find out what was really in the wind, and when he did find out he was obliged to revise his plans.

What was in the wind was an ambitious attempt by one Major General John A. McClernand to find and to use a new route to victory. McClernand had been prominent in Democratic politics in Illinois before the war, and as a prominent "War Democrat" his standing with the administration was very high; he had been given a brigadier general's commission and then he had been made major general, and he had led troops under Grant at Fort Donelson and at Shiloh. He was not a West Pointer, and Grant considered him too erratic and opinionated for independent command, but he was a good fighter and leader of men, and on the whole his combat record was good. He had taken leave of absence late in September and had gone to Washington to see Lincoln and Stanton, and he had persuaded them that unless a conclusive victory were won soon in the Mississippi Valley, the whole Northwest might fall out of the war. Since this jibed with what they already had been told, the President and the Secretary of War listened attentively.

McClernand's proposal was unorthodox but direct. He had a solid following among the Democrats of the Northwest. He believed that he could organize enough fresh troops in that area to form a new army. With such an army, he believed, he could go straight down the Mississippi, and while Grant and the others were threshing about inland he could capture Vicksburg, opening the waterway to the sea and providing the victory which would inspire the Northwest and make possible a final Federal triumph. Lincoln and Stanton liked the idea and gave McClernand top-secret orders to go ahead. In these orders, however, they wrote an escape clause which McClernand seems not to have noticed; what McClernand did was to be done in Grant's department, and if Halleck and Grant saw fit, Grant could at any time assume over-all command over McClernand, McClernand's troops, and the entire venture.

McClernand went back to Illinois and began to raise troops, and rumors of the project trickled out. Halleck could not tell Grant just what was up, but he did his best to warn him by indirection: also, he saw to it that as McClernand's recruits were formed into regiments the regiments were sent downstream to Grant's department. In one way and another, Grant finally came to see what was going on. There was going to be an advance on Vicksburg by water, and Halleck wanted him to assume control of it; wanted him, apparently, to get it moving at once, before McClernand (for whose abilities Halleck had an abiding distrust) could himself reach the scene and take charge.

The upshot of all this was that in December Grant recast his plans. He sent his most trusted subordinate, William T. Sherman, back to Memphis, with orders to organize a striking force out of Sherman's own troops and the new levies that were coming downstream from Illinois, and to proceed down the river with it at the earliest possible date and put his men ashore a few miles north of Vicksburg. Grant, meanwhile, would bring his own army down the line of the railroad, and Pemberton could not possibly meet both threats; if he concentrated against one Federal force, the other would strike him in the rear, and since he would be outnumbered he could not possibly meet both threats at once. Sherman hurried to get things in motion, and Grant went on with his own advance.

At this point the Confederates took a hand. The General Van Dorn who had been beaten at Corinth took a cavalry force, swung in behind Grant, and captured the vast Federal supply base at Holly Springs; and at the same time Bedford Forrest rode up into western Tennessee, cutting railroads and telegraph lines, seizing enough Federal weapons, horses, and equipment to outfit the new recruits who joined him in that stoutly secessionist area, and creating vast confusion and disorganization deep in the Federal rear. In consequence,

Typical of the hardened Southerners who fought in the West were these men of the 9th Mississippi Infantry, photographed in 1861 in Florida.

Grant was brought to a standstill, and he could not get word of this to Sherman, who by now was en route to Vicksburg with 30,000 men, many of whom belonged to the absent McClernand.

So Sherman ran into trouble, because Pemberton was able to ignore Grant and give Sherman all of his attention. The Federals attacked on December 29 and were decisively repulsed, losing more than 1,700 men. Sherman withdrew to the Mississippi River, and on January 2 he was joined there by the indignant McClernand, who was beginning to realize that things were not working out quite as he had hoped. McClernand assumed command, and—for want of anything better to do—he and Sherman, with the help of the navy's gunboats, went up the Arkansas River to capture Confederate Fort Hindman: a nice little triumph, but not precisely what had been contemplated earlier. From Fort Hindman they returned to make camp on the west shore of the Mississippi at Young's Point and Milliken's Bend, some dozen miles above Vicksburg.

There, at the end of the month, Grant showed up, bringing with him most of the men with whom he had attempted the advance down the railroad. His arrival reduced McClernand to the position of a corps commander—a demotion which McClernand protested bitterly but in vain—and gave

Grant a field force which numbered between 40,000 and 50,000 men. It also gave Grant a position from which it was all but impossible even to get at the Confederate stronghold, let alone capture it.

Grant's move to the river had been inevitable. There was going to be a Federal column operating on the river, whether Grant liked it or not—Washington had settled that, and the decision was irreversible—and it was clearly unsound to try to co-ordinate that column's movements with the movements of a separate army operating in the interior of the state of Mississippi. The only sensible thing to do was concentrate everything along the river and make the best of it. But in this area geography was on the side of the Confederates.

Vicksburg occupied high ground on the east bank of the Mississippi, and it could be attacked with any chance of success only from the east or southeast. The Yazoo River entered the Mississippi a short distance north of Vicksburg, with steep bluffs along its left bank, and Pemberton had entrenched these bluffs and put troops in them; Sherman's December experience had shown the futility of trying an assault in that area. North of there, the fertile low country of the Yazoo delta ran for two hundred miles, cut by innumerable rivers, creeks, and bayous—fine land for farming, almost impossible land for an army of invasion to cross with all of its guns and supplies.

To the south things looked little better. The Louisiana shore of the Mississippi was low, swampy, intersected like the Yazoo delta by many streams, and if the army did go south it could not cross the river without many steamboats, and there did not seem to be any good way to get these past the Vicksburg batteries. Even if steamboats were available, Confederates had mounted batteries to cover most of the downstream places where a crossing might be made.

What all of this meant was that the army must somehow get east of Vicksburg in order to assault the place, and there did not seem to be any way to get east without going all the way back to Memphis and starting out again on the overland route which Grant had tried in December. This was out of the question because it would be an obvious, unmitigated confession of defeat, and an unhappy Northern public which was trying to digest the bad news from Fredericksburg and Murfreesboro probably could not swallow one more defeat.

Apparently, then, the Northern war machine was stalled, on dead center. It was perfectly possible that the Federals had broken the great Confederate counteroffensive in the fall only to let their hopes of victory die of sheer inanition during the winter. The Army of the Potomac had a new commander—Major General Joseph Hooker, handsome, cocky, a hard drinker and a hard fighter—and Hooker was doing his best to get the army back into shape. By reorganizing his supply and hospital services, shaking up the chain of command, overhauling his cavalry, and instituting a program of constant drills, Hooker was restoring morale, but it would be the middle of the spring before the army could be expected to do anything. (No one except Hooker himself was really prepared to bet that it would then fare any better against Lee than McClellan, Pope, and Burnside had fared.) At Murfreesboro lay the Army of the Cumberland, licking its wounds and recuperating. It had suffered no decline in morale, but it had been cruelly racked at Stones River, and Rosecrans was going to take his time about resuming the offensive.

It was up to Grant, even though he did seem to be stymied. He had hardly reached the Mississippi before he began to try every possible means to solve the problem which faced him. There seemed to be four possibilities. He would try them all.

Opposite Vicksburg the Mississippi made a hairpin turn. If a canal could be cut across the base of the narrow finger of land that pointed north on the Louisiana side, the Mississippi might pour through it, bypassing the city entirely. Then gunboats, transports, and everything else could float downstream unhindered, and Vicksburg would be a problem no longer. Dredges were brought down, and Sherman's corps was put to work with pick and shovel, and the canal was

The engraving above from Leslie's *magazine shows Grant's attempt to divert the Mississippi to bypass Vicksburg, an imposing but unsuccessful project.*

dug. (In the end it did not work; perversely, the Mississippi refused to enter it in any volume, and Sherman's men had done their work for nothing.)

Fifty miles upstream from Vicksburg, on the Louisiana side, a backwater known as Lake Providence lay near the river. It might be possible to cut a channel from river to lake and to deepen the chain of streams that led south from Lake Providence. If that worked, steamers could go all the way down to the Red River, coming back to the Mississippi 150 miles below Vicksburg. Using this route, the army could get east of the river, roundabout but unhindered; it also could draw supplies and substantial reinforcements from New Orleans. So this too was tried; after two months it could be seen that this was not quite going to work, partly because the shallow-draft steamers needed could not be obtained in quantity.

A good 300 miles north of Vicksburg, streams tributary to the Yazoo flowed from a deep-water slough just over the levee from the Mississippi. Cut the levee, send transports and gunboats through, get into the Yazoo, and cruise down to a landing point just above the fortified chain of bluffs;

put troops ashore there, take the fortifications in flank—and Vicksburg is taken. Engineer troops cut the levee, gunboats and transports steamed through: and where the Tallahatchie and Yalobusha rivers unite to form the Yazoo, they ran into Confederate Fort Pemberton, which was not particularly strong but was situated in a place that made it practically impregnable. It was surrounded by water, or by half-flooded bottom land, and could be attacked only from the river, and the river just here came up to the fort in a straight, narrow reach which was fully controlled by the fort's guns. The gunboats moved in to bombard, got the worst of it—and the whole expedition had to go ignominiously back to the Mississippi. The Yazoo venture was out.

A fourth possibility involved a fearfully complicated network of little streams and backwaters which could be entered from the Mississippi near the mouth of the Yazoo. Gunboats and transports might go up this chain for a hundred miles or more and, if their luck was in, safely below Fort Pemberton go on over to the Yazoo, coming down thereafter to the same place which the other expedition had tried to reach. This too was tried, with troops under Sherman and gunboats under the David Porter who had commanded Farragut's mortar boats below New Orleans. This move was a total fiasco. Porter's gunboats got hung up in streams no wider than the boats were, with an infernal tangle of willows growing up ahead to block further progress, and with busy Confederates felling trees in the rear to cut off escape. The whole fleet narrowly escaped destruction. It finally got back to the Mississippi, but it had demonstrated once and for all that this route to Vicksburg was no good.

Four chances, and four failures: and as spring came on Grant sat in the cabin of his headquarters steamer at Milliken's Bend, stared into the wreaths of cigar smoke which surrounded him, and worked out the means by which he would finally be enabled to attack Vicksburg. If he failed, his army would probably be lost, and with it the war; if he succeeded, the North would at last be on the road to victory. Either way, everything was up to him.

THE
SOUTH'S LAST
OPPORTUNITY

In the spring of 1863 the Northern grip on the Confederacy was slowly tightening; yet there was still a chance for the South to upset everything, and for a few unendurably tense weeks that chance looked very good. With Rosecrans inactive in Tennessee, and with Grant seemingly bogged down hopelessly in the steaming low country north of Vicksburg, attention shifted to the East, and it appeared that a Southern victory here might restore the bright prospects that had gone so dim in the preceding September. Robert E. Lee set out to provide that victory; winning it, he then made his supreme effort to win the one final, unattainable triumph that would bring the new nation to independence. He never came quite as close to success as men supposed at the time, but he did give the war its most memorable hour of drama.

Joe Hooker had done admirably in repairing the Army of the Potomac. He displayed genuine talents as an organizer and an executive, which was something of a surprise, for he

The painting at left by E. B. F. Julio shows the last meeting of Lee and Jackson. That evening Jackson was mortally wounded at Chancellorsville.

was believed to be a dashing heads-down fighter and nothing more. He saw to it that the routine chores of military housekeeping were performed properly, so that the men got enough to eat and lived in decent camps; he turned his cavalry corps into an outfit that could fight Jeb Stuart's boys on something like even terms; and he restored the weary army's confidence in itself. He himself had abundant confidence— too much, Mr. Lincoln suspected, for Hooker's jaunty remark that the question was not whether he could take Richmond, but simply when he would take it, struck the President as a little too optimistic. But when April came, and the spring winds dried the unpaved roads so that the armies could use them, Hooker led his troops off on a new offensive with the highest hopes.

Hooker had a greater advantage in numbers than McClellan had ever had. The manpower shortage was beginning to handicap the Confederacy. Union troops were moving about the Virginia landscape on the south side of the lower James River, apparently with aggressive intent; to hold them in check, and to keep that part of the country open so that its bacon and forage could be used, Lee had had to detach James Longstreet and most of Longstreet's army corps early that spring, and when Hooker began to move, Lee's army in and around Fredericksburg numbered hardly more than 60,-000 men of all arms. Hooker had more than twice that many, and he was handling them with strategic insight.

He would not repeat Burnside's mistake, butting head-on against the stout Confederate defenses at Fredericksburg. Instead, he left a third of his army at Fredericksburg to hold Lee's attention, and took the rest on a long swing up the Rappahannock, planning to cross that river and the Rapidan twenty-five miles away, and then march in on Lee's unprotected left and rear. He made the move competently and swiftly, and he sent his cavalry on ahead to make a sweep across Lee's lines of communication near Richmond. He would compel Lee to retreat, his own army would lie on Lee's flank when the retreat began, Lee would have to attack this army on ground of Hooker's choice—and, all in all, this might be the recipe for a resounding Union victory.

It might have worked, except for two things. At the critical moment Hooker lost his nerve—and Lee refused to act by the script which Hooker had written. What followed was one more dismal Union defeat, and the end of another of those "on to Richmond" drives that never seemed to get anywhere.

The first part of Hooker's plan went very smoothly. Hooker got more than 70,000 men established around Chancellorsville, a crossroads a dozen miles back of Lee's left flank, and his cavalry went swooping down to cut the Richmond, Fredericksburg, and Potomac Railroad farther south. But Lee ignored the cavalry raid and used Stuart's cavalry to control all of the roads around Chancellorsville, so that Hooker could not find out where the Confederates were. Worried and somewhat bewildered, Hooker called a halt and put his troops in sketchy fieldworks near Chancellorsville, instead of pushing on to the more open country half a dozen miles to the east, which was where he had originally planned to take position. Then Lee, in the most daring move of his whole career, split his army into three pieces and gave Joe Hooker an expensive lesson in tactics.

Lee left part of his men at Fredericksburg to make sure that the massed Federals there did not do anything damaging. With 45,000 men he went to Chancellorsville to face Hooker; and after making a quick size-up of the situation he gave Stonewall Jackson 26,000 of these and sent him on a long swing around Hooker's exposed right. Two hours before dusk on May 2 Jackson hit that right flank with piledriver force, shattering it to pieces, driving a whole Yankee army corps in wild rout, and knocking Hooker's army completely loose from its prepared position. Two or three days of confused and desperate fighting ensued—around Chancellorsville clearing and back at Fredericksburg, where the Federals forced a crossing and then found they could accomplish nothing in particular—and in the end Hooker beat an ignominious retreat, pulling all of his troops north of the Rappahannock. He had lost 17,000 men, he had let an army

Alfred Waud sketched the Union II Corps advancing to meet Jackson's flank attack of May 2 as the tangled remnants of the XI Corps retreat.

half the size of his own cut him to pieces, and he had handled his men so poorly that a very substantial part of his immense host had never been put into action at all. Chancellorsville was Lee's most brilliant victory. It had been bought at a heavy cost, however, for Stonewall Jackson was mortally wounded, shot down by his own troops in the confused fighting in the thickets on the night of May 2.

Once more, Lee had taken the initiative away from his Federal opponent. The next move would be his, and after conferences with President Davis and his cabinet in Richmond, that move was prepared: Lee would invade Pennsylvania, trying in the early summer of 1863 the move that had failed in the fall of 1862.

This decision may have been a mistake: a thing which is more easily seen now than at the time it was made. It would be a gamble, at best—a bet that the magnificent Army of Northern Virginia could somehow win, on Northern soil, an offensive victory decisive enough to bring the war to a close. The army was certain to be outnumbered. The thrust into the Northern heartland was certain to stir the Federals to a new effort. The business would have to be a quick, one-punch affair—a raid, rather than a regular invasion—for Confederate resources just were not adequate to a sustained campaign in Northern territory. If it failed, the Confederacy might lose its army and the war along with it. When he marched for Pennsylvania, Lee would be marching against long odds. He would have Longstreet and Longstreet's soldiers, which he had not had at Chancellorsville, but he would greatly miss Stonewall Jackson.

But the fact is that no really good move was available to him. If he stayed in Virginia, holding his ground, the North would inevitably refit the Army of the Potomac and in a month or so would come down with another ponderous offensive. That offensive might indeed be beaten back, but the process would be expensive, and the campaign would further consume the resources of war-racked Viriginia. European recognition and intervention—that will-o'-the-wisp which still flickered across the Confederate horizon—could never be won by defensive warfare. A good Confederate victory in Pennsylvania might, just possibly, bring it about.

Furthermore, the Confederacy was beginning to feel the

When Jackson made his flank attack, Hooker sent for General Sedgwick, who was at Fredericksburg with 25,000 men. Sedgwick fought his way through the Confederate lines to reach Chancellorsville. Below is a rare action photograph of a Union battery taken during the fight; at bottom is the Sunken Road near Fredericksburg after Sedgwick broke through.

To make boggy roads passable for guns and wagons, men felled trees and laid the logs side by side across them to create a corduroy surface.

pressure which Grant was applying in the Vicksburg area. An invasion of the North might very well compel the Federals to pull troops away from the Mississippi Valley; certainly a Southern victory in Pennsylvania would offset anything that might be lost in the West . . . for it was beginning to be obvious that a great deal was likely to be lost in the West, and fairly soon at that.

For Grant, having tried all of the schemes that could not work, had finally hit upon one that would work, and he was following it with an energy and a daring fully equal to Lee's own.

To get east of the river, where he could force his enemy to give battle, Grant had followed the simplest but riskiest plan of all. He would march his troops downstream on the Louisiana side of the river; he would use gunboats and transports —which first must run the gantlet of the powerful Vicksburg batteries—to get the soldiers over to the eastern shore; and then he could march to the northeast, destroying any field army that might come to face him, cutting Pemberton's lines of communication with the rest of the Confederacy, herding Pemberton's troops back inside of the Vicksburg entrenchments, and then laying siege to the place and capturing army, fortress, and all. Like Lee's move at Chancellorsville, this would be a dazzling trick if it worked. If it did not

In the Currier and Ives print above, Admiral Porter's gunboats, with transports and barges lashed to their sides, run Vicksburg's defenses.

work, the North would lose much more than it could afford to lose.

As the month of May wore on, Grant was making it work.

The area which his army would have to traverse on the Louisiana side was swampy, with a tangle of bayous and lakes in the way. The western pioneers in Grant's army were handy with the axe and the spade, and they built roads and bridges with an untaught competence that left the engineer officers talking to themselves. Downstream the army went; and downstream, too, came Admiral Porter's gunboats and enough transports to serve as ferries, after a hair-raising midnight dash past the thundering guns along the Vicksburg waterfront. The navy proved unable to beat down the Confederate defenses at Grand Gulf, twenty-five miles below Vicksburg, but Grant got his troops across a few miles farther down, flanked the Grand Gulf defenses, beat an inadequate force which Pemberton had sent down to check him, and then started out for the Mississippi state capital, Jackson, forty miles east of Vicksburg. Jackson was a supply base and railroad center; if the Richmond government sent help to Vicksburg, the help would come through Jackson, and Grant's first move was to take that piece off the board before it could be used.

Grant made his river crossing with some 33,000 men. (He

A remarkable photograph taken by a Confederate secret service agent shows Grierson's cavalry on review after the brigade reached Baton Rouge.

had more soldiers in the general area, and would have many more than 33,000 before long, but that was what he had when he started moving across the state of Mississippi.) At this time the Confederates had more troops in the vicinity than Grant had, but they never could make proper use of them; Grant's swift move had bewildered Pemberton much as Lee's had bewildered Hooker. Just before he marched downstream, Grant had ordered a brigade of cavalry to come down from the Tennessee border, riding between the parallel north-south lines of the Mississippi Central and the Mobile and Ohio railroads. This brigade was led by Colonel Benjamin H. Grierson, and it was eminently successful; it went slicing the length of the state, cutting railroads, fighting detachments of Confederate cavalry, and reaching Union lines finally at Baton Rouge. For the few days that counted most, it drew Pemberton's attention away from Grant and kept him from figuring out what the Yankees were driving at.

From Port Gibson, a town in the rear of Grand Gulf, Grant moved on Jackson. Joe Johnston was at Jackson. He had recovered from his wounds, and Davis had sent him out to take general command in the West—an assignment which Johnston did not care for, because Pemberton's and Bragg's armies, for which he now had responsibility, were widely separated, and Johnston did not see how he could control both of them at once. He was trying now to assemble enough of a force to stave Grant off and then, with Pemberton, to defeat him outright, but Grant did not give him time enough. On May 14, having driven off a Confederate detachment at the town of Raymond, Grant occupied Jackson, and Johnston, moving north, sent word to Pemberton to come east and join him. (It was clear enough to Johnston that Pemberton would lose both his army and Vicksburg if he were ever driven into his entrenchments and compelled to stand siege.)

Pemberton was in a fix. From Richmond, Davis was ordering him to hold Vicksburg at any cost; Johnston, meanwhile, was telling him to leave the place and save his army; and Pemberton, trying to do a little of both, came quickly to grief. He marched east to find Grant, heeded Johnston's orders too late and tried to swing to the northeast, and on May 16 he was brought to battle on the rolling, wooded plateau known as Champion's Hill, halfway between Vicksburg and Jackson. Grant beat him and drove him back to the west, followed hard and routed his rear guard the next day at the crossing of the Big Black River, and sent him headlong into his Vicksburg lines. Grant's army followed fast, occupying the high ground along the Yazoo River—the ground that had been the goal of all the winter's fruitless campaigning—and establishing there a secure base, where steamboats from

The water color below, by an unknown artist, is a primitive view of Grant's first unsuccessful attack on Vicksburg, shown in the background.

the North could reach it with all the supplies and reinforcements it might need. On May 19 and again on May 22 Grant made an attempt to take Vicksburg by storm. He was repulsed both times, with heavy loss, so he resorted to siege warfare. He drew lines of trenches and redoubts to face the entire length of the Confederate lines—all in all, Grant's entrenched line was fifteen miles long by the time it was finished—he detached a sufficient force eastward to hold Joe Johnston at bay, and then he settled down grimly to starve the place into submission. Johnston was building up his relieving army, but he never could make it strong enough. He had perhaps 25,000 men, and Pemberton had 30,000, but Grant was reinforced until he had 75,000, and he could handle both Pemberton and Johnston without difficulty. By the first of June, Pemberton was locked up, Johnston was helpless, and it seemed likely that Vicksburg's fall would only be a question of time.

So when Lee prepared for his own campaign, the inexorable pressure of Grant's grip on Vicksburg was an important

This photograph shows the dugouts behind the Union lines encircling Vicksburg from which sapping operations under a Rebel fort were begun.

factor in his plans. It may be that his best move then would have been to stay on the defensive in Virginia and send troops west so that Johnston could beat Grant and raise the siege of Vicksburg, but to argue so is to indulge in the second-guessing that is so simple long after the event. The move would have been very chancy, at best, and there was no guarantee that the Federals in Virginia would permit it. The Army of the Potomac had been disgracefully beaten at Chancellorsville, but it had not been disorganized, and the battle somehow had not left the depression and low morale which had followed Second Bull Run and Fredericksburg. The army would be ready for action very soon, and if it began a new campaign of invasion, Lee would need every man he could get. To send west enough troops to turn the tables on Grant might be to invite a disastrous defeat in Virginia . . . and so, in the end, the idea was dropped, and Lee prepared to head north.

Lee began his move on June 3, shifting his troops northwest from Fredericksburg behind the line of the Rappahannock River, aiming to reach the Shenandoah Valley and cross the Potomac west of the Blue Ridge. His army was divided into three corps, now: one led by the redoubtable Longstreet (who took a very dim view, incidentally, of this invasion of Pennsylvania), and the others commanded by two new lieutenant generals, Richard S. Ewell and A. P. Hill. Longstreet's corps led off, pausing at Culpeper Court House while Ewell's corps leapfrogged it and went on to drive scattered Federal detachments out of the lower Valley. Hill stayed in Fredericksburg to watch the Yankees.

The movement was made with skill, and Hooker was given no real opening for an attack on the separated segments of Lee's army. Hooker did propose, once he saw what was going on, that he himself simply march toward Richmond, in the belief that that would force Lee to return quickly enough. But Washington did not approve. Hooker's mishandling of the army at Chancellorsville had aroused the gravest distrust of his abilities; and although the administration could not quite nerve itself to remove him (he enjoyed the powerful backing of Secretary of the Treasury Salmon P. Chase), it apparently was unwilling to let him try a new offensive. Hooker was told to act strictly on the defensive, and to follow Lee wherever Lee might go.

By June 14 Lee had pulled Hill out of Fredericksburg, and the whole army was on the move, with Longstreet holding the gaps in the Blue Ridge, and Ewell, behind him, moving toward the Potomac crossings. Hooker's army was sidling toward the northwest, determined, whatever happened, to keep between Lee and Washington. Between the two armies the rival cavalry sparred and skirmished, each commander trying to get news of the enemy's army and deny to the enemy news of his own. Out of all of this sparring came a moment of inspiration to Jeb Stuart. He acted on it, and thereby helped Lee lose the campaign.

As Lee's army crossed the Potomac and wheeled eastward, Stuart and his cavalry were to move on its right flank and front, keeping Lee informed about the Union army's movements. It occurred to Stuart that he could best get his horsemen across the Potomac by riding all the way around Hooker's army—a feat which would bring Stuart much acclaim—and so Stuart, with Lee's permission, undertook to do it that way. But the Federal army occupied more ground and was much more active than Stuart had supposed, and

Hooker skillfully kept the Federal army within striking distance of Lee. Here General Doubleday's division crosses the Potomac in pursuit.

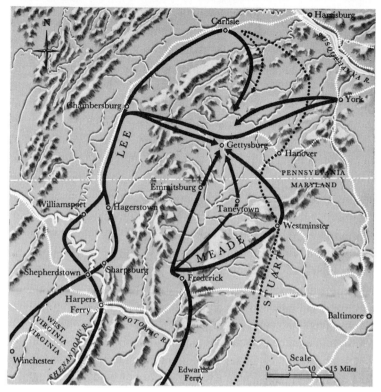

*Lee's army was spread out over 100 miles, and before concentrating at
Gettysburg some of his advance elements were as far east as York. Stuart's
ride around the Union army left Lee without a scouting force.*

Stuart, driven far to the east, was completely out of touch
with Lee for ten days. Lacking Stuart, Lee during those ten
days was completely out of touch with Hooker. Invading the
enemy's country, Lee was in effect moving blindfolded.

Lee got his army into Pennsylvania, its three corps widely
separated—the advance of the army, as June neared its end,
was at York, and the rear was at Chambersburg—and he believed that this dispersion was proper, since, as far as he
knew, Hooker had not yet come north of the Potomac.
(Stuart surely would have notified Lee if the Federals had
moved.) But the Army of the Potomac had actually crossed
the river on June 25 and 26, and on June 28 Lee learned
that the whole Yankee army was concentrated around Frederick, Maryland, squarely on his flank. He also learned that
it was Hooker's army no longer. Hooker had at last been re-

lieved, and the command had gone to the short-tempered, grizzled, and competent Major General George Gordon Meade.

Lee hastened to concentrate, and the handiest place was the town of Gettysburg. Moving north to bring him to battle, Meade collided with him there, and on July 1, 2, and 3 there was fought the greatest single battle of the war— Gettysburg, a terrible and spectacular drama which, properly or not, is usually looked upon as the great moment of decision.

In the fighting on July 1 the Federals were badly outnumbered, only a fraction of their army being present, and they were soundly beaten. On the next two days Lee attacked, striking at both flanks and at the center in an all-out effort to crush the Army of the Potomac once and for all. Nothing quite worked. The climactic moment came in the afternoon of July 3, when 15,000 men led by a division under Major General George Pickett made a gallant but doomed assault on the central Federal position on Cemetery Ridge. The assault almost succeeded, but "almost" was not good enough. Broken apart and staggered by enormous losses, the assaulting column fell back to the Confederate lines, and the Battle of Gettysburg was over. The Federals had lost 23,000 men, and the Confederates very nearly as many—which meant that Lee had lost nearly a third of his whole army. He could do nothing now but retreat. Meade followed, but his own army was too mangled, and Meade was too cautious to try to force another battle on Lee north of the Potomac. Lee got his army back into Virginia, and the campaign was over.

Stuart's absence had been expensive. (He finally reached Lee on the evening of the second day of the battle.) Lee had been forced to fight before he was ready for it, and when the fighting began he had not felt free to maneuver because, with Stuart away, he could never be sure where the Yankees were. At the close of the first day's fighting Longstreet had urged Lee to move around the Federal left flank and assume a position somewhere in the Federal rear that would force Meade to do the attacking, but with the knowledge he then

In Alexander Gardner's photograph, a dead Southern sharpshooter lies behind a stone breastwork he has built in Devil's Den, near Gettysburg. Below, Meade's trains are approaching the Potomac long after Lee has crossed the river and gotten his troops back into Virginia.

An army private made this drawing of Vicksburg's capture. White flags fly from the Confederate works as Union troops form to march into the city and the Rebel defenders march out to stack their arms.

had Lee could not be sure that such a move would not take him straight to destruction. He had felt compelled to fight where he was, and when the fighting came he desperately missed Stonewall Jackson: Ewell, leading Jackson's old troops, proved irresolute and let opportunities slip, while Longstreet was sulky and moved with less than his usual speed. All in all, Lee was poorly served by his lieutenants in the greatest battle of his career.

But if Gettysburg was what took the eye, Vicksburg was probably more important; and the climax came at Vicksburg, by odd chance, at almost exactly the same time that it came at Gettysburg. Grant's lines had grown tighter and tighter, and Pemberton's army was strained to the breaking

On November 19 Abraham Lincoln dedicated a part of the Gettysburg battlefield as a national cemetery for those who died in the battle. In this

point; and on July 3, just about the time when Pickett's men were forming for their hopeless charge, Pemberton sent a white flag through the lines and asked for terms. Grant followed the old "unconditional surrender" line, but receded from it quickly enough when Pemberton refused to go for it; and on July 4 Pemberton surrendered the city and the army, on terms which permitted his men to give their paroles and go to their homes. Halleck, back in Washington, complained that Grant should have insisted on sending the whole army north as prisoners of war, but Grant believed that this was not really necessary. The 30,000 soldiers whom Pemberton had surrendered were effectively out of the war. Vicksburg itself was taken, within a week the Confederates would surrender the downstream fortress at Port Hudson—and, as Lincoln put it, the Father of Waters would roll unvexed to the sea.

Gettysburg ruined a Confederate offensive and demonstrated that the great triumph on Northern soil which the South had to win if it was to gain recognition abroad could not be won. But Vicksburg broke the Confederacy into halves, gave the Mississippi Valley to the Union, and inflicted a wound that would ultimately prove mortal. Losing at Gettysburg, the Confederates had lost more than they could well afford to lose; at Vicksburg, they lost what they could not afford at all.

photograph, Lincoln and Edward Everett, who gave the principal address, are seated at the speakers' table, Lincoln at left of center.

THE ARMIES

The statesmen and the diplomats did their best to control and direct the war, but the real load was carried from first to last by the ordinary soldier. Poorly trained and cared for, often very poorly led, he was unmilitary but exceedingly warlike. A citizen in arms, incurably individualistic even under the rod of discipline, combining frontier irreverence with the devout piety of an unsophisticated society, he was an arrant sentimentalist with an inner core as tough as the heart of a hickory stump. He had to learn the business of war as he went along because there was hardly anyone on hand qualified to teach him, and he had to pay for the education of his generals, some of whom were all but totally ineducable. In many ways he was just like the G.I. Joe of modern days, but he lived in a simpler era, and when he went off to war he had more illusions to lose. He lost them with all proper speed, and when the fainthearts and weaklings had been winnowed out, he became one of the stoutest fighting

Their capture at Gettysburg in the summer of 1863 ended the fighting days of these three lean, tough Confederate soldiers.

men the world has ever seen. In his own person he finally embodied what the war was all about.

The first thing to remember about him is that, at least in the beginning, he went off to war because he wanted to go. In the spring of 1861 hardly any Americans in either section had any understanding of what war really was like. The Revolution was a legend, and the War of 1812 had been no more than an episode, and the war with Mexico had never gone to the heart. Right after Fort Sumter war looked like a great adventure, and the waving flags and the brass bands and the chest-thumping orators put a gloss of romance over everything; thousands upon thousands of young Northerners and Southerners hastened to enlist, feeling that they were very lucky to have the chance. Neither government was able to use all of the men who crowded the recruiting stations in those first glittering weeks, and the boys who were rejected went back home with bitter complaints. Men who went off to camp were consumed with a fear that the war might actually be over before they got into action—an emotion which, a year later, they recalled with wry grins.

In the early part of the war the camps which received these recruits were strikingly unlike the grimly efficient training camps of the twentieth century. There were militia regiments which hired civilian cooks and raised mess funds to buy better foods than the government provided. In the South a young aristocrat would as likely as not enlist as a private and enter the army with a body servant and a full trunk of spare clothing; and in the North there were volunteer regiments which were organized somewhat like private clubs—a recruit could be admitted only if the men who were already in voted to accept him. In both sections the early regiments were loaded down with baggage, as well as with many strange notions. These sons of a rawboned democracy considered it degrading to give immediate and unquestioning obedience to orders, and they had a way of wanting to debate things, or at least to have them explained, before they acted. In the South a hot-blooded young private might challenge a company officer to a duel if he felt that such a course was

Servants relieved most officers of such tiresome chores as preparing food and washing clothes. This group stopped moving long enough to pose for a photographer at Yorktown in May, 1862.

called for, and if the Northern regiments saw no duels, they at least saw plenty of fist fights between officers and men. The whole concept of taut, impersonal discipline was foreign to the recruits of 1861, and many of them never did get the idea.

The free and easy ways of the first few months were substantially toned down, of course, as time went on, and in both armies it presently dawned on the effervescent young volunteer that his commanders quite literally possessed the power of life and death over him. Yet the Civil War armies never acquired the automatic habit of immediate, unquestioning obedience which is drilled into modern soldiers. There was always a quaint touch of informality to those regiments; the men did what they were told to do, they saluted and said "Sir" and adjusted themselves to the army's eternal routine, but they kept a loose-jointed quality right down to the end, and they never got or wanted to get the snap and precision which European soldiers considered essential. The Prussian General von Moltke remarked in the 1870's that he saw no point in studying the American Civil War, because it had been fought by armed mobs, and in a way—but only in a way—he was quite right. These American armies simply did not follow the European military tradition.

One reason why discipline was imperfect was the fact that company and regimental officers were mostly either elected by the soldiers or appointed by the state governor for reasons of politics: they either were, or wanted to be, personally liked by the men they commanded, and an officer with political ambitions could see a postwar constituent in everybody in the ranks. Such men were not likely to bear down very hard, and if they did the privates were not likely to take it very well. On top of this, neither North nor South had anything resembling the officer-candidate schools of the present day. Most officers had to learn their jobs while they were performing them, and there is something pathetic in the way in which these neophytes in shoulder straps bought military textbooks and sat up nights to study them. They might be unqualified for military command, but as a general thing they were painfully conscientious, and they did their best. A regiment which happened to have a West Pointer for a colonel, or was assigned to a brigade commanded by a West Pointer, was in luck; such an officer was likely to devote a good deal of time to the instruction of his subordinates.

There is one thing to remember about Civil War discipline. In camp it was imperfect, and on the march it was seldom tight enough to prevent a good deal of straggling, but in battle it was often very good. (The discipline that will take soldiers through an Antietam, for instance, has much to be said for it, even though it is not recognizable to a Prussian martinet.) The one thing which both Northern and Southern privates demanded from their officers was the leadership and the physical courage that will stand up under fire, and the officers who proved lacking in either quality did not last very long.

The training which a Civil War soldier got included, of course, the age-old fundamentals—how to stand at attention, how to pick up and shoulder a musket, how to do a right face, and so on—but beyond this it was designed largely to teach him how to get from a formation in which he could

Above, three Union soldiers play cards. The first war sketch received by
Harper's (at center) shows Confederates at Camp Las Moras, Texas, in
March, 1861. At bottom, a shaven Union soldier is drummed out of camp.
The placard states that he stole money from a wounded friend.

march into a formation in which he could fight. A division moving along a country road would go, generally, in column of fours; moving thus, it would be a spraddled-out organism eight feet wide and a mile long. When it reached the battle-field, this organism had to change its shape completely, transforming length into width, becoming, on occasion, six feet long and a mile wide. It might form a series of lines, each line one or more regiments in width; it might temporarily throw its regiments into boxlike shapes, two companies marching abreast, while it moved from road to fighting field; if the ground was rough and badly wooded, the ten companies of a regiment might go forward in ten parallel columns, each column two men wide and forty or fifty men deep; and the fighting line into which any of these formations finally brought itself might lie at any conceivable angle to the original line of march, with underbrush and gullies and fences and swamps to interfere with its formation. Once put into action, the fighting line might have to shift to the right or left, to swing on a pivot like an immense gate, to advance or to retreat, to toss a swarm of skirmishers out in its front or on either flank—to do, in short, any one or all of a dozen different things, doing them usually under fire, and with an infernal racket making it almost impossible to hear the words of command.

A regiment which could not do these things could not

The New York Excelsior Brigade, formed in long lines, charges Rebel troops at Fair Oaks; Alfred Waud sketched the action from a description.

Edwin Forbes sketched Union artillery impeded by mud in the Wilderness.

fight efficiently, as the First Battle of Bull Run had abundantly proved. To do them, the men had to master a whole series of movements as intricate as the movements of a ballet; had to master them so that doing them became second nature, because they might have to be done in the dark or in a wilderness and almost certainly would have to be done under great difficulties of one sort or another. As a result an immense amount of drill was called for, and few generals ever considered that their men had had enough.

Oddly enough, the average regiment did not get a great deal of target practice. The old theory was that the ordinary American was a backwoodsman to whom the use of a rifle was second nature, but that had never really been true, and by 1861 it was very full of holes. (Here the Confederacy tended to have an advantage. A higher proportion of its men had lived under frontier conditions and really did know something about firearms before they entered the army.) In some cases—notably at Shiloh—green troops were actually sent into action without ever having been shown how to load their muskets; and although this was an exceptional case, very few regiments ever spent much time on a rifle range. As late as the summer of 1863 General George Gordon Meade, commanding the Army of the Potomac, felt compelled to call regimental officers' attention to the fact

The 12-pound, smoothbore, muzzle-loading cannon was the basic artillery piece on both sides. The photograph above shows the Keystone Battery.

that the army contained many soldiers who apparently had never fired their weapons in action. On the field at Gettysburg his ordnance officers had collected thousands of muskets loaded with two, three, or even ten charges; in the excitement of the fight many men had feverishly loaded and reloaded without discharging the pieces.

This musket was one great source of woe for the Civil War soldier. It looked like the old weapon of infantry tradition, but in actual fact it was a new piece, and it compelled a radical change in infantry tactics. The change was made late and slowly, and thousands of lives were lost as a result.

Infantry tactics at that time were based on the use of the smoothbore musket, a weapon of limited range and accuracy. Firing lines that were much more than a hundred yards apart could not inflict very much damage on each other, and so troops which were to make an attack would be massed together, elbow to elbow, and would make a run for it; if there were enough of them, and they ran fast enough, the defensive line could not hurt them seriously, and when they got to

Horses with their carts of ammunition chests are placed safely to the rear, and guns (one being loaded) are at ready in the foreground.

close quarters the advantage of numbers and the use of the bayonet would settle things. But the Civil War musket was rifled, which made an enormous difference. It was still a muzzle-loader, but it had much more accuracy and a far longer range than the old smoothbore, and it completely changed the conditions under which soldiers fought. An advancing line could be brought under killing fire at a distance of half a mile, now, and the massed charge of Napoleonic tradition was miserably out of date. When a defensive line occupied field entrenchments—which the soldiers learned to dig fairly early in the game—a direct frontal assault became almost impossible. The hideous casualty lists of Civil War battles owed much of their size to the fact that soldiers were fighting with rifles but were using tactics suited to smoothbores. It took the generals a long time to learn that a new approach was needed.

Much the same development was taking place in the artillery, although the full effect was not yet evident. The Civil War cannon, almost without exception, was a muzzle-loader, but the rifled gun was coming into service. It could reach farther and hit harder than the smoothbore, and for counter-battery fire it was highly effective—a rifled battery could hit a battery of smoothbores without being hit in return, and the new three-inch iron rifles, firing a ten-pound conoidal shot, had a flat trajectory and immense penetrating power. But the old smoothbore—a brass gun of four-and-one-half-inch caliber, firing a twelve-pound spherical shot—remained popular to the end of the war; in the wooded, hilly country where so many Civil War battles were fought, its range of slightly less than a mile was about all that was needed, and for close-range work against infantry the smoothbore was better than the rifle. For such work the artillerist fired canister—a tin can full of lead slugs, with a propellant at one end and a wooden disk at the other—and the can disintegrated when the gun was fired, letting the lead slugs be sprayed all over the landscape. In effect, the gun then was a huge sawed-off shotgun, and at ranges of 250 yards or less it was in the highest degree murderous.

The rifled cannon had a little more range than was ordinarily needed. No one yet had worked out any system for indirect fire; the gunner had to see his target with his own eyes, and a gun that would shoot two miles was of no especial advantage if the target was less than a mile away. Shell fuzes were often defective, and most gunners followed a simple rule: never fire over your own infantry, except in an extreme emergency. (The things were likely to go off too soon, killing friends instead of enemies.) Against fixed fortifications, or carefully prepared fieldworks, the gunners liked to use mortars, which gave them a high-angle fire they could not get from fieldpieces. They would also bring up siege guns—ponderous rifled pieces, too heavy to be used in ordinary battles, but powerful enough to flatten parapets or to knock down masonry walls. These large guns were somewhat dangerous to the user. They tended to be weak in the breech, and every now and then one of them would explode when fired.

The Federals had a big advantage in artillery, partly because of their superior industrial plant and partly because, having larger armies, they could afford to use more batteries. On most fields they had many more guns than the Confederates, with a much higher percentage of rifled pieces. (An important factor at Antietam was that Federal artillery could overpower the Confederate guns, and Southern gunners for the rest of the war referred to that fight as "artillery hell.") It appears too that Northern recruits by and large had a little more aptitude for artillery service, just as Southerners outclassed Northerners in the cavalry.

For at least the first half of the war Confederate cavalry was so much better than that of the Federals that there was no real comparison. Here the South was helped both by background and tradition. Most of its recruits came from rural areas and were used to horses; and the legends of chivalry were powerful, so that it seemed much more knightly and gallant to go off to war on horseback than in the infantry. Quite literally, the Confederate trooper rode to the wars on his own charger, cavalry horses not being government issue with the Richmond administration. In the beginning this was an advantage, for many Confederate squadrons were mounted on blooded stock that could run rings around the nags which sharpshooting traders were selling to the Yankee government. In the long run, though, the system was most harmful. A trooper who lost his horse had to provide an-

Jeb Stuart's horse artillery comes into action against an advance of Federals in Virginia. Union skirmishers are in the field at top right.

other one all by himself, and he usually could get a furlough so that he might go home and obtain one. Toward the end of the war replacements were hard to come by.

In any case, both horses and riders in the Confederate cavalry were infinitely superior to anything the Yankees could show for at least two years. There were plenty of farm boys in the Federal armies, but they did not come from a horseback country; most horses on Northern farms were draft animals, and it never occurred to a Northern farm boy that he could acquire social prestige simply by getting on a horse's back. Being well aware that it takes a lot of work to care for a horse, the Northern country boy generally enlisted in the infantry. The Union cavalry got its recruits mostly from city boys or from nonagricultural groups; and before this cavalry could do anything at all, its members had first to be taught how to stay in the saddle. Since Jeb Stuart's troopers could have taught circus riders tricks, the Yankees were hopelessly outclassed. Not until 1863 was the Army of the Potomac's cavalry able to meet Stuart on anything like even terms.

In the West matters were a little different. Here the Confederacy had a very dashing cavalry raider in the person of John Hunt Morgan, who made a number of headlines without particularly affecting the course of the war, and it had the youthful Joe Wheeler, who performed competently; but most of all it had Nathan Bedford Forrest, an untaught genius who had had no military training and who never possessed an ounce of social status, but who was probably the best cavalry leader in the entire war. Forrest simply used his horsemen as a modern general would use motorized infantry. He liked horses because he liked fast movement, and his mounted men could get from here to there much faster than any infantry could; but when they reached the field they usually tied their horses to trees and fought on foot, and they were as good as the very best infantry. Not for nothing did Forrest say that the essence of strategy was "to git thar fust with the most men." (Do not, under any circumstances whatever, quote Forrest as saying "fustest" and "mostest." He did not say it that way, and nobody who knows anything

Even the horses are in step in this painting of the 4th Pennsylvania Cavalry. The cavalry was the glamorous branch of the land services.

about him imagines that he did.) The Yankees never came up with anybody to match Forrest, and tough William T. Sherman once paid him a grim compliment: there would never be peace in western Tennessee, said Sherman, until Forrest was dead.

Aside from what a man like Forrest could do, cavalry in the Civil War was actually of secondary importance as far as fighting was concerned. It was essential for scouting and for screening an army, but as a combat arm it was declining. Cavalry skirmished frequently with other cavalry, and the skirmishes at times rose to the level of pitched battles, but it fought infantry only very rarely. It enjoyed vast prestige with the press and with back-home civilians, but neither infantry nor artillery admired it. The commonest infantry wisecrack of the war was the bitter question: "Who ever saw a dead cavalryman?"

Infantry, artillery, cavalry—these were the three major subdivisions of a Civil War army. Numerically very small, but of considerable value, were the engineer troops. They built bridges, opened roads, laid out fortifications, and performed other technical chores; pontoon trains were in their care, and they were supposed to do any mining or countermining that was done, although in actual practice this was

161

Union engineers, here building a pontoon bridge at Fredericksburg, were targets for sharpshooters, whom Longstreet called Confederate hornets.

frequently done by troops of the line. Indeed, it was the engineer officer rather than the engineer battalion that was really important. In the Northern armies the average regiment contained men of so many different skills that with proper direction they could do almost anything an engineer outfit could do; it was the special skill and ability of the trained officer that really counted. The Confederate regiments contained fewer jacks-of-all-trades, but this shortage never proved a serious handicap. At the top the South had the best engineer officer of the lot in the person of Robert E. Lee.

It is hard to get an accurate count on the numbers who served in the Civil War armies. The books show total enlistments in the Union armies of 2,900,000 and in the Confederate armies of 1,300,000, but these figures do not mean what they appear to mean. They are fuzzed up by a large number of short-term enlistments and by a good deal of duplication, and the one certainty is that neither side ever actually put that many individuals under arms. One of the best students of the matter has concluded that the Union had the equivalent of about 1,500,000 three-year enlistments, from first to last, and that the Confederates had the equivalent of about 1,000,000. Anyone who chooses may quarrel with these figures. Nobody will ever get an exact count, because the records are very confusing, and some figures are missing altogether. In any case, approximately 359,000 Federal soldiers and 258,000 Confederate soldiers lost their lives in the course of the war. These figures, to be sure, include deaths from disease as well as battle casualties, but a young man who died of dysentery is just as dead as the one who stopped a bullet, and when these figures are matched against the total possible enrollment, they are appalling.

For the unfortunate Civil War soldier, whether he came from the North or from the South, not only got into the army just when the killing power of weapons was being brought to a brand-new peak of efficiency; he enlisted in the closing years of an era when the science of medicine was woefully, incredibly imperfect, so that he got the worst of it in two ways. When he fought, he was likely to be hurt pretty badly; when he stayed in camp, he lived under conditions that were very likely to make him sick; and in either case he had almost no chance to get the kind of medical treatment which a generation or so later would be routine.

Both the Federal and Confederate governments did their best to provide proper medical care for their soldiers, but even the best was not very good. This was nobody's fault. There simply was no such thing as good medical care in that age—not as the modern era understands the expression.

Few medical men then knew why wounds become infected or what causes disease; the treatment of wounds and disease,

Below, Alfred Waud shows the grisly aftermath of war: dead soldiers are being buried and dead horses burned in the fires in the background.

Sometimes, as at top left, kindness was the only medicine available to the wounded man. At bottom left is a two-wheeled ambulance; a ride in one of these often proved fatal to the badly wounded. The hospital steward at right dispensed powders, a remedy for all ailments.

consequently, ranged from the inadequate through the useless to the downright harmful. When a man was wounded and the wound was dressed, doctors expected it to suppurate; they spoke of "laudable pus" and supposed that its appearance was a good sign. The idea that a surgical dressing ought to be sterilized never entered anyone's head; for that matter, no physician would have known what the word "sterilized" meant in such a connection. If a surgeon's instruments were so much as rinsed off between operations at a field hospital, the case was an exception.

In camp, diseases like typhoid, dysentery, and pneumonia were dreaded killers. No one knew what caused them, and

Soldiers of both armies learned to relieve the monotony of salt pork, hard-tack, and coffee by foraging, which often was simply looting and pillaging. The men above, yearning for a taste of sweet, have been routed by a swarm of bees while trying to seize the hive.

no one could do much for them when they appeared. Doctors had discovered that there was some connection between the cleanliness of a camp and the number of men on sick call, but sanitation was still a rudimentary science, and if a water supply was not visibly befouled or odorous, it was thought to be perfectly safe. The intestinal maladies that took so heavy a toll were believed due to "miasmic odors" or to even more subtle emanations in the air.

So the soldier of the 1860's had everything working against him. In his favor there was a great deal of native toughness, and a sardonic humor that came to his rescue when things were darkest; these, and an intense devotion to

Off-duty Confederate soldiers (above) entertain themselves during one of the many long waits between battles. In the center is the kitchen of Frémont's Dragoons, set up on the fairgrounds at Tipton, Missouri. At bottom, Rebel soldiers watch with interest as a bullock is killed; the animal may or may not have been confiscated from a Southern farmer.

the cause he was serving. Neither Yank nor Reb ever talked very much about the cause; to listen to eloquence on the issues of the war, one had to visit cities behind the lines, read newspapers, or drop in on Congress, either in Washington or in Richmond, because very little along that line was ever heard in camp. The soldier had ribald mockery for high-flown language, and he cared very little for the patriotic war songs which had piped him down to the recruiting office in the first place. In his off hours, at camp or in bivouac, he was a sentimentalist, and one of the most typical of all Civil War scenes is the campfire group of an evening, supper finished, chores done, darkness coming on, with dim lights flickering and homesick young men singing sad little songs like "Lorena" or "Tenting Tonight." No matter which army is looked at, the picture is the same. On each side the soldier realized that he personally was getting the worst of it, and when he had time he felt very sorry for himself. . . . But mostly he did not have the time, and his predominant mood was never one of self-pity. Mostly he was ready for whatever came to him.

A Confederate picket watches for the enemy, bayonetted gun at the ready.

TWO
ECONOMIES
AT WAR

The inner meaning of Gettysburg was not immediately visible. It had been a fearful and clamorous act of violence, a physical convulsion that cost the two armies close to 50,000 casualties, the most enormous battle that had ever been fought on the North American continent, and all men knew that; but the deep mystic overtones of it, the qualities that made this, more than any other battle, stand for the final significance of the war and the war's dreadful cost— these were realized slowly, fully recognized only after Abraham Lincoln made them explicit in the moving sentences of the Gettysburg Address.

In that speech Lincoln went to the core of the business. The war was not merely a test of the Union's cohesive strength, nor was it just a fight to end slavery and to extend the boundaries of human freedom. It was the final acid test of the idea of democracy itself; in a way that went far beyond anything which either government had stated as its war aims,

Some 3,000 cannon for the Union armies were manufactured at the West Point foundry at left, painted by John Ferguson Weir.

the conflict was somehow a definitive assaying of the values on which American society had been built. The inexplicable devotion which stirred the hearts of men, displayed in its last full measure on the sun-scorched fields and slopes around Gettysburg, was both the nation's principal reliance and something which must thereafter be lived up to. Gettysburg and the war itself would be forever memorable, not merely because so many men had died, but because their deaths finally did mean something that would be a light in the dark skies as long as America should exist.

. . . Thus Lincoln, considering the tragedy with the eyes of a prophet. Yet while the mystical interpretation may explain the meaning of the ultimate victory, it does not explain the victory itself. The Confederate soldier had fully as much selfless devotion as the Unionist, and he risked death with fully as much heroism; if the outcome had depended on a comparison of the moral qualities of the men who did the fighting, it would be going on yet, for the consecration that rests on the parked avenues at Gettysburg derives as much from the Southerner as from the Northerner. The war did not come out as it did because one side had better men than the other. To understand the process of victory it is necessary to examine a series of wholly material factors.

Underneath everything there was the fact that the Civil War was a modern war: an all-out war, as that generation understood the concept, in which everything that a nation has and does must be listed with its assets or its debits. Military striking power in such a war is finally supported, conditioned, and limited by the physical scope and vitality of the basic economy. Simple valor and devotion can never be enough to win, if the war once develops past its opening stages. And for such a war the North was prepared and the South was not prepared: prepared, not in the sense that it was ready for the war—neither side was in the least ready—but in the resources which were at its disposal. The North could win a modern war and the South could not. Clinging to a society based on the completely archaic institution of slavery, the South for a whole generation had been making a valiant attempt to reject the industrial revolution, and this attempt had involved it at last in a war in which the industrial revolution would be the decisive factor.

To a Southland fighting for its existence, slavery was an asset in the farm belt. The needed crops could be produced even though the army took away so many farmers, simply because slaves could keep plantations going with very little help. But in all other respects the peculiar institution was a terrible handicap. Its existence had kept the South from developing a class of skilled workers; it had kept the South rural, and although some slaves were on occasion used as factory workers, slavery had prevented the rise of industrialism. Now, in a war whose base was industrial strength, the South was fatally limited. It could put a high percentage of its adult white manpower on the firing line, but it lacked the economic muscle on which the firing line ultimately was based. Producing ample supplies of food and fibers, it had to go hungry and inadequately clad; needing an adequate distributive mechanism, it was saddled with railroads and highways which had never been quite good enough and which now could not possibly be improved or even maintained.

The North bore a heavy load in the war. The proliferating casualty lists reached into every community, touching nearly every home. War expenditures reached what then seemed to be the incomprehensible total of more than two million dollars a day. Inflation sent living costs rising faster than the average man's income could rise. War profiteers were numerous and blatant, and at times the whole struggle seemed to be waged for their benefit; to the very end of the war there was always a chance that the South might gain its independence, not because of victories in the field but because the people in the North simply found the burden too heavy to carry any longer.

Yet with all of this the war brought to the North a period of tremendous growth and development. A commercial and industrial boom like nothing the country had imagined before took place. During the first year, to be sure, times were hard: the country had not entirely recovered from the Panic

171

of 1857, and when the Southern states seceded the three hundred million dollars which Southerners owed to Northern businessmen went up in smoke, briefly intensifying the depression in the North. But recovery was rapid; the Federal government was spending so much money that no depression could endure, and by the summer of 1862 the Northern states were waist-deep in prosperity.

In the twentieth century boom times often leave the farmer out in the cold, but it was not so during the Civil War. The demand for every kind of foodstuff seemed insatiable. Middle-western farmers, who used to export corn and hogs to Southern plantation owners, quickly found that government requirements more than offset the loss of that market—which, as a matter of fact, never entirely vanished; a certain amount of intersectional trade went on throughout the war, despite efforts by both governments to check it.

Not only were grain and meat in demand, but the government was buying more leather than ever before—marching armies, after all, need shoes, and the hundreds of thousands of horses and mules used by the armies needed harness—and the market for hides was never better. A textile industry which could not get a fraction of all the cotton it wanted turned increasingly to the production of woolen fabrics (here likewise government requirements had skyrocketed), and the market for raw wool was never livelier. Taking everything into consideration, there had never before been such a prodigious rise in the demand for all kinds of Northern farm produce.

This increased demand Northern farms met with effortless ease. There might have been a crippling manpower shortage, because patriotic fervor nowhere ran stronger than in the farm belt and a high percentage of the able-bodied men had gone into the army. But the war came precisely when the industrial revolution was making itself felt on the farm. Labor-saving machinery had been perfected and was being put into use—a vastly improved plow, a corn planter, the two-horse cultivator, mowers and reapers and steam-driven threshing machines—all were available now, and under the

The North raised more corn and wheat than it could use, so the excess was shipped to Europe. In this photograph a forest of masts, symbolic of the Union's commerce, chokes New York's East River waterfront.

pressure of the war the farmer had to use them. Until 1861 farm labor had been abundant and cheap, and these machines made their way slowly; now farm labor was scarce and high-priced, and the farmer who turned to machinery could actually expand his acreage and his production with fewer hands.

The expansion of acreage was almost automatic. All along the frontier, and even in the older settled areas of the East, there was much good land that had not yet been brought into agricultural use. Now it was put into service, and as this happened the government confidently looked toward the future. It passed, in 1862, the long-sought Homestead Act, which virtually gave away enormous quantities of land, in family-sized chunks, to any people who were willing to cultivate it. (The real effect of this was felt after the war rather than during it, but the act's adoption in wartime was symptomatic.) Along with this came the Morrill Land Grant Act, which offered substantial Federal support to state agricultural colleges, and which also was passed in 1862. In the

In the woodcut above, John Bull vainly attempts to retain British labor. During the war the pace of immigration slowed but never halted as hundreds of thousands of Europeans sought a new life in America.

middle of the war the government was declaring that all idle land was to be made available for farming, and that the American farmer was going to get the best technical education he could be given.

As acreage increased, with the aid of laborsaving machinery, the danger of a really crippling manpower shortage vanished; indeed, it probably would have vanished even without the machinery, because of the heavy stream of immigration from Europe. During 1861 and 1862 the number of immigrants fell below the level of 1860, but thereafter the European who wanted to come to America apparently stopped worrying about the war and concluded that America was still the land of promise. During the five years 1861–65 inclusive, more than 800,000 Europeans came to America; most of them from England, Ireland, and Germany. In spite of heavy casualty lists, the North's population increased during the war.

With all of this, the Northern farm belt not only met wartime needs for food and fibers, but it also helped to feed Great Britain. More than 40 per cent of the wheat and flour imported into Great Britain came from the United States. The country's wheat exports tripled during the war, as if it was Northern wheat rather than Southern cotton that was king.

But if the farms enjoyed a war boom, Northern industry had a growth that was almost explosive. Like the farmer, the manufacturer had all sorts of new machinery available—new machinery, and the mass-production techniques that go with machinery—and the war took all limits off his markets. The armies needed all manner of goods: uniforms, underwear, boots and shoes, hats, blankets, tents, muskets, swords, revolvers, cannon, a bewildering variety of ammunition, wagons, canned foods, dressed lumber, shovels, steamboats, surgical instruments, and so on. During the first year industry was not geared to turn out all of these things in the quantities required, and heavy purchases were made abroad while new factories were built, old factories remodeled, and machinery acquired and installed. By 1862 the government practically stopped buying munitions abroad, because its own manufacturers could give it everything it wanted.

The heavy-goods industries needed to support all of this production were available. One of the lucky accidents that worked in favor of American industry in this war was the fact that the canal at Sault Sainte Marie, Michigan, had been built and put into service a few years before the war, and the unlimited supply of iron ore from the Lake Superior ranges could be brought down to the furnaces inexpensively. Pittsburgh was beginning to be Pittsburgh, with foundries that could turn out cannon and mortars, railroad rails, iron plating for warships or for locomotives—iron, in short, for every purpose, iron enough to meet the most fantastic demands of wartime.

There was a railroad network to go with all of this. Dur-

Herman Haupt served as chief of U.S. military rail transportation. An expert on railroad construction, Haupt scorned military red tape to get his job done. He stands at right, directing work on a Virginia line.

ing the 1850's the Northern railroad network had been somewhat overbuilt, and many carriers had been having a hard time of it in 1860, but the war brought a heavy traffic that forced the construction of much new mileage. New locomotives and cars were needed, and the facilities to build them were at hand. The Civil War was the first of the "railroad wars," in a military sense, and the Northern railway nexus enabled the Federal government to switch troops back and forth between the Eastern and Western theaters of action with a facility the South could never match.

Altogether, it is probable that the Civil War pushed the North into the industrial age a full generation sooner than would otherwise have been the case. It was just ready to embrace the factory system in 1861, but without the war its development would have gone more slowly. The war provided a forced draft that accelerated the process enormously. By 1865 the northeastern portion of America had become an industrialized nation, with half a century of development compressed into four feverish years.

One concrete symbol of this was the speedy revision of tariff rates. Southern members had no sooner left the Congress than the low tariff rates established in 1857 came in for revision. A protective tariff was adopted, partly to raise money for war purposes but chiefly to give manufacturers what they wanted, and the policy then adopted has not since been abandoned.

The North had little trouble in financing the war. As in more modern times, it relied heavily on war loans, to float which Secretary Chase got the aid—at a price—of the Philadelphia banker Jay Cooke. Cooke sold the bonds on commission, with a flourish very much like the techniques of the 1940's, and during the war more than two billion dollars' worth were marketed. Congress also authorized the issuance of some four hundred and fifty million dollars in "greenbacks"—paper money, made legal tender by act of Congress but secured by no gold reserve. The value of these notes fluctuated, dropping at times to no more than forty cents in gold, but the issue did provide a circulating medium of exchange. More important was the passage in 1863 of a National Bank Act, which gave the country for the first time a national currency.

Wartime taxes were moderate by present-day standards, but the Federal government had never before levied many taxes, and at the time they seemed heavy. There was a long string of excise taxes on liquor, tobacco, and other goods; there were taxes on manufacturers, on professional men, on railroads and banks and insurance companies, bringing in a total of three hundred million dollars. There was also an income tax, although it never netted the Federal treasury any large sums. One point worth noting is that the supply of precious metals in the country was always adequate, thanks to the California mines and to lodes developed in other parts of the West, notably in Colorado and Nevada.

It remains to be said that the North's war-born prosperity was not evenly distributed. Prices, as usual, rose much faster than ordinary incomes: in the first two years of the war wages rose by 10 per cent and prices by 50 per cent, and people who lived on fixed incomes were squeezed by wartime inflation. In such places as the Pennsylvania coal fields there was a good deal of unrest, leading to labor troubles which, in the eyes of the government, looked like outbreaks of secessionist sympathy, but which actually were simply protests

A Union construction corps sets up a bakery at City Point, Virginia, for the siege of Petersburg. The North supplied its troops generously.

against intolerable working conditions. There were many war profiteers, some of them men apparently devoid of all conscience, who sold the government large quantities of shoddy uniforms, cardboard shoes, spavined horses, condemned weapons imperfectly reconditioned, and steamboats worth perhaps a tenth of their price, and these men did not wear their new wealth gracefully. The casualty lists produced by such battles as Stones River and Gettysburg were not made any more acceptable by the ostentatious extravagance with which the war contractors spent their profits. Yet it was not all ugly. Some of the war money went to endow new colleges and universities, and such war relief organizations as the U.S. Sanitary Commission and the Christian Commission got millions to spend on their work for the soldiers.

Thus it was in the North, where an economy capable of supporting a modern war was enormously expanded by war's stimulus. In the South the conditions were tragically reversed. Instead of expanding under wartime pressures, the Southern economy all but collapsed. When the war began, the Confederacy had almost nothing but men. The men were as good as the very best, but their country simply could not support them, although the effort it made to do so was heroic and ingenious. The South was not organized for war or for independent existence in any of the essential fields—not in manufacturing, in transportation, or in finance—and it never was able during the course of the war to remedy its deficiencies.

Until 1861 the South had been almost strictly an agricultural region, and its agricultural strength rested largely on cotton. The vain hope that England and France would intervene in order to assure their own supplies of raw cotton— the hoary "cotton is king" motif—kept the Confederacy from sending enough cotton overseas during the first year of the war to establish adequate credit, and the munitions and other manufactured goods that might have been imported then appeared only in a trickle. When the government finally saw that its rosy expectations were delusions and changed its policy, the blockade had become effective enough to thwart its aims. As a result the South was compelled to remake its entire economy. It had to achieve self-sufficiency, or something very close to it, and the job was humanly impossible.

A valiant effort was made, and in retrospect the wonder is not that it failed but that it accomplished so much. To a great extent the South's farmers shifted from the production of cotton to the growth of foodstuffs. Salt works were established (in the days before artificial refrigeration salt was a military necessity of the first importance, since meat could not be preserved without it), and textile mills and processing plants were built. Powder mills, armories, and arsenals were constructed, shipyards were established, facilities to make boiler plate and cannon were expanded, and the great Tredegar Iron Works at Richmond became one of the busiest factories in America. Moonshiners' stills were collected for the copper they contained, sash weights were melted

A symbol of Richmond's industrial importance was the Virginia Armory. Its capacity was 5,000 small arms per month, the largest in the South.

down to make bullets, all sorts of expedients were resorted to for saltpeter; and out of all these activities, together with the things that came in through the blockade and war material which not infrequently was captured from the Yankee soldiers and supply trains, the South managed to keep its armies in the field for four years.

But it was attempting a job beyond its means. It was trying to build an industrial plant almost from scratch, without enough capital, without enough machinery or raw materials, and with a desperate shortage of skilled labor. From first to last it was hampered by a badly inadequate railway transportation network, and the situation here got progressively worse because the facilities to repair, to rebuild, or even properly to maintain the railroads did not exist. From the beginning of the war to the end, not one mile of railroad rail was produced in the Confederacy; when a new line had to be built, or when war-ruined track had to be rebuilt, the rails had to come from some branch line or side track. The situation in regard to rolling stock was very little better. When 20,000 troops from the Army of Northern Virginia were sent to northern Georgia by rail in the fall of 1863, a Confederate general quipped that never before had such good soldiers been moved so far on such terrible railroads. Much of the food shortage which plagued Confederate armies and civilians alike as the war grew old came not from any lack of production but from simple inability to move the products from farm to ultimate consumer.

To make matters worse, there was constant and increasing

Federal interference with the resources the South did have. The Union armies' advance up the Tennessee and Cumberland rivers in the winter of 1862 meant more than a simple loss of territory for the Confederacy. It put out of action a modest industrial network; there were ironworks, foundries, and small manufacturing plants in western Tennessee which the South could not afford to lose. The early loss of such cities as New Orleans, Nashville, and Memphis further reduced manufacturing capacity. Any Union army which got into Confederate territory destroyed railway lines as a matter of course. If the soldiers simply bent the rails out of shape, and then went away, the rails could quickly be straightened and re-used; as the war progressed, however, the Federals developed a system of giving such rails a spiral twist, which meant that they were of no use unless they could be sent to a rolling mill . . . of which the Confederacy had very few.

Increasingly, the war for the Confederates became a process of doing without. Until the end the soldiers had the guns and ammunition they needed, but they did not always have much of anything else. Confederate soldiers made a practice of removing the shoes, and often the clothing, of dead or captured Federals out of sheer necessity, and it was frequently remarked that the great *élan* which the Southern soldier displayed in his attacks on Federal positions came at least partly from his knowledge that if he seized a Yankee camp he would find plenty of good things to eat.

As in the North, there were war profiteers in the South, although there were not nearly so many of them, and they

Workers repair an Orange and Alexandria Railroad bridge at Bull Run. The bridge had been destroyed by Jackson to cut Pope's supply line.

put on pretty much the same sort of display. The blockade-runners brought in luxury goods as well as necessities, and the Southerner who had plenty of money could fare very well. Few people qualified in this respect, but the ones who did qualify and who chose to spend their money on themselves found all kinds of things to buy.

Perhaps the shortage that hit the Confederacy hardest of all was the shortage—or, rather, the absolute lack—of a sound currency. This compounded and intensified all of the other shortages; to a nation which could neither produce all it needed nor get the goods which it did produce to the places where they were wanted, there came this additional, crushing disaster of leaping inflation. As a base for Confederate currency the new government possessed hardly more than one million dollars in specie. Credit resources were strictly limited, and an adequate system of taxation was never devised. From the beginning the nation put its chief reliance on printing-press money. This deteriorated rapidly, and kept on deteriorating, so that by 1864 a Confederate dollar had a gold value of just five cents. (By the end of 1864 the value had dropped very nearly to zero.) Prices went up, and wages and incomes were hopelessly outdistanced. It was in the South during the Civil War that men made the wisecrack that was re-used during Germany's inflation in the 1920's—that a citizen went to market carrying his money in a basket and came home with the goods he had bought in his wallet.

Under such conditions government finances got into a hopeless mess. One desperate expedient was a 10 per cent "tax in kind" on farm produce. This did bring needed corn and pork in to the armies, but it was one of the most unpopular taxes ever levied, and it contributed largely to the progressive loss of public confidence in the Davis administration. To supply its armies, the government at times had to wink at violations of its own laws. It strictly prohibited the export of raw cotton to Yankee consumers, for instance, but now and then it carefully looked the other way when such deals were made: the Yankees might get the cotton, but in

Adalbert Volck drew Confederates smuggling medicines across the lines; they could sometimes be obtained from Rebel sympathizers in the North.

return the Southern armies could sometimes get munitions and medicines which were otherwise unobtainable.

By the spring of 1865, when the military effort of the Southland was at last brought to a halt, the Confederate economy had suffered an all but total collapse. The nation was able to keep an army in the field at all only because of the matchless endurance and determination of its surviving soldiers. Its ability to produce, transport, and pay for the necessities of national life was almost entirely exhausted; the nation remained on its feet only by a supreme and despairing effort of will, and it moved as in a trance. Opposing it was a nation which the war had strengthened instead of weakened —a nation which had had much the greater strength to begin with and which had now become one of the strongest powers on the globe. The war could end only as it did end. The Confederacy died because the war had finally worn it out.

THE

DESTRUCTION

OF SLAVERY

A singular fact about modern war is that it takes charge.
Once begun it has to be carried to its conclusion, and
carrying it there sets in motion events that may be beyond
men's control. Doing what has to be done to win, men perform acts that alter the very soil in which society's roots are
nourished. They bring about infinite change, not because
anyone especially wants it, but because all-out warfare destroys so much that things can never again be as they used to
be.

In the 1860's the overwhelming mass of the people, in the
North and in the South, were conservatives who hated the
very notion of change. Life in America had been good and it
had been fairly simple, and most people wanted to keep it
that way. The Northerner wanted to preserve the old Union,
and the Southerner wanted to preserve the semifeudal society in which he lived; and the unspoken aim in each section was to win a victory which would let people go back to

*The precipitous summit of Lookout Mountain, overlooking Chattanooga,
was photographed after its capture by Union troops in November, 1863.*

what they had had in a less turbulent day. But after a war which cuts as deeply and goes on as long as the Civil War, no one "goes back" to anything at all. Everybody goes on to something new, and the process is guided and accelerated by the mere act of fighting.

One trouble was that once this war was well begun there was no way, humanly speaking, to work out a compromise peace. The thing had to end in total victory for one side or the other: in a completely independent Confederacy, or in a completely restored Union and the final evaporation of the theory of the right of secession. The longer the war went on and the more it cost, the less willing were patriots on either side to recede from this position. The heroic dead, who were so tragically numerous and who had died for such diametrically opposite causes, must not have died in vain, and only total victory would justify what had been done. And because total victory was the only thinkable outcome, men came to feel that it was right to do anything at all that might bring victory nearer. It was right to destroy railroads, to burn factories and confiscate supplies of food or other raw materials, to seize or ruin any kind of property which was helpful to the enemy.

This feeling rested with especial weight on the North because the North was of necessity the aggressor. The Confederacy existed and it had to be destroyed—not merely brought to the point where its leaders were willing to talk about peace, but destroyed outright. It had to be made incapable of carrying on the fight; both its armies and the industrial and economic muscle which supported them must be made helpless. And so the North at last undertook to wipe out the institution of human slavery.

Lincoln had made this official with the Emancipation Proclamation, but that strange document had to be ratified by the tacit consent of the people at home and by the active endorsement of the soldiers in the field. And most of the soldiers had not, in the beginning, felt very strongly about slavery. There were, to be sure, many regiments of solid antislavery sentiment: New Englanders, many of the German

Wesley Merritt's Union cavalry raids a farm in Virginia east of the Shenandoah Valley, burning buildings and confiscating livestock.

levies, and certain regiments from abolitionist areas in the Middle West. But these were in a minority. The average Federal soldier began his term of service either quite willing to tolerate slavery in the South or definitely in sympathy with it. He was fighting for the Union and for nothing more. Lincoln's proclamation was not enthusiastically accepted by all of the troops. A few regiments, from border states or from places like southern Illinois and Indiana where there were close ties of sentiment and understanding with the South, came close to mutiny when the document was published, and a good many more grew morose with discontent.

Yet in the end all of the army went along with the new program; became, indeed, the sharp cutting edge that cut slavery down. This happened, quite simply, because the Federal armies that were being taught to lay their hands on any property which might be of service to the Confederate nation realized that the most accessible and most useful property of all was the Negro slave. They had little sympathy with the slave as a person, and they had no particular objection to the fact that he was property; indeed, it was his very status as property which led them to take him away from his owners and to refer to him as "contraband." As property, he supported the Southern war effort. As property, therefore, he was to be taken away from his owners, and when he was taken away, the only logical thing to do with him was to set him free.

The war, in other words, was taking charge. To save the Union the North had to destroy the Confederacy, and to destroy the Confederacy it had to destroy slavery. The Federal armies got the point and behaved accordingly. Slavery was doomed, not so much by any proclamation from Washington as by the necessities of war. The soldiers killed it because it got in their way. Perhaps the most profound miscalculation the Southern leaders ever made was that slavery could be defended by force of arms. By the middle of the nineteenth century slavery was too fragile for that. It could exist only by the tolerance of people who did not like it, and war destroyed that tolerance.

So where the Northern armies went, slavery went out of existence. In Virginia this meant little, partly because in

Slaves with their belongings flee a Tennessee manor house in order to follow a column of the Army of the Cumberland, visible in the distance.

Virginia the Federal armies did not go very far, and partly because in the fought-over country most Southerners got their slaves off to safety as fast as they could. But in the West, in Tennessee and northern Mississippi and Alabama, Federal armies ranged far, destroying the substance of the land as they ranged. They burned barns, consuming or wasting the contents. They burned unoccupied homes, and sometimes rowdy stragglers on the fringes of the armies burned occupied homes as well; they seized any cotton that they found, they broke bridges and tore up railway tracks and ruined mills and ironworks and similar installations . . . and they killed slavery. Grim General Sherman, the author of so much of this destruction, remarked not long after the victory at Vicksburg that all the powers of the earth could no more restore slaves to the bereaved Southerners than they could restore their dead grandfathers. Wherever Union armies moved, they were followed by long lines of fugitive slaves— unlettered folk who did not know what the war was about and could not imagine what the future held, but who dimly sensed that the road trodden by the men in blue was the road to freedom.

Neither the soldiers nor the generals were entirely happy about this increasing flood of refugees. In a clumsy, makeshift manner camps were set up for them; thousands of the refugees died, of hunger or disease or simple neglect, but most of them survived—survived in such numbers that the Federals had to do something about them. Negro labor could be used to build roads or fortifications, to harvest cotton in plantations that lay inside the Union lines, to perform all manner of useful military chores about the camps.

The refugee camps needed guards, to keep intruders out and to police the activities of the refugees themselves, and the Federal soldiers almost unanimously objected to performing such service. (They had enlisted to save the Union, not to guard a milling herd of bewildered Negroes.) It seemed logical, after a time, to raise guard detachments from among the Negroes themselves, outfitting them with castoff army uniforms. Then it appeared that the immense reserve of manpower represented by the newly freed slaves might be put to more direct use, and at last the government authorized, and even encouraged, the organization of Negro regiments, to be officered by whites but to be regarded as troops of the line, available for combat duty if needed.

To this move the soldiers made a good deal of objection —at first. Then they began to change their minds. They did not like Negroes, for race prejudice of a malignity rarely seen today was very prevalent in the North at that time, and they did not want to associate with them on anything remotely like terms of equality, but they came to see that much might be said for Negro regiments. For one thing, a great many enlisted men in the Northern armies could win officers' commissions in these regiments, and a high private who saw a chance to become a lieutenant or a captain was likely to lose a great deal of his antagonism to the notion of Negro soldiers. More important than this was the dawning realization that the colored soldier could stop a Rebel bullet just as well as a white soldier could, and when he did so, some white soldier who would otherwise have died would go on living. . . . And so by the middle of 1863 the North was raising numbers of Negro regiments, and the white soldiers who had been so bitter about the idea adjusted themselves rapidly.

All told, the Federals put more than 150,000 Negroes into uniform. Many of these regiments were used only for garrison duty, and in many other cases the army saw to it that the colored regiments became little more than permanent fatigue details to relieve white soldiers of hard work, but some units saw actual combat service and in a number of instances acquitted themselves well. And there was an importance to this that went far beyond any concrete achievements on the field of battle, for this was the seed of further change. The war had freed the slave, the war had put freed slaves into army uniforms—and a permanent alteration in the colored man's status would have to come out of that fact. A man who had worn the country's uniform and faced death in its service could not, ultimately, be anything less than a full-fledged

This guard detail of the 107th U.S. Colored Infantry posed at Fort Corcoran, near Washington. The regiment saw action late in the war.

citizen, and it was going to be very hard to make citizens out of some Negroes without making citizens out of all.

The armies moved across the sun-baked American landscape in the summer of 1863, trying to preserve the cherished past and actually breaking a way into the unpredictable future; and after Gettysburg and Vicksburg the center of attention became central Tennessee and northern Georgia, where the chance of war gave the South one more opportunity to restore the balance.

Nothing of much consequence would happen just now in Virginia. Both armies had been badly mangled at Gettysburg, and the rival commanders were being very circumspect. Lee had not the strength to make a real offensive campaign, and Meade was little better off; the two maneuvered up and down around the Orange and Alexandria Railroad, sparring for position, neither one willing to bring on a stand-up fight unless he could do so to real advantage, each one careful to give the other no opening. There were skirmishes, cavalry engagements, and now and then sharp actions between parts of the armies, but nothing really important took place, and as the summer gave way to fall it became apparent that there would not be a really big campaign in Virginia before 1864.

In Mississippi there was a similar lull. After the capture of

Vicksburg, Grant wanted to go driving on. There was nothing in the South that could stop his army, and he believed that he could sweep through southern Mississippi and Alabama, taking Mobile and compelling Bragg to hurry back from in front of Chattanooga. The authorities in Washington, however, clung to the notion that the important thing in this war was to occupy Southern territory, and Grant was compelled to scatter his trooops. Some of them he had to send to Louisiana, where Major General Nathaniel P. Banks was preparing to invade Texas. Others went to Missouri and to Arkansas, and those that were left were engaged in garrison duty in western Tennessee and Mississippi, occupying cities and guarding railroad lines, effectively immobilized.

Virginia and Mississippi were, so to speak, the wings of the war front. The center was in middle Tennessee, where Rosecrans with the Army of the Cumberland faced Bragg with the Army of Tennessee; and at the end of June Rosecrans at last began to move, hoping to seize Chattanooga and thus to make possible Federal occupation of Knoxville and eastern Tennessee—a point in which President Lincoln was greatly interested, because eastern Tennessee was a stronghold of Unionist sentiment.

Rosecrans made his move late, but when he did so he moved with much skill. Bragg, covering Chattanooga, had weakened his force sending troops to Joe Johnston, and in his position around the town of Tullahoma he had perhaps 47,000 men, of which a disproportionate number were cavalry. (Forrest's cavalry though, mostly, and hence of value against infantry.) The Confederates held good defensive ground, and considering everything Rosecrans' field force of 60,000 was none too large for the job at hand.

Old Rosy, as his troops called him, feinted smartly and moved with speed. He made as if to swing around Bragg's left flank, then sliced off in the opposite direction, and despite seventeen consecutive days of rain his troops got into the rear of Bragg's right before Bragg realized what was going on. Rosecrans bluffed an attack and then slipped off on another flanking movement, and Bragg found himself

Closing in on Chattanooga, the Federals cross the Tennessee River near Stevenson, Alabama. Rosecrans is shown at left, waving his sword.

compelled to retreat. By July 4 the Confederate army was back in Chattanooga, and Rosecrans, calling in vain for reinforcements (the government was sending pieces of Grant's army off in all directions, but somehow it could not spare any for Rosecrans), was trying to find a line of advance that would force Bragg to retreat still farther. He presently found it, and in August he made an unexpected crossing of the Tennessee River thirty miles west of Chattanooga. Establishing a base of supplies at Bridgeport, Alabama, on the Tennessee, Rosecrans moved over into a mountain valley with nothing between him and Chattanooga but the long rampart of Lookout Mountain. Refusing to make a frontal assault on Bragg's defensive position, he then went southeast, going through a series of gaps in Lookout Mountain and heading for the Western and Atlantic Railroad, which ran from Chattanooga to Atlanta and was Bragg's supply line. Bragg had to evacuate Chattanooga, Union troops entered the place, and Old Rosy had completed a brilliant and virtually bloodless campaign.

The only trouble was that Rosecrans did not know that he had completed it. He might have concentrated in Chattanooga, paused to renew his supplies and let his hard-marching army catch its breath, and then he could have advanced down the railroad line to good effect. Instead, he tried to keep on going, and as he moved through the mountain passes his three army corps became widely separated. Furthermore, Bragg had stopped retreating and was making a stand at La Fayette, Georgia, about twenty-five miles from Chattanooga, awaiting reinforcements. These he was getting; troops from Knoxville, from Mississippi, and two divisions from the Army of Northern Virginia itself, led by James Longstreet. (The move the Richmond government had refused to make in June was being made now, with troops from Lee going to fight in the West.) Thus reinforced, Bragg moved in for a counterattack, and Rosecrans, waking up in the nick of time, hastily pulled his troops together to meet him. On the banks of Chickamauga Creek, about twelve miles below Chattanooga, Bragg made his attack, and on September 19 and 20 he fought and won the great Battle of Chickamauga. Part of Rosecrans' army was driven from the field in wild rout, and only a last-ditch stand by George Thomas saved the whole army from destruction. The Union troops retreated to Chattanooga, Bragg advanced and en-

Alfred Waud's drawing shows Hood's division, rushed west from Lee's army, driving Yankee cavalry away from a Chickamauga Creek bridge. The smoke of Rebel gunfire can be seen in the background.

William Travis painted the Union and Confederate lines at Chickamauga in hand-to-hand combat, with Union reinforcements rushing up at left.

trenched his men on high ground in a vast crescent, and the Army of the Cumberland found itself besieged.

The name Chickamauga was an old Cherokee word, men said, meaning "river of death," and there was an awful literalness to its meaning now. Each army had lost nearly a third of its numbers, Bragg's casualty list running to 18,000 or more, and Rosecrans' to nearly 16,000. Rosecrans' campaign was wrecked, and his own career as a field commander was ended; he was relieved and assigned to duty in St. Louis, and Rock-of-Chickamauga Thomas took his place. Bragg, the victor, had not added greatly to his reputation. He had made the Federals retreat, but if he had handled his army with more energy he might have destroyed the whole Army of the Cumberland, and his subordinates complained bitterly about his inability to make use of the triumph the troops had won. Their complaints echoed in Richmond, and President Davis came to Tennessee to see whether Bragg ought to be replaced; concluded, finally, that he should remain, and went back to Richmond without ordering any change.

Chickamauga was a Union disaster, but at least it jarred the Federal campaign in the West back onto the rails. It forced the government to drop the ruinous policy of dispersion and concentrate its forces, and in the end this was all to the good. Additionally, it gave new powers and a new opportunity to U. S. Grant, who knew what to do with both. Thus it may have been worth what it cost, although the soldiers of the Army of the Cumberland probably would have had trouble seeing it that way.

As September ended these soldiers were in serious trouble. They held Chattanooga, but they seemed very likely to be starved into surrender there. The Confederate line, unassailable by any force George Thomas could muster, ran in a vast semicircle, touching the Tennessee River upstream from Chattanooga, following the high parapet of Missionary Ridge to the east and south, anchoring itself in the west on the precipitous sides of Lookout Mountain, and touching the Tennessee again just west of Lookout. The Confederates had no troops north of the river, nor did they need any there; that country was wild, mountainous, and all but uninhabited, and no military supply train could cross it. Supplies could reach Thomas only by the river itself, by the railroad which ran along the river's southern bank, or by the roads which similarly lay south of the river, and all of these were firmly controlled by Bragg. The Union army could not even retreat. (No army under Thomas was likely to retreat, but physical inability to get out of a trap is a handicap any way you look at it.) As far as Bragg could see, he need only keep his army in position for a month or two longer, and the Unionists would have to give up.

Neither by a military nor a political calculation could the Federal cause afford a catastrophe like the outright loss of the Army of the Cumberland, and the crisis at Chattanooga had a galvanic effect on the Federal nerve center in Washington. Two army corps were detached from Meade, placed under the command of Joe Hooker, and sent west by rail. This was the most effective military use of railroads yet made anywhere, and the soldiers were moved with surprising speed; leaving the banks of the Rappahannock on September 24, they reached Bridgeport, Alabama, just eight days later. Sherman was ordered to move east from Memphis with part of the Army of the Tennessee, and Grant was put in command of all military operations west of the Alleghenies (except for Banks' venture in the New Orleans-Texas area) and was ordered over to Chattanooga to set things straight.

On the night of October 26 William Hazen's brigade from Thomas' army drifted down the Tennessee on pontoon rafts (painted above by Travis) to take Brown's Ferry, key to the Chattanooga supply line.

This Grant proceeded to do, his contribution being chiefly the unflagging energy with which he tackled the job. Plans for loosening the Confederate strangle hold had already been made, and what Grant did was to make certain that they were put into effect speedily. He brought Hooker east from Bridgeport, used a brigade of Thomas' men in a sudden thrust at the Confederate outpost on the Tennessee River west of Lookout Mountain, and presently opened a route through which supplies could be brought to Chattanooga. The route combined the use of steamboats, scows, a pontoon bridge, and army wagons, and it could not begin to supply the army with everything it needed, but at least it warded off starvation. Thomas' men dubbed it "the cracker line" and began to feel that life might be worth living after all.

Sherman, leaving Memphis, had about three hundred miles to march, and for some reason Halleck had given him orders to repair the line of the Memphis and Charleston Railroad as he moved, so his progress was glacial. Grant told him to forget about the track-gang job and to come as fast as he could; and by early November the Federal force in Chattanooga, no longer-half-starved, had powerful reinforcements at hand and was ready to try to break the ring that was around it. Bragg, meanwhile, acted with incredible obtuseness. A Federal force under General Burnside had come

Grant regarded Hooker's capture of Lookout Mountain as simply a first step in his general assault on Bragg's main Missionary Ridge line.

down through the Kentucky-Tennessee mountain country to occupy Knoxville, and although it had got into the place it was not, for the moment, doing any particular harm there; but Bragg sent Longstreet and 12,000 men away to try to dislodge this force, and he detached his cavalry and still more infantry to help—so that when it came time for the big fight Bragg would be badly outnumbered, facing the best generals the Federals could muster, Grant, Sherman, and Thomas.

The big fight came on November 24 and 25. Hooker with his men from the Army of the Potomac drove the Confederate left from Lookout Mountain—less of an achievement than it looked, since Bragg had only a skeleton force there, which was dug in along the slopes rather than on the crest, but it was one of the war's spectacular scenes for all that. There had been low-lying clouds all day, and when these finally lifted and the sun broke through, the Northern flag was on the top of Lookout, and war correspondents wrote enthusiastically about the "battle above the clouds." Sherman took his Army of the Tennessee units upstream and attacked the Confederate right. He made some progress but not enough, and was getting not much more than a bloody nose for his pains; and on the afternoon of November 25 Grant told Thomas to push his Army of the Cumberland forward and

Late in the day a heavy mist shrouded the action until only the gun flashes, "like swarms of fireflies," could be seen by those below.

take the Rebel rifle pits at the base of Missionary Ridge. This pressure might force Bragg to recall troops from Sherman's front.

At this point Thomas' soldiers took things into their own hands. They had been suffering a slow burn for a month; both Hooker's and Sherman's men had jeered at them for the Chickamauga defeat and had reminded them that other armies had to come to their rescue, and the Cumberlands had had all they cared to take. Now they moved forward, took the Confederate rifle pits as ordered—and then, after a brief pause for breath, went straight on up the steep mountain slope without orders from either Grant or Thomas, broke Bragg's line right where it was strongest, drove the Confederate army off in complete retreat, and won the Battle of Chattanooga in one spontaneous explosion of pent-up energy and fury.

Chattanooga was decisive. The beaten Confederates withdrew into Georgia. Burnside's position in Knoxville was secure. Grant, with new laurels on his unassuming head, was very clearly going to become general in chief of the Union armies, the South had definitely lost the war in the West—and, when spring came, the Federals would have a chance to apply more pressure than the Confederacy could resist.

THE
NORTHERN
VISE TIGHTENS

O n the ninth of March, 1864, U. S. Grant was made lieutenant general and given command of all the Union
armies, and the hitherto insoluble military problem of the
Federal government was at last on its way to solution. President Lincoln had learned that it took a soldier to do a soldier's job, and he had at last found the soldier who was capable of it: a direct, straightforward man who would leave high
policy to the civilian government and devote himself with
unflagging energy to the task of putting Confederate armies
out of action. There would be no more side shows: from
now on the whole weight of Northern power would be applied remorselessly, with concentrated force.

There had been a number of side shows during the last
year, and the net result of all of them had been to detract
from the general effectiveness of the Union war effort. An
army and navy expedition had tried throughout the preceding summer to hammer its way into Charleston, South Caro-

*Lieutenant General Ulysses S. Grant poses for his portrait outside his tent
at Cold Harbor, Virginia, before the siege of Petersburg.*

201

lina. It had reduced Fort Sumter to a shapeless heap of rubble, but it had cost the North a number of ships and soldiers and had accomplished nothing except to prove that Charleston could not be taken by direct assault. In Louisiana, General Banks was trying to move into Texas, partly for the sake of the cotton that could be picked up along the way and partly because the government believed that Napoleon III would give up his Mexican adventure if a Northern army occupied Texas and went to the Rio Grande. The belief may have been justified, but Banks never came close, and his campaign was coming to grief this spring. Early in April he was beaten at Mansfield and Pleasant Hill, Louisiana, far up the Red River, and he retreated with such panicky haste that Admiral Porter's accompanying fleet of gunboats narrowly escaped complete destruction. (The water level in the Red River was falling, and for a time it seemed that the gunboats could never get out; they were saved at the last when a backwoods colonel in the Union army took a regiment of lumbermen and built dams that temporarily made the water deep enough for escape.) In Florida a Union expedition in which white and Negro troops were brigaded together attempted a conquest that would have had no important results even if it had succeeded; it had failed dismally, meeting defeat at Olustee late in February. Union cavalry under William Sooy Smith had tried to sweep across Mississippi during the winter and had been ignominiously routed by Bedford Forrest.

All of these ventures had dissipated energy and manpower that might have been used elsewhere. (Banks' Texas expedition had been the chief reason why Grant had not been allowed to exploit the great opportunity opened by the capture of Vicksburg.) They had won nothing, and they would not have won the war even if all of them had succeeded. Now, it was hoped, there would be no more of them. Grant had intense singleness of purpose, and the government was giving him a free hand. He would either win the war or be the man on the spot when the Union confessed that victory was unattainable.

Grant considered the military problem to be basically quite simple. The principal Confederate armies had to be destroyed. The capture of cities and "strategic points" and the occupation of Southern territory meant very little; as long as the main Confederate armies were in the field the Confederacy lived, and as soon as they vanished the Confederacy ceased to be. His objectives, therefore, would be the opposing armies, and his goal would be to put them out of action as quickly as possible.

There were two armies that concerned him: the incomparable Army of Northern Virginia, led by Robert E. Lee, and the Army of Tennessee, commanded now by Joseph E. Johnston. Bragg's inability to win had at last become manifest even to Jefferson Davis, who had an inexplicable confidence in the man. Bragg had made a hash of his Kentucky invasion in the late summer of 1862, he had let victory slip through his grasp at Murfreesboro, and he had utterly failed to make proper use of his great victory at Chickamauga. After Chattanooga, Davis removed him—bringing him to Richmond and installing him as chief military adviser to the President—and Johnston was put in his place.

Davis had scant confidence in Johnston and had grown to dislike the man personally, and Johnston felt precisely the same way about Davis. But the much-abused Army of Tennessee, which had fought as well as any army could fight but which had never had adequate leadership, revered and trusted Johnston profoundly, and his appointment had been inevitable. His army had recovered its morale, and it was strongly entrenched on the low mountain ridges northwest of Dalton, Georgia, a few miles from the bloodstained field of Chickamauga. It contained about 60,000 men, and Lee's army, which lay just below the Rapidan River in central Virginia, was about the same size.

These armies were all that mattered. The Confederacy had sizable forces west of the Mississippi, under the over-all command of Edmund Kirby Smith, but the trans-Mississippi region was effectively cut off now that the Federals controlled the great river, and what happened there was of minor importance. The Southern nation would live or die depending on the fate of Lee's and Johnston's armies. Grant saw it so, and his entire plan for 1864 centered on the attempt to destroy those two armies.

In the West everything would be up to Sherman. Grant had put him in control of the whole Western theater of the war, with the exception of the Banks expedition, which was flickering out in expensive futility. Sherman was what would now be called an army group commander. In and around Chattanooga he had his own Army of the Tennessee, under Major General James B. McPherson; the redoubtable Army of the Cumberland, under Thomas; and a small force called the Army of the Ohio—hardly more than an army corps in actual size—commanded by a capable regular with pink cheeks and a flowing beard, Major General John M. Schofield. All in all, Sherman had upwards of 100,000 combat men with him. When he moved, he would go down the Western and Atlantic Railroad toward Atlanta; but Atlanta, important as it was to the Confederacy, was not his real objective. His objective was the Confederate army in his front. As he himself described his mission after the war, "I was to go for Joe Johnston."

Grant, meanwhile, would go for Lee.

Although he was general in chief, Grant would not operate from headquarters in Washington. The demoted Halleck was retained as chief of staff, and he would stay in Washington to handle the paper work; but Grant's operating headquarters would be in the field, moving with the Army of the Potomac. General Meade was kept in command of that army. With a fine spirit of abnegation, Meade had offered to resign, suggesting that Grant might want some Westerner in whom he had full confidence to command the army; but Grant had told him to stay where he was, and he endorsed an army-reorganization plan which Meade was just then putting into effect. Grant made no change in the army's interior chain of command, except that he brought a tough infantry officer, Phil Sheridan, from the Army of the Cumberland and put him in charge of the Army of the Potomac's

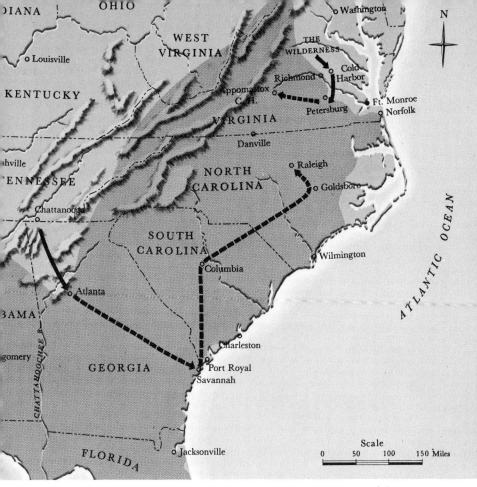

The map shows the 1864 Federal thrusts into the shrinking Confederacy. The dotted lines are the ultimate courses of Sherman and Grant.

cavalry corps. But if Grant considered Meade a capable officer who deserved to retain his command, he himself would nevertheless move with Meade's army, and he would exercise so much control over it that before long people would be speaking of it as Grant's army.

Grant's reasons were simple enough. The Army of the Potomac had much the sort of record the Confederate Army of Tennessee had—magnificent combat performance, brought to nothing by repeated failures in leadership. It had been unlucky, and its officer corps was badly clique-ridden, obsessed by the memory of the departed McClellan, so deeply

205

impressed by Lee's superior abilities that its talk at times almost had a defeatist quality. The War Department had been second-guessing this army's commanders so long that it probably would go on doing it unless the general in chief himself were present. All in all, the Army of the Potomac needed a powerful hand on the controls. Grant would supply that hand, although his presence with the army would create an extremely difficult command situation.

This army was in camp in the general vicinity of Culpeper Court House, on the northern side of the upper Rapidan. (A measure of its lack of success thus far is the fact that after three years of warfare it was camped only a few miles farther south than it had been camped when the war began.) Facing it, beyond the river, was the Army of Northern Virginia. Longstreet and his corps were returning from an unhappy winter in eastern Tennessee. When the spring campaign opened, Lee would have rather more than 60,000 fighting men. The Unionists who had called up Burnside and his old IX Corps to work with the Army of the Potomac, would be moving with nearly twice that number.

The mission of the Army of the Potomac was as simple as Sherman's: it was to head for the Confederate army and fight until something broke. It would move toward Richmond, just as Sherman was moving toward Atlanta, but its real assignment would be less to capture the Confederate capital than to destroy the army that was bound to defend that capital.

Grant was missing no bets. The irrepressible Ben Butler commanded a force of some 33,000 men around Fort Monroe, denominated the Army of the James, and when the Army of the Potomac advanced, Butler was to move up the south bank of the James River toward Richmond. At the very least his advance would occupy the attention of Confederate troops who would otherwise reinforce Lee; and if everything went well (which, considering Butler's defects as a strategist, was not really very likely), Lee would be compelled to retreat. On top of this there was a Union army in the Shenandoah, commanded by the German-born Franz

Sigel, and this army was to move down to the town of Staunton, whence it might go east through the Blue Ridge in the direction of Richmond. All in all, three Federal armies would be converging on the Confederate capital, each one with a powerful numerical advantage over any force that could be brought against it.

Everybody would move together. Sherman would march when Grant and Meade marched, and Butler and Sigel would advance at the same time. For the first time in the war the Union would put on a really co-ordinated campaign under central control, with all of its armies acting as a team.

On May 4, 1864, the machine began to roll.

Public attention on both sides was always centered on the fighting in Virginia. The opposing capitals were no more than a hundred miles apart, and they were the supremely sensitive nerve centers. What happened in Virginia took the eye first, and this spring it almost seemed as if all of the fury and desperation of the war were concentrated there.

The Army of the Potomac crossed the Rapidan and started to march down through a junglelike stretch of second-growth timber and isolated farms known as the Wilderness, with the hope that it could bring Lee to battle in the open country farther south. But one of Lee's distinguishing characteristics was a deep unwillingness to fight where his opponent wanted to fight. He liked to choose his own field, and he did so now. Undismayed by the great disparity in

In Timothy O'Sullivan's photograph, Union artillery crosses the Rapidan on May 4, 1864, at the opening of Grant's campaign against Richmond.

A soldier said that the battle in the Wilderness (above) was "simply bush-whacking on a grand scale." Another called it "a blind and bloody fight to the death, in bewildering thickets, rather than a battle."

numbers, he marched straight into the Wilderness and jumped the Federal columns before they could get across. Grant immediately concluded that if Lee wanted to fight here, he might as well get what he wanted, and on May 5 an enormous two-day battle got under way.

The Wilderness was a bad place for a fight. The roads were few, narrow, and bad, and the farm clearings were scarce; most of the country was densely wooded, with under-brush so thick that nobody could see fifty yards in any direction, cut up by ravines and little watercourses, with brambles and creepers that made movement almost impossible. The Federal advantage in numbers meant little here, and its advantage in artillery meant nothing at all, since few guns could be used. Because a much higher percentage of its men came from the country and were used to the woods, the Confederate army was probably less handicapped by all of this than the Army of the Potomac.

The Battle of the Wilderness was blind and vicious. The woods caught fire, and many wounded men were burned to death, and the smoke of this fire together with the battle smoke made a choking fog that intensified the almost impenetrable gloom of the woods. At the end of two days the Federals had lost more than 17,000 men and had gained not one foot. Both flanks had been broken in, and outright disaster had been staved off by a narrow margin. By any indicator one could use, the Army of the Potomac had been beaten just as badly as Hooker had been beaten at Chancellorsville a year earlier. On May 7 the rival armies glowered at each other in the smoldering forest, and the Federal soldiers assumed that the old game would be repeated: they would retreat north of the Rapidan, reorganize and refit and get reinforcements, and then they would make a new campaign somewhere else.

That night, at dusk, the Army of the Potomac was pulled back from its firing lines and put in motion. But when it moved, it moved south, not north. Grant was not Hooker. Beaten here, he would sideslip to the left and fight again; his immediate objective was a crossroads at Spotsylvania Court House, eleven miles southwest of Fredericksburg. It was on Lee's road to Richmond, and if Grant got there first, Lee would have to do the attacking. So the army moved all night, and as the exhausted soldiers realized that they were not retreating but were actually advancing they set up a cheer.

Grant had made one of the crucial decisions of the war, and in retrospect the Battle of the Wilderness became almost a Federal victory. This army was not going to retreat, it was not even going to pause to lick its wounds; it was simply going to force the fighting, and in the end Lee's outnumbered army was going to be compelled to play the sort of game which it could not win.

It was not going to be automatic, however. Lee saw what

Grant was up to and made a night march of his own. His men got to Spotsylvania Court House just ahead of the Federals, and the first hot skirmish for the crossroads swelled into a rolling battle that went on for twelve days, from May 8 to May 19. No bitterer fighting than the fighting that took place here was ever seen on the American continent. The Federals broke the Southern line once, on May 12, at a spot known ever after as "Bloody Angle," and there was a solid day of hand-to-hand combat while the Federals tried unsuccessfully to enlarge the break and split Lee's army into halves. There was fighting every day, and Grant kept shifting his troops to the left in an attempt to crumple Lee's flank, so that Federal soldiers who were facing east when the battle began were facing due west when it closed. Phil Sheridan took the cavalry off on a driving raid toward Richmond, and Jeb Stuart galloped to meet him. The Unionists were driven off in a hard fight at Yellow Tavern, in the Richmond suburbs, but Stuart himself was killed.

This Rebel was killed in Ewell's attack on the Union right on May 19.

Ben Butler, trapped on the Peninsula, tried to cut a channel to bypass a loop in the James River. His aim was to enable Yankee gunboats to reach Richmond, but the war was almost over before the work was done.

Elsewhere in Virginia things went badly for the Federals. Sigel moved up the Shenandoah Valley, was met by a scratch Confederate force at New Market, and was routed in a battle in which the corps of cadets from Virginia Military Institute greatly distinguished itself. Ben Butler made his advance up the James River most ineptly and was beaten at Bermuda Hundred. He made camp on the Bermuda Hundred peninsula, the Confederates drew a fortified line across the base of the peninsula, and in Grant's expressive phrase Butler was as much out of action as if he had been put in a tightly corked bottle. He would cause Lee no worries for some time, and from the army which had beaten him Lee got reinforcements that practically made up for his heavy battle losses thus far.

There were brief lulls in the campaign but no real pauses. From Spotsylvania the Army of the Potomac again moved by its left, skirmishing every day, looking for an opening and not quite finding one. It fought minor battles along the North Anna and on Totopotomoy Creek, and it got at last to a crossroads known as Cold Harbor, near the Chickahominy River and mortally close to Richmond; and here, because there was scant room for maneuver, Grant on June 3 put on a tremendous frontal asault in the hope of breaking the Confederate line once and for all. The assault failed, with fearful losses, and the Union and Confederate armies remained in contact, each one protected by impregnable trenches, for ten days more. Then Grant made his final

The top photograph shows a pontoon bridge over the North Anna River, where part of Grant's army crossed on the way to Cold Harbor. Above, seated on pews from a nearby church, the Union high command plans the Cold Harbor assault. Grant is at left, leaning over the back of a pew.

move—a skillful sideslip to the left, once more, and this time he went clear across the James River and advanced on the town of Petersburg. Most of the railroads that tied Richmond to the South came through Petersburg, and if the Federals could occupy the place before Lee got there, Richmond would have to be abandoned. But General William F.

Smith, leading the Union advance, fumbled the attack, and when the rest of the army came up, Lee had had time to man the city's defenses. The Union attacks failed, and Grant settled down to a siege.

The campaign thus far had been made at a stunning cost. In the first month the Union army had lost 60,000 men. The armies were never entirely out of contact after the first shots were fired in the Wilderness; they remained in close touch, as a matter of fact, until the spring of 1865, and once they got to Petersburg they waged trench warfare strongly resembling that of World War I. Across the North people grew disheartened. Lee's army had not been broken, Richmond had not been taken, and no American had ever seen anything like the endless casualty lists that were coming out. At close range the achievement of the Army of the Potomac was hard to see. Yet it had forced Lee to fight continuously on the defensive, giving him no chance for one of those dazzling strokes by which he had disrupted every previous Federal of-

Fouled water stands in the trenches of Grant's Petersburg lines. After a heavy rain, the men often stood waist-deep in water all day.

fensive, never letting him regain the initiative. He tried it once, sending Jubal Early and 14,000 men up on a dash through the Shenandoah Valley into Maryland. Early brushed aside a small Federal force that tried to stop him on the Monocacy River and got clear to the Washington suburb of Silver Spring, less than a dozen miles from the Capitol building; but at the last minute Grant sent an army corps north from the Army of the Potomac, and after a skirmish at Silver Spring (witnessed by a worried Abraham Lincoln, in person) Early had to go back to Virginia. No longer could a threat to Washington induce the administration to recall an army of invasion. Early's march had given the government a severe case of nerves, but it had been barren of accomplishment.

Sherman's campaign in Georgia followed a different pattern from Grant's. Sherman had both the room and the inclination to make it a war of maneuver, but Johnston was an able strategist who could match paces with him all the way. Maneuvered out of his lines at Dalton, Johnston faded back, Sherman following. Often the Confederates would make a stand; when they did, Sherman would confront them with Thomas' Army of the Cumberland, using McPherson's and Schofield's troops for a wide flanking maneuver, and while these tactics usually made Johnston give ground, they never compelled him to fight at a disadvantage, and Sherman's progress looked better on the map than it really was. He had been ordered to go for Joe Johnston, and he could not quite crowd the man into a corner and bring his superior weight to bear. There were several pitched battles and there were innumerable skirmishes, and both armies had losses, but there was nothing like the all-consuming fighting that was going on in Virginia. Johnston made a stand once, on the slopes of Kennesaw Mountain, and Sherman tired of his flanking operations and tried to crack the center of the Confederate line. It refused to yield, and Sherman's men were repulsed with substantial losses; then, after a time, the war of movement was resumed, like a formalized military dance performed to the rhythmic music of the guns.

Sherman's artillery faces Rebel batteries on top of Kennesaw Mountain.

By the middle of July Sherman had crossed the Chattahoochee River and reached the outskirts of Atlanta, but he
had by no means done what he set out to do. Johnston's
army, picking up reinforcements as it retreated, was probably stronger now than when the campaign began, and Sherman for the moment was at a standstill. Grant and Meade
were stalled in front of Petersburg, and Sherman was stalled
in front of Atlanta. The Confederate strongholds were un-
conquered, and Northerners began to find the prospect dis-
couraging.

A Federal column scrambles up the precipitous face of the mountain.

They became even more discouraged late in July, when Grant's army failed in a stroke that should have taken Petersburg. Frontal attacks on properly held entrenchments were doomed to failure, and even Grant, not easily convinced, had had to admit this. But at Petersburg a new chance offered itself. A regiment of Pennsylvania coal miners dug a five-hundred-foot tunnel under the Confederate lines, several tons of powder were planted there, and at dawn on July 30 the mine was exploded. It blew an enormous gap in the defensive entrenchments, and for an hour or more the way was open for the Federal army to march almost unopposed into Petersburg.

Burnside's corps made the attempt and bungled it fearfully; the assault failed, and Grant's one great chance to end the war in one day vanished.

The people of the North were getting very war-weary as

The moment the mine exploded, demolishing Confederate entrenchments in "an enormous whirlwind," Federal artillery opened a heavy bombardment.

The armies' entrenchments scarred the land around Petersburg. These rugged outer works were abandoned by the Rebels early in the siege.

the month of July ended. Grant did not seem to be any nearer the capture of Richmond than he had been when the campaign began; Sherman was deep in Georgia, but he had neither whipped the Confederate army which faced him nor taken Atlanta. The pressure which the Confederacy could not long endure was being applied relentlessly, but it was hard for the folks back home to see that anything was really being accomplished. They only knew that the war was costing more than it had ever cost before, and that there seemed to be nothing of any consequence to show for it; and that summer President Lincoln privately wrote down his belief that he could not be re-elected that fall. If the electorate should repudiate him, the North would almost certainly fall out of the war, and the South would have its independence.

THE
POLITICS
OF WAR

O n each side there was one man who stood at storm center, trying to lead a people who would follow no leader for long unless they felt in him some final embodiment of the deep passions and misty insights that moved them. This man was the President, given power and responsibility beyond all other men, hemmed in by insistent crowds yet always profoundly alone—Abraham Lincoln, in Washington, and Jefferson Davis, in Richmond.

They were very different, these two, alike only in their origins and in the crushing weight of the burdens they carried. On each rested an impossible imperative—to adjust himself to fate and yet at the same time somehow to control it. Miracles were expected of them by an age which had lost its belief in the miraculous.

Davis was all iron will and determination, a rigid man who might conceivably be broken but who could never be bent, proud almost to arrogance and yet humbly devoted to

General Butler's highhanded administration of captured New Orleans earned him the nickname "Beast Ben Butler" in the Southern states.

a cause greater than himself. Of the rightness of that cause he had never a doubt, and it was hard for him to understand that other men might not see that rightness as easily as he did. Essentially a legalist, he had been put in charge of the strangest of revolutions—an uprising of conservatives who would overturn things in order to preserve a cherished *status quo*—and he would do his unwavering best to make the revolution follow the proper forms. He had had much experience with politics, yet it had been the experience of the aristocrat-in-politics. He had never known the daily immersion in the rough-and-tumble of ward and courthouse politics, where the candidate is hammered into shape by repeated contact with the electorate.

There were other handicaps, the greatest being the fact that the kind of government Southerners wanted was not the kind that could fight and win an extended war. The administration had to have broad wartime powers, but when Davis tried to get and use them he was bitterly criticized; fighting against strong centralized government, he had to create such a government in order to win. States' rights made an impossible base for modern war. The doctrinaire was forever tripping up the realist.

Nor was that all. Davis' cabinet gave him little help. It contained some good men, the ablest perhaps being Judah P. Benjamin, a lawyer and former senator from Louisiana. He served, successively, as Attorney General, Secretary of War, and Secretary of State. He was a brilliant man and a hard worker, wholly devoted to the cause, and Davis trusted him and relied on him as much as a man of Davis' bristling independence could be said to rely on anyone. Other men, in the cabinet and out of it, seemed to feel that Benjamin was just a little too clever, and he was never able to bring a broad national following to the President's support. Another good man, underestimated at the time, was Stephen Mallory of Florida, the Secretary of the Navy. Mallory had very little to work with, and the Confederacy's total inability to break the strangling blockade brought him much unjust criticism, but he did a good deal better with the materials at hand than there was any reason to expect. He and John H. Reagan of Texas, the Postmaster General, were the only two who held their cabinet posts from the Confederacy's birth to its death. There were six secretaries of war, and the one who held the job longest was James A. Seddon of Virginia; like those who preceded and followed him, Seddon found his path made difficult by the fact that Davis to all intents and purposes was his own Secretary of War.

Broadly speaking, the cabinet was undistinguished, and it never contained the South's strongest men. Alexander Stephens was Vice-President, as isolated in that office as an American Vice-President invariably is; Howell Cobb was never a member, Robert Toombs was in the Cabinet only briefly, and as a general thing the cabinet did not contain the men who had been most influential in bringing about secession in the first place—the men who, just before the separation took place, would have been regarded as the South's strongest leaders. More and more as the war went on the Confederate government was a one-man show.

In the sense that the President was always dominant, the Northern government too was a one-man show, but in reality it was a team of powerful men—a team which was unruly, stubborn, and hard to manage, but which provided a great deal of service. Lincoln put in his cabinet men of force and ability, and although some of them fought against him at times and tried to wrest leadership from him, they added strength to his administration. Lincoln had a suppleness which Davis lacked, his political experience had taught him how to win a political fight without making personal enemies out of the men he defeated, and he had as well the ability to use the talents of self-assured men who considered themselves his betters.

William H. Seward, his Secretary of State, had opposed him for the Republican Presidential nomination, entered the cabinet reluctantly, and believed that he rather than Lincoln would actually run the show. Lincoln quickly disillusioned him on this point and then made a loyal supporter of him. Edwin M. Stanton, who became Secretary of War after Simon Cameron had demonstrated his own abysmal unfitness for the post, was harsh, domineering, ruthless, forever conniving with the radical Republicans to upset Lincoln's control of high policy; yet he, like Seward, finally came to see that the President was boss, and he was an uncommonly energetic and able administrator. Salmon P. Chase, Secretary of the Treasury, was another man who had sought the Republican Presidential nomination in 1860 and who, failing to get it, believed firmly that the better man had lost. He had no conception of the loyalty which a cabinet member might be supposed to owe to the President who had appointed him, and in 1864 he tried hard, while still in Lincoln's cabinet, to take the nomination away from him. But if he was a difficult man to get along with, he ran the Treasury Department ably; after removing him for unendurable political insubordination in 1864, Lincoln a few months later showed how highly he regarded Chase's services by making him Chief Justice of the United States.

Thus both Lincoln and Davis had to face intense political opposition as the war progressed. To sum up the quality of their respective cabinets, it can only be said that in the face of this opposition Lincoln's cabinet was in the long run a help to him, and that Davis' cabinet was not.

One queer aspect of the political phase of the war was the fact that it was the government at Richmond which was first and boldest in its assertion of centralized control over the armies. Despite the states' rights theory, the Confederate government became a truly national government, as far as matters like conscription were concerned, much earlier and much more unequivocally than the government at Washington.

When the war began, Confederate soldiers were enlisted for a term of twelve months, which meant that in the spring of 1862 the Confederate armies were in danger of dissolving. The administration and the Congress met this problem head-on, putting through a conscription act which placed exclusive control over all male citizens between eighteen and thirty-five in the hands of the Confederate President. With

THE VOLUNTARY MANNER IN WHICH SOME OF THE SOUTHERN VOLUNTEERS ENLIST.

The cartoon above mocks the Confederate system of recruiting soldiers.

certain specified exceptions and exemptions, all men within those age limits were conscripted for the duration of the war. Some of the state governors, most notably the egregious Joseph E. Brown of Georgia, complained bitterly that this was a body blow at constitutional liberties, but the President and Congress were unmoved. There might be widespread complaint about the exemptions under the law—the owner or overseer of twenty slaves, for instance, could not be called into military service—and in the latter part of the war there was trouble enforcing the conscription act properly, but the act itself was courageous and straightforward, and it went unmodified.

It was the Northern government that found itself unable to assert adequate central control over the lives of its citizens, and although it was driven to conscription in 1863, it never was as bold or direct about it as the government at Richmond had been, and it never adopted as good a law.

Northern armies were composed of regiments raised by the several states, and the volunteer signed up, usually, for a three-year term. When new men were needed the Federal government set a total and assigned a quota to each state, and each state quota in turn was broken down into quotas for the separate Congressional districts. If any district or state could fill its quota with volunteers, there would be no draft, and since the draft was extremely unpopular, every state, town, and county did its best to promote volunteering. This led to the indefensible bounty system, which was enormously expensive and did the Union armies more harm than good. A state would offer a cash bounty for enlistments, cities and townships and counties would add their own contribution, the Federal government would make a further offer —and by 1864 there were many areas in which a man could receive more than a thousand dollars simply for joining the army.

The man responding to this appeal could bring his horse—and welcome.

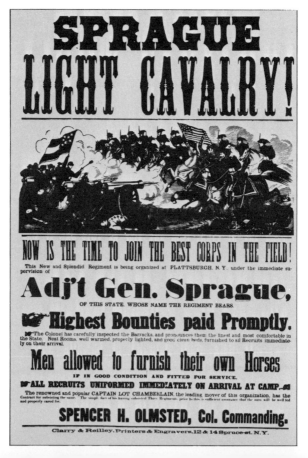

Above is Adalbert Volck's comment on the Northern substitute broker; this one is offering the timid man at right his choice of derelicts.

The results were almost uniformly vicious. Men who had no intention of rendering any service at the front would enlist, collect their bounty, desert at the first opportunity, reenlist under another name in some other locality, collect another bounty, desert again, and go on with the process indefinitely—the "bounty jumpers," who were detested by the veteran soldiers and who brought the very dregs of society into the army. Even when the high-bounty man did not desert, he did the cause little good; he was in the army because he was offered a great deal of money, not because of any patriotic impulse, and late in the war General Grant estimated that not one in eight of the high-bounty recruits ever did any useful service at the front.

On top of this, the draft act contained a couple of grotesque monstrosities. A drafted man could obtain exemption by paying a commutation fee of three hundred dollars; or, if he preferred—as well he might, since the exemption thus gained would last only until a new draft was called—he could hire a substitute to go to war in his place, thus obtaining permanent release from military service. The government could hardly have devised a worse law. It put the load on the poor man and gave special favors to the well-to-do, and it brought some very poor material into the army. The substitute broker—the dealer who, for a price, would find substitutes for well-heeled draft dodgers—would take any men he could get, and some of them were mentally or physically defective. Through bribery, the broker could often get these men accepted, but they were not of much use to the army.

All in all, the conscription law was an atrocity. Comparatively few men were actually drafted; the one virtue of the law was that it stimulated recruiting, and although the volunteers it brought in were by no means the equals of the men who had enlisted in 1861 and 1862, the army could make do with them. The high-bounty laws did have one good effect. Veteran soldiers whose three-year terms were expiring often re-enlisted because the proffered bounty and the furlough that went with re-enlistment looked attractive. In the final year of the war the heaviest part of the military load was carried by the old regiments which were entitled to denominate themselves "veteran volunteers."

That he accepted things like the bounty system and the conscription law simply indicates that Lincoln was always prepared to make political compromises to keep the war machine moving. He managed to keep his cabinet under moderately good control, and all things considered he got along with the Congress and with the state governors a good deal better than Davis was able to do. But the road was never smooth, and his problems multiplied as the war progressed. There were recurring cabinet crises. Lincoln had to hold the support of the radicals who followed Chase and Stanton and of the moderates who followed Seward, and there were times when it seemed all but impossible to head off an open break between the leaders of these factions. The innumerable political generals raised similar problems. Such men as Ben Butler, Nathaniel P. Banks, Franz Sigel, and John Charles Frémont were very poor generals indeed, but they held the confidence of large groups of citizens, and in the intricate game of war-plus-politics which Lincoln had to play it seemed, rightly or wrongly, that these generals must be re-

The poster on this recruiting station offers county, state, and federal bounties, extra for veterans, and cash for anyone bringing a recruit.

tained in the government's service. The fearsome Congressional Joint Committee on the Conduct of the War was forever trying to interfere in the setting of administration policy and in the control of the armies; it was necessary for Lincoln to retain control without driving the energetic spellbinders who composed this committee into open opposition.

Lincoln was an adroit politician of extraordinary suppleness and agility. He had to be one, in 1864 especially, because there was about to be a Presidential election, and in the history of the world there had never been a canvass quite like this one. Never before had a democratic nation prepared to hold free elections while it was in the midst of a bloody attempt to win a violent civil war, and the results were unpredictable. As spring gave way to summer and autumn drew near it became increasingly apparent that when it voted on the Presidency, the nation might in effect be voting whether to drop out of the war or carry on to victory at any cost.

The Republicans would of course support Lincoln, even though the party's radicals wanted someone who would wage war with more vigor and with more bitterness. Secretary

Chase's bid for the nomination had failed, and although a third party tried to advance General Frémont, it got nowhere, and Frémont presently withdrew. Lincoln was renominated, by a party which called itself the Union party in deference to the support it was getting from the War Democrats, and Andrew Johnson of Tennessee was named as his running mate. Lincoln would make no election campaign. What had been done in the war would, of necessity, be the principal issue. Fighting to defeat him for re-election, the Democrats would have great difficulty to keep from fighting for a different sort of war effort; and since the people who wanted a harder war were bound to support Lincoln, the Democrats were apt to speak, or at least to appear to speak, for a softer war—which, under the circumstances, would be likely to mean no war at all.

A great many people in the North were completely disillusioned about the war. Federal troops had to be used, in Ohio and Illinois and elsewhere, to put down uprisings provoked by the draft act; and New York City went through a few bloody days just after the Battle of Gettysburg when mobs stormed draft offices, killed or beat up any Negroes they could find, battled police and soldiers, and in general

A Southerner eggs on New York rioters from a rooftop on 46th Street.

McClellan, as Hamlet, holds the skull of Lincoln, saying, "I knew him, Horatio; a fellow of infinite jest . . . where be your jibes now?"

acted like revolutionists. The riots were at last suppressed, after combat troops had been sent in from the Army of the Potomac, but a thousand civilians had been killed or wounded and an immense amount of property had been destroyed, and the riots were a fearful symptom of deep underlying unrest and discontent. The 1864 Presidential election offered this discontent a chance to show its full strength.

In August the Democrats held their convention in Chicago, and the Copperhead wing was, if not in full control, very active and exceedingly vocal. (Copperhead: one of the anti-war Democrats, who wore in their lapels Indian heads cut from copper pennies.) They dictated a platform which declared the war a failure and called for re-establishment of the Union on the old basis, which amounted to an open confession of lack of will to go on fighting. They accepted the nomination of General McClellan as Presidential candidate, while George H. Pendleton of Ohio, friend of the Copperhead leader, Clement Vallandigham, was named for the Vice-Presidency. Then they sat back and waited for nationwide war weariness and disillusionment to do the job.

It appeared that they might have things figured correctly. With the summer coming to a close, the campaigns that had been begun in the spring did look like failures. Neither Lee nor Johnston had been beaten, neither Richmond nor Atlanta had been taken, a Confederate army had recently menaced Washington itself, casualty lists were higher than they had ever been before, the administration had recently called for a new draft of 500,000 men, and Lincoln himself privately believed that he could not be re-elected. He believed, additionally, that if he were defeated, the man who beat him would win the election on terms which would make it humanly impossible to win the war; and although McClellan disavowed the peace plank in the Democratic platform and refused to say that the war was a failure, the Lincoln-McClellan contest was generally accepted as a test of the North's willingness to go on with the fight.

One factor in the public's war weariness was the presence of many thousands of Northern soldiers in Southern prison camps, where living conditions were atrocious and the death rate was alarmingly high. In the first years of the war the opposing governments had operated on a system of prisoner exchanges, by which prisoners were periodically repatriated on a man-for-man basis. This system had broken down by the time 1864 began, and when Grant took control of the Union armies he refused to put it in repair. The North now held more prisoners than the South held, and the manpower shortage was hurting the Confederacy much more than it hurt the Union. With lucid but pitiless logic Grant argued that to resume exchanges would simply reinforce the Confederate armies. (It would also reinforce Federal armies, but these would be reinforced anyway, and the Confederate armies would not.) Unionists in Southern prison camps, therefore, would have to stay there, and if they died like flies—from dysentery, typhoid, malnutrition, and homesick despair

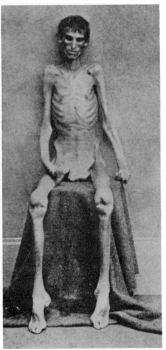

The photograph at top shows the Andersonville stockade in Georgia; the 26-acre plot, bisected by a dismal, sluggish stream, held nearly 32,000 Union prisoners, whose death rate rose to 3,000 per month by August, 1864. Pictures of Andersonville captives, like that at left, horrified the North. Above, disconsolate Iowa prisoners pose in a New Orleans yard after their release; they were lucky, however, to have been imprisoned for only ten months.

A Rebel confined at Point Lookout Prison, Maryland, showed the catching and cooking of rats for meals with considerable humor. Volck's drawing below of prisoners at Camp Douglas, near Chicago, was grimmer.

complicated by infected quarters—that was regrettable but unavoidable.

In actual fact the Union prisoners of war were very little worse off than the Southerners who were held in Northern prisons, but most people in the North did not realize this and would not have been consoled if they had realized it. All prison camps were death traps in that war. They were overcrowded, reeking from lack of sanitation, badly policed; housing was bad, food was worse, and medical care was sometimes worst of all. This was due less to any active ill-will on either side than to the general, unintended brutality and heartlessness of war. Army life in those days was rough, even under the best conditions, and disease killed many more men than bullets killed; in a prison camp this roughness was inevitably intensified (26,436 Southerners and 22,576 Northerners died in prison camps) even though nobody really meant it so.

No one in the North tried to analyze any of this in the summer of 1864. Heartsick parents could see only that their boys were dying in prisons because the administration, for some inscrutable reason, was refusing to bring them home. Grant was fighting the war on the theory that the North could stand heavier losses than the South could stand, and Lincoln was supporting him, but the immediate fruits of this policy did not make good election-campaign material.

Davis had no campaign problems that summer. The Confederate Constitution set the President's term at six years and ruled out a second term, and Davis did not need to ask for anybody's vote. He was devoting a good part of his attention, with a good deal of skill, to the task of making war-weary Northerners feel the burden of the war, and he was using for this purpose a device which a later generation would know as a fifth column.

This fifth column was directed from bases in neutral Canada, where certain Confederate emissaries, their operations amply financed by the sale of cotton, kept in touch with agents in the Northern states. They were in touch also with a good many of the Copperhead leaders, and they worked closely with a strange, amorphous, and slightly unreal secret society known variously as the Order of American Knights or the Sons of Liberty; a pro-Confederate peace organization which had proliferated all across the Middle West, claiming hundreds of thousands of members and supposedly preparing to take up arms against the Federal government. The plots that were laid for armed uprisings never came to anything—there was one scheme for a wholesale prison delivery in the Northern states, but it died a-borning—but their existence was an open secret, and the whole business tended to spread defeatist talk and defeatist feelings across the North as nothing else could have done. The fifth column attempted other things—to burn New York City, to capture a warship on the Great Lakes, to destroy railroad bridges, and to enrich the Confederacy with money taken from Yankee banks—and although the actual results were small, the program itself was as desperate as anything a modern fifth columnist would be likely to attempt.

Although Jefferson Davis lacked Lincoln's political ad-

Ladies played spectacular roles as spies. Mrs. Rose Greenhow, at left with her daughter in Old Capitol Prison, supplied the Rebels with information about Union troops before First Bull Run. At right is the actress Pauline Cushman, who was captured and sentenced to death as a Federal agent but returned North when her captors retreated.

"Major Allen," seated at right, was the detective Allan Pinkerton, who often supplied McClellan with exaggerated reports of enemy strength.

dress, he was adapting himself to the war situation with real skill. He was, to repeat, a legalist, insisting that the revolution which he led was in fact no revolution at all but something fully sanctioned by constitution and law; but he was laying his hands on a revolutionary weapon with genuine earnestness and ruthless energy, and it was no fault of his that the great fifth-column movement of 1864 came to so little. If the Northern Copperhead leaders had been able to deliver on a fifth of their promises, the Confederacy might that summer have given the Northern home front a good deal more than it could conveniently handle.

The Presidential campaign of 1864 was, all in all, about the most crucial political contest in American history, but it was a campaign in which what men said made very little difference. Speeches were of small account. It was what the men in uniform did that mattered. The war effort was alleged to be a failure; if most people felt, by election day, that it really was a failure, then it would in fact become one through the defeat of the candidate and the party which had had direction of the war effort. On the other hand, if by election day the war was clearly being won, the Democratic campaign would inevitably come to nothing. Everything depended on the fighting men. If they should start to win, Lincoln would win. He would not win otherwise.

TOTAL
WARFARE

In the early summer of 1864 General Joseph E. Johnston understood the military situation very clearly. Sherman had driven him from the Tennessee border to the edge of Atlanta, and in Richmond this looked like the equivalent of a Confederate disaster; but to Johnston it looked very different. Sherman had done a great deal, but he had neither routed Johnston's army nor taken Atlanta, and until he did at least one of these things the Northern public would consider his campaign a failure. Feeling so, it might very well beat Lincoln at the polls—and this, as things stood in the fourth year of the war, represented the Confederacy's last and best hope for victory. As Johnston appraised things, his cue was to play a waiting game; stall for time, avert a showdown at all costs, let Sherman dangle ineffectually at the end of that long, tenuous supply line, and count on Northern depression and weariness to turn the tide.

But Davis saw it otherwise, and Davis had the final re-

The photograph opposite shows the last train from Atlanta, piled high with refugees and their belongings; Sherman had ordered the evacuation.

237

sponsibility. He was a man beset by rising shadows, and as he struggled gallantly to keep life in a dying cause, refusing to recognize the omens of doom, he looked about him with the eyes of a soldier rather than with the eyes of a politician. What might happen in the November elections was a politician's concern; to Davis the victories that would save the Confederacy must be won in the field, and they would never be won unless the Confederate armies turned and fought the invader until the invader had had enough. So Davis relieved Johnston of his command and put General John Bell Hood in his place. Doing so, he made one of the fateful decisions of the war.

Hood was a combat soldier of proved effectiveness. He had commanded a brigade and then a division in Lee's army, fighting with great dash and valor; had been badly wounded in the arm at Gettysburg, had recovered in time to fight at Chickamauga, and there had lost a leg. Patched up, and riding strapped to his saddle, he had been given corps command under Johnston, and he had been bitterly critical of Johnston's series of feints and retreats. He understood stand-up fighting, and now Davis wanted a stand-up fighter and gave Hood Johnston's job. Unfortunately, Hood was suited for subordinate command but not for the top job. The transfer worked to Sherman's immense advantage.

Hood was aware that he had been put in charge of the army to fight, and he lost no time in getting at it. Sherman had crossed the Chattahoochee River and was moving so as to come down on Atlanta from the north and east. Atlanta was ringed with earthworks, and Sherman had no intention of attacking these. He hoped to cut the four railroad lines that converged on the city and thus compel the Confederates either to retreat or to come out and make a stand-up fight in the open. Moving out to attack, Hood was doing just what Sherman wanted.

Hood was not being stupid, for Sherman had in fact incautiously left an opening. McPherson, with Schofield and rather less than half of the Federal troops, had moved to a point on the Georgia Railroad, east of the city, and was

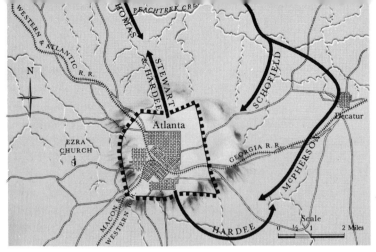

The map shows the July 20 thrust by Confederates Stewart and Hardee toward Peachtree Creek, and Hardee's attack on Schofield two days later.

marching in, tearing up the railroad as he advanced. Thomas, with the rest of the army, was crossing Peachtree Creek, and there was a gap of several miles between his forces and the men of McPherson and Schofield; and on July 20 Hood attacked Thomas savagely, hoping to destroy him before Sherman could reunite his forces.

Hood's troops attacked with spirit, but there never was a better defensive fighter than George Thomas, and his troops were as good as their general. Hood's attack was beaten off, the Confederates had substantial losses, and Thomas was able to re-establish contact with McPherson and Schofield.

Two days later Hood struck again. This time he swung east, seeking to hit McPherson in the flank the way Jackson had hit Hooker at Chancellorsville. The fight that resulted, known as the Battle of Atlanta, was desperate, and it came fairly close to success. McPherson himself was killed, and for a time part of his army was being assailed from front and rear simultaneously. But the Unionists rallied at last, the Confederate assaults failed, and Hood pulled his men back inside the fortified lines. The two battles together had cost him upward of 13,000 men, and Sherman now was pinning him in his earthworks. The railroads that came to Atlanta from the north and east had been cut, and Sherman began to swing ponderously around by his right, hoping to reach the Macon and Western that ran southwest from Atlanta. Once

General John A. Logan gallops forward to urge the restoration of the broken Union line at Atlanta. Sherman's headquarters were at top left.

more Hood came out to attack him, and there was a hard fight at Ezra Church west of the city; once again the Confederates were repulsed, with losses heavier than they could afford, and Sherman was a long step nearer the capture of Atlanta.

It was Atlanta that he wanted, now. He had started out to destroy the Confederate army in his front, and this he had never been able to do; since Hood replaced Johnston that army had been badly mangled, but it still existed as an effective fighting force, and Sherman had been changing his objective. If he could get the city, the campaign would be a success, even though it would not be the final, conclusive success he had hoped to win. Hood alone could not keep him out of Atlanta indefinitely; Sherman had more than a two-to-one advantage in numbers now, and he could reach farther and farther around the city, snipping the railroad connections and compelling the defenders at last to evacuate. Sherman's chief worry now was his own rear—the railroad that went back to Chattanooga, down the Tennessee Valley to Bridgeport, and up through Nashville to Kentucky. There was in the Confederacy one man who might operate on that line so effectively that Sherman would have to retreat—Bedford Forrest—and as the siege of Atlanta began, Sherman's great concern was to put Forrest out of action.

Unfortunately for Sherman, all attempts to do this ended in ignominious defeat; the Federal army, apparently, contained no subordinate general capable of handling this self-taught soldier. Early in June, Sherman sent a strong cavalry column under Major General Samuel D. Sturgis down into Mississippi from Memphis, in the hope that Forrest could be forced into a losing battle. It did not work out as he hoped. Forrest met Sturgis, who had twice his strength, at Brice's Crossroads, Mississippi, on June 10, and gave him one of the classic beatings of the Civil War. Sturgis drew off in disgrace, and Sherman had to make another effort.

He made it in July. With his own army nearing Atlanta, Sherman ordered a powerful expedition under Major General A. J. Smith to move down from Memphis into Mississippi to keep Forrest busy. Top Confederate commander in that area was General Stephen D. Lee, and he and Forrest with a mixed force ran into Smith's expedition near the town of Tupelo. There was a brisk fight in which Forrest was wounded and the Confederates were driven off, a clear tactical victory for the Unionists; but Smith did not like the looks of things, and he beat a hasty retreat to Memphis, his withdrawal badly harassed by Forrest's cavalry. In August he was sent out to try again; and this time Forrest slipped past him and rode into Memphis itself—he was traveling in a buggy just now, his wounded foot propped up on a special rack, but he could still move faster and more elusively than any other cavalry commander. He could not stay in Memphis more than a moment, and he did no especial harm there, but he did force the authorities to recall Smith's expedition. The moral apparently was that no one could invade the interior of Mississippi as long as Forrest was around.

Brilliant as Forrest's tactics had been, however, the Federal moves had done what Sherman wanted done; that is, they had kept Forrest so busy in the deep South that he had not been able to get into Tennessee and strike the sort of blow against Sherman's long supply line that would have pulled Sherman back from Atlanta. With Forrest otherwise engaged, Hood could not hold the place forever. On August

The painting above shows the torn battleground behind the Union lines at Atlanta, with the Georgia Railroad destroyed by Sherman's troops.

25 Sherman broke off his intermittent bombardment of the Confederate lines and began another circling movement to the southwest and south of the city. Hood's efforts to drive the advancing columns back failed, and it was clear now that Atlanta was going to fall. Hood got his army out smartly, and on September 2 the Federals occupied the city.

Here was a victory which the administration could toss into the teeth of the Democrats who were basing their Presidential campaign on the assertion that the war was a failure. (The fact that this was not the kind of victory Sherman and Grant had hoped for in the spring was irrelevant; the fragmentation of the Confederacy was visibly progressing, and the capture of Atlanta was something to crow about.) The victory came on the heels of another one, at Mobile Bay, where tough old Admiral Farragut on August 5 had hammered his way past the defending forts and, after a hard fight, had taken the ironclad ram *Tennessee.* This victory effectively closed the port of Mobile, and although that city itself would hold out for months to come, it would receive and dispatch no more blockade-runners. One more Confederate gate to the outer world had been nailed shut, and there had been a spectacular quality to Farragut's victory that took men's imaginations. He had steamed in through a Confederate mine field (they called mines "torpedoes" in those days) and one of his monitors had run on one of the mines and had been lost, whereat the rest of the battle line hesitated and fell into confusion; but Farragut bulled his way in, and his "Damn the torpedoes—full speed ahead!" was a battle cry that stuck in the public's mind as if robust confidence in ultimate victory had been reborn.

Not long after this a third Federal triumph was recorded, and Northern spirits rose still higher.

Jubal Early had led his diminutive Confederate army to the very suburbs of Washington, but he had not been able to force his way in or to stay where he was, and he had retreated to the upper end of the Shenandoah Valley. The War Department had assembled troops to drive him away, but although Early was very badly outnumbered—he had about 15,000 men with him, and the Federals mustered three army corps and a good body of cavalry, 45,000 men or more—everybody was being very cautious, and Grant in front of Petersburg found it impossible to get aggressive action by remote control. He finally put Phil Sheridan in charge of the operation, went to the scene himself long enough to make sure that Sheridan understood what he was supposed to do, and returned to Petersburg to await results.

Sheridan was supposed to do two things—beat Early and take the Shenandoah Valley out of the war. This valley, running southwest from the Potomac behind the shield of the Blue Ridge, had been of great strategic value to the Confederacy ever since Stonewall Jackson had demonstrated its possibilities. A Confederate army moving down the Valley was heading straight for the Northern heartland, threatening both the capital and such cities as Philadelphia and Balti-

Jubal Early demands $200,000 from the citizens of Frederick, Maryland. He also collected a levy from Hagerstown on his way toward Washington.

more, to say nothing of the North's east-west railway connections; but a Northern army moving up the Valley was heading nowhere in particular, since the Valley went off into mountain country and led the invader far away from Richmond. The Valley was immensely fertile, producing meat and grain that were of great importance to Lee's army defending Richmond, and a Confederate army operating in the lower Valley could supply itself with food and forage from the Valley itself. All in all, a Federal army trying to take Richmond could never be entirely secure until the Confederates were deprived of all use of the Shenandoah Valley, and it was up to Sheridan to deprive them of it.

Grant's instructions were grimly specific. He wanted the rich farmlands of the Valley despoiled so thoroughly that the place could no longer support a Confederate army; he told Sheridan to devastate the whole area so thoroughly that a crow flying across over the Valley would have to carry its own rations. This work Sheridan set out to do.

And now, in September of 1864, total war began to be waged in full earnest. Grant and Sheridan were striking directly at the Southern economy, and what happened to Early's army was more or less incidental; barns and corncribs and gristmills and herds of cattle were military objectives now, and if thousands of civilians whose property this was had to suffer heartbreaking loss as a result, that also was incidental. A garden spot was to be turned into a desert in order that the Southern nation might be destroyed.

Sheridan began cautiously. Early was a hard hitter, and although his army was small, it was lean and sinewy, composed of veterans—altogether, an outfit to be treated with much respect. Sheridan did not really make his move until September, and on the nineteenth of that month he fought Early near the town of Winchester, Virginia. The battle began before half of Sheridan's army had reached the scene, and the morning hours saw a Union repulse, but by midafternoon Sheridan had all of his men in hand, and Early was badly beaten and compelled to retreat. Sheridan pursued, winning another battle at Fisher's Hill three days later, and Early continued on up the Valley while Sheridan's men got on with the job of devastation Grant had ordered.

Few campaigns in the war aroused more bitterness than

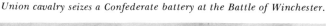
Union cavalry seizes a Confederate battery at the Battle of Winchester.

Phil Sheridan rides through his cheering troops as cattle are driven off and burning farm buildings send up columns of smoke behind them.

this one. The Union troopers carried out their orders with a heavy hand, and as they did so they were plagued by the attacks of bands of Confederate guerrillas—irregular fighters who were of small account in a pitched battle, but who raided outposts, burned Yankee wagon trains, shot sentries and couriers, and compelled Sheridan to use a sizable percentage of his force for simple guard duty. The Federal soldiers considered the guerrillas no better than highwaymen, and when they captured any of them they usually hanged them. The guerrillas hanged Yankees in return, naturally enough; and from all of this there was a deep scar, burned into the American memory, as the romanticized "war between brothers" took on an ugly phase.

Guerrilla warfare tended to get out of hand. Most bands were semi-independent, and in some areas they did the Confederacy harm by draining able-bodied men away from the regular fighting forces and by stimulating the Federals to vicious reprisals. Best of the guerrilla leaders was Colonel John S. Mosby, who harassed Sheridan's supply lines so effectively that substantial numbers of Sheridan's troops had to be kept on duty patrolling roads back of the front, but most partisan leaders were far below Mosby's stature. In Missouri

A Union cavalryman drew this picture of Quantrill's raid on Lawrence. A survivor said, "Bodies of dead men . . . were laying in all directions."

guerrilla warfare was especially rough; neighborhood feuds got all mixed in with the business of fighting the Yankees, and the notorious W. C. Quantrill, whose desperadoes sacked Lawrence, Kansas, in 1863, killing about 150 citizens, often looked more like an outlaw than a soldier.

The middle of October found Sheridan's army encamped near Cedar Creek, twenty miles south of Winchester. Early was not far away, but he had been beaten twice and it seemed unlikely that he retained any aggressive intentions, and Sheridan left the army briefly to visit Washington. At dawn on the morning of October 19, just as Sheridan was preparing to leave Winchester and return to camp, Early launched a sudden attack that took the Union army completely by surprise, broke it, and drove various fragments down the road in a highly disordered retreat. Sheridan met these fragments as he was riding back to camp, hauled them back into formation, got them to the battle front, put them in line with the soldiers who had not run away, and late in the afternoon made a fuious counterattack which was overwhelmingly successful. Early was driven off, his army too badly manhandled to be a substantial menace any longer, and it was plain to all men that the Confederacy would

Sheridan, on his black, Reinzi, rallies his soldiers at Cedar Creek.

never again threaten the North by way of the Shenandoah Valley.

This victory aroused much enthusiasm. Like Farragut's fight, it was intensely dramatic; men made a legend out of Sheridan's ride from Winchester and about the way his rallied troops broke the Confederate line, and a catchy little ballad describing the business went all across the North. Coming on the heels of Mobile Bay and Atlanta, Sheridan's conquest was a tonic that checked war weariness and created a new spirit of optimism. No longer could the Democrats make an effective campaign on the argument that the war was a failure. The war was visibly being won, and although the price remained high it was obvious that the last crisis had been passed. Sherman, Farragut, and Sheridan were winning Lincoln's election for him.

Which is to say that they were winning it in part. The victory which Lincoln was to gain when the nation cast its ballots in November was fundamentally of his own making. In his conduct of the war he had made many mistakes, especially in his handling of military matters in the first two years. He had seemed, at times, to be more politician than statesman, he had been bitterly criticized both for moving too fast on the slavery question and for not moving fast enough, and there had always been sincere patriots to complain that he had lacked drive and firmness in his leader-

Soldiers vote in camp; the military vote went heavily for Lincoln.

ship. But he had gained and kept, somehow, the confidence of the average citizen of the North. If his leadership had at times been tentative, almost fumbling, it had firmly taken the mass of the people in the direction they themselves deeply wanted. The determination and the flexible but unbreakable will that kept on waging war in the face of all manner of reverses had been his. The military victories won in the late summer and early fall of 1864 did reverse an unfavorable political current, but in the last analysis it was a majority belief in Lincoln himself that carried the day.

While these triumphs were being won, Grant's army was still dug in at Petersburg. It had had a fearful campaign. Coming to grips with Lee's army in the first week of May, it had remained in daily contact with its foes (except for the two-day interlude provided by the shift from Cold Harbor to Petersburg) for more than five months. It had fought the hardest, longest, costliest battles ever seen on the American continent, and its casualties had been so heavy that it was not really the same army it had been in the spring; most of the veterans were gone now, and some of the most famous fighting units had ceased to exist, and in all of this wearing fighting there had been nothing that could be pointed to as a clear-cut victory. The Army of the Potomac had won no glory, and it had been chewed up almost beyond recognition. It had done just one thing, but that one thing was es-

In Frank Bellew's cartoon, a giant "Majority" bears a well-satisfied President through troubled waters, with Little Mac swamped in the rear.

sential to the final Union triumph: it had compelled Lee to stay in the immediate vicinity of Richmond and fight a consuming defensive fight which he could not win.

For the Army of Northern Virginia, doggedly barring the way to Richmond, had paid a price in this campaign too. It had been worn down hard, and if its losses were not nearly as heavy as the losses which it had inflicted, its numbers had never been as great, and the capacity to recuperate quickly from a hard blood-letting was gone. In all previous campaigns in Virginia this army, under Lee's direction, had been able to make a hard counterblow that robbed the Federals of the initiative and restored the offensive to the Confederacy. That had not happened in the 1864 campaign, partly because Grant had crowded Lee too hard, but even more because the Army of Northern Virginia was not quite the instrument it had been. The razor-sharp edge was gone.

The army was still unconquerable on the defensive, and it was still knocking back offensive thrusts made by its rival, but it was no longer up to the kind of thing that had made Second Bull Run and Chancellorsville such triumphs.

In plain words, these two armies had worn each other out. The significance of this was the fact that the really decisive campaigns—the campaigns which would determine the outcome of the war—would therefore be made far to the south and west, where the Confederacy operated at a ruinous disadvantage. A stalemate in Virginia meant victory for the North. Only when the Army of Northern Virginia had the room and the strength to maneuver as of old could the nation which it carried on its shoulders hope to survive. Crippled and driven into a corner, it could do no more than protect the capital while the overwhelming weight of other Federal armies crushed the life out of the Confederacy.

Lincoln's re-election was the clincher. It meant that the pressure would never be relaxed; that Grant would be sustained in his application of a strategy that was as expensive as it was remorseless, and that no loss of spirit back home would cancel out what the armies in the field were winning. It should be pointed out that the Federal government used every political trick at its command to win the election; many soldiers were permitted to cast their ballots in camp, and where this was not possible, whole regiments were furloughed so that the men could go home and vote. However, Lincoln would have won even without the soldier vote. He got 2,203,831 votes to McClellan's 1,797,019, winning 212 electoral votes to 21 for his rival. In some states, notably New York, the winning margin was painfully narrow, and the fact that McClellan could get as much as 45 per cent of the total vote indicates that a surprisingly large number in the North were not happy about the course of events since March 4, 1861. However, 45 per cent remains a losing minority. By a substantial majority the people of the North had told Lincoln to carry the war on to a victorious conclusion. After November, triumph for the Union could only be a question of time.

THE
FORLORN
HOPE

The Federal occupation of Atlanta led to a brief lull—a final intermission, so to speak, before the curtain should rise for the last act in the war. Sherman undertook to make a fortress out of Atlanta, and he ordered all noncombatants to leave—one of the harsh acts for which Georgians never forgave him. There was a brief truce, and Union army teamsters helped the exiles get their pathetic bundles of personal property south of the city and inside the Confederate lines. Not all civilians left Atlanta, but a great many did. The town was more than half depopulated, and many abandoned homes were looted or destroyed outright. Meanwhile, the rival commanders tried to devise new strategic plans.

Sherman welcomed the breathing spell. His army needed rest and a refit, and he himself needed time to decide on his next step. Under the program Grant had laid down in the spring, Sherman had not yet attained his true objective, the destruction of Hood's army; but as he studied the situation

Tennessee's imposing marble capitol appeared as a grim fortress during the Union's 1864 defense of Nashville against Hood's forces.

now he began to realize that the whole nature of the war had changed, and that a radical reconsideration of possible objectives might be necessary. He was in the very heart of the South, and he had subject to his orders many more soldiers than his foe could bring against him. He could go anywhere he chose to go, and when he selected his goal he might not be bound by the tenets of military orthodoxy. He had broken the shell of the Confederacy, and—as he was to remark —he was finding hollowness within. His problem was to find the best way to exploit that hollowness.

Hood's problem was to get Sherman out of the South. The Confederate could hardly hope to do this by a direct attack. The inequality of the opposing forces ruled this out, and the battles around Atlanta had hurt Hood far more than they had hurt Sherman. If Sherman was to be dislodged, it must be by maneuver, and Hood concluded that his best hope was to go west of Atlanta, swing north, and attack Sherman's communications. This would force Sherman to follow him, and in the tangled country of northern Georgia an opportunity for a winning battle might somehow be developed.

So Hood put his army on the march, and as he did so Forrest went up into Tennessee and broke an important section of the railroad between Nashville and the Tennessee River. If this move had been made before the capture of Atlanta, it would have given Sherman serious trouble; even as it was, the Federals assembled 30,000 men to get Forrest out of Tennessee, and Sherman sent his ablest subordinate, Thomas, back to Nashville to make Tennessee secure. Forrest escaped the Federal net and withdrew to northern Mississippi. He got there early in October, just as Hood began his operations against Sherman's railroad line in Georgia.

Sherman left an army corps to hold Atlanta and set out after Hood, and for a fortnight or more the two armies sparred at long range and maneuvered for position. At Allatoona Pass on October 5 Hood saw an opportunity to capture large Federal stores of supplies, which were lightly guarded by a detachment under Brigadier General John M. Corse. The Confederates sent Corse a demand for immediate

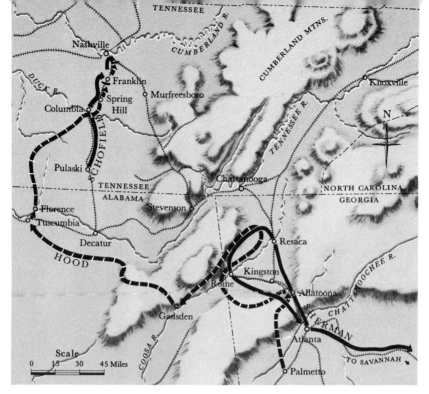

The map shows the maneuvers at Allatoona, Hood's long, looping route from Atlanta to Nashville, and the fencing with Schofield at Franklin.

surrender "to avoid a needless effusion of blood," but the Unionist stoutly replied that he was ready for just such an effusion "whenever it is agreeable to you." From nearby Kennesaw Mountain, Sherman signaled Corse—an interchange of messages which inspired a popular patriotic ballad entitled "Hold the Fort"—and in the fight that followed Corse stubbornly held on, and the Rebels were eventually forced to retire.

Hood could never quite make a real break in Sherman's railroad, and Sherman could never pin the elusive Confederate down for a finish fight; and late in October the two armies turned their backs on one another and set off in opposite directions, each general having at last evolved a new program. Taken together, the decisions of Hood and Sherman put the war into its concluding phase.

Hood had settled on a bold and desperate gamble. He would go over into northern Alabama, and from that area he would march his entire army into Tennessee, in the belief that this would force Sherman to evacuate Atlanta and come after him. Joe Wheeler, with Hood's cavalry, would remain in Georgia to keep an eye on Sherman and hurt him as much as possible. When Hood crossed the Tennessee River and started north, Forrest would go with him in Wheeler's stead. Even if this move did not persuade the Federal authorities to call off Sherman's gigantic raid, Hood might possibly overwhelm Thomas and regain Tennessee for the Confederacy, and after refitting at Nashville, he could drive north into Kentucky. From that state, Hood reasoned, he could threaten Cincinnati, and he might even cross the Cumberland Mountains to fall upon Grant's rear and thus come to the aid of Lee before Richmond. It was a plan born of desperation, and, as it turned out, it was a strategic error of the first magnitude, but the plain fact of the matter was that Hood had no good choice to make.

Sherman, meanwhile, was looking southeast to the sea, meditating a bold gamble of his own—a gamble all the more remarkable in that it involved a complete reversal of the strategic plan laid down by Grant six months earlier. Grant had insisted that Confederate armies were the chief objectives for Union strategy. What Sherman was saying now was that he would completely ignore the Confederate army which was supposed to be his target, and that he would go instead for a military intangible—the spirit that sustained the Confederate nation itself. He would march for Savannah and the seacoast, abandoning his own line of supply, living off the lush Georgia country—the harvest was in, there was corn in the bins and forage in the barns, plantation smokehouses were crammed with bacon and ham, and there were hogs and cattle in the fields. If 60,000 Union soldiers (Sherman argued) could go anywhere in the South they wanted to go, making the South support them as they moved and paying no attention to anything the South's army might try to do, they would prove once and for all that the Confederate nation was too weak to live. Lee and Hood might make war along the Southland's frontier; Sherman would make the Southern heartland his own, proving that the Confederacy could not protect the homes, the property, or the families of its own defenders. Grant was skeptical at first, but he finally approved Sherman's plan, and Sherman set off to implement it.

By November 16 the strangest movements of the war were under way: Hood was going north, striking for Nashville, and Sherman was marching southeast for Savannah. Atlanta Sherman left in flames: he had ordered that only buildings of some military potentiality should be destroyed, but his soldiers were careless with matches, and the place was full of empty dwellings, and as the Union army left most of Atlanta went up in smoke. With some 60,000 men Sherman set out for the sea.

Nowhere in Georgia was there any force that could give him serious opposition, and the march seemed to the soldiers more like a prolonged picnic than like regular war. The march was leisurely, and as it moved the army fanned out widely, covering a front sixty miles from wing to wing; and, by orders and by the inclination of its imperfectly disciplined soldiers, the army laid waste the land as it moved, doing much the same thing Sheridan had done in the Shenandoah Valley but doing it jocosely, like Halloween rowdies on a spree, rather than with the cold grimness of Sheridan's troopers. Regular foraging parties were sent out by each brigade, every morning, to bring in supplies, and these brought in far more than the army needed. Soldiers used to a diet of salt pork and hardtack ate chicken and sweet potatoes, fresh beef and southern ham, anything and everything that a rich agricultural region could provide. The supply wagons were always full, and when the army moved on, it destroyed or gave away to the runaway slaves who clustered about it more food than it had eaten.

In addition, the army was preceded, surrounded, and followed by a destructive horde of lawless stragglers. These included outright deserters, who had abandoned their regiments and had no intention of returning to them, and who were going along now on the fringe of the army just for the fun of it; they included, also, men temporarily absent without

A Yankee soldier drew this bummer, one of swarms of looters who trailed after the Union troops in Georgia.

leave, who would return to duty later but who were free-wheeling it for the time being; and they included, oddly enough, certain numbers of deserters from the Confederate army, who found kindred spirits among these lawless marauders and went with them for the sake of the loot. All of these characters, out from under anyone's control, went under the generic name of "bummers," and they made Georgia's lot far more grievous than Sherman's orders intended. They robbed and pillaged and burned all the way from Atlanta to the sea, not because they had anything against the people they were afflicting, but simply because they had gone outside of all normal controls—including their own.

Sherman probably could have suppressed them if he had tried hard. He did not try. He argued, with some justification, that his responsibility was to get his army safely to the sea, and that he could spare neither the manpower nor the energy to protect the people of Georgia while he got it there. But in point of plain fact the bummers were doing pretty largely what Sherman wanted done. They were undoubtedly being a great deal more brutal and wanton than he would have wanted them to be, but they were effectively laying waste the Confederate homeland, and that was all that mattered—to Sherman. He had said that he would make Georgia howl; Georgia was howling to the high heavens, and much of the impetus was coming from the work of the bummers. It is hard to imagine Sherman making a really serious effort to put all of these characters under proper restraint.

For this, again, was total war. Sherman's march to the sea

was the demonstration that the Confederacy could not protect its own; it was also the nineteenth-century equivalent of the modern bombing raid, a blow at the civilian underpinning of the military machine. Bridges, railroads, machine shops, warehouses—anything of this nature that lay in Sherman's path was burned or dismantled. Barns were burned, with their contents; food to feed the army and its animals was taken, and three or four times as much as the army needed was simply spoiled . . . and partly because of all of this, Lee's soldiers would be on starvation rations, and the whole Confederate war effort would become progressively weaker. Wholesale destruction was one of the points of this movement. The process through which that destruction was brought about was not pretty to watch, nor is it pleasant to read about today.

Sherman went on toward the sea, taking his time about it, and the Confederacy could do nothing to stop him. Hood, who might have engaged his attention, was going on into central Tennessee, his gamble a failure before it was made. Thomas was assembling an army of more than 50,000 men at Nashville, and Hood was a great deal weaker. The odds were great, and the fact that they were so great was a conclusive demonstration of the North's overwhelming power; the Federal government could take Sherman's army clear off the board and still outnumber the best force Hood could bring to the field.

Sherman's railroad wreckers, shown at work during the march to the sea

It took Thomas a certain amount of time, however, to get all of his forces together, and Hood was an aggressive fighter who would use his hitting power to the utmost. He was moving up from the Muscle Shoals crossing of the Tennessee, heading for Nashville by way of Franklin, and Federal General Schofield, commanding two army corps, was falling back from in front of him. Hood outmaneuvered Schofield and at Spring Hill had a chance to cut in behind him and put his whole force out of action—a blow which would have compelled the Federal high command to take Hood's movement very seriously indeed. Hood had particular admiration for the fighting qualities and generalship of the late Stonewall Jackson, and his move was now patterned after Jackson's spectacularly successful flanking march and attack at Chancellorsville. At Spring Hill he came very close to duplicating it, but at the last minute his command arrangements got completely snarled, in one way or another he failed to take advantage of his opportunity, and Schofield's army marched unmolested across the Confederate front, wagon trains and all, to escape the trap. On November 30 Hood overtook him at Franklin; furious because of the chance he had missed, Hood ordered a frontal assault on the Federal line, sending 18,000 men forward through the haze of an Indian-summer afternoon in an attack as spectacular, and as hopeless, as Pickett's famous charge at Gettysburg.

Never was a charge driven home more heroically, or at greater cost—to a more dismal defeat. In a few hours' time Hood's army lost 6,252 men, including five generals killed. The Union lines held firmly, and Hood gained nothing whatever by the assault. After dark Schofield drew away and continued his retreat to Nashville, and Hood was left in possession of the field, which he would have gained without fighting at all because Schofield had no intention of remaining there. Weaker than Thomas to begin with, Hood had further weakened his army; worse yet, his men had lost confidence in him, realizing that the whole battle had been useless.

No army in the war was unluckier than Hood's army, the

An endless line of Union tents faced Hood when he reached Nashville.

gallant Army of Tennessee. It had fought as well as any army ever fought, but mistakes in leadership always intervened to cancel out gains that were won on battlefields. Bragg had taken it far up into Kentucky and then had been able to do nothing better than lead it back south again, its mission unaccomplished. The army had nearly destroyed Rosecrans at Murfreesboro only to see its near-victory turned into defeat. It had completely routed Rosecrans at Chickamauga, but Bragg's inept handling of it thereafter had made the victory barren. It had lost more men than it could afford to lose in the heroic assaults on Sherman's troops around Atlanta, and now, at Franklin, it had almost wrecked itself in an attack that should never have been ordered. It was at a dead end. It could continue to advance, but it was on the road to nowhere.

Hood followed hard, once the Battle of Franklin was over. The Federals in Nashville were solidly entrenched; they had been occupying the city for three years, and by now it was one of the best-fortified places in the country, and Thomas had put together a force at least twice the size of Hood's. Hood put his men in camp on high ground a few miles south of Nashville and waited—for what, it is hard to determine, since he had nothing to gain by hanging on in front of Nashville. He could not conceivably take the place by storm, his force was altogether too small for him to lay siege to it, he could not side-step and march north without inviting Thomas to attack his flank and rear, and he believed that if he tamely retreated his army would disintegrate. In simple fact he had run out of strategic ideas, even of strategic possibilities, and as he waited he was no better than a sitting duck for the ablest Federal commander in the West.

Thomas was still holding back, preferring not to strike until everything was ready. Just when he completed his preparations a hard sleet storm came down, sheathing the roads and hills with glare ice and making movement impossible, so Thomas waited a few days longer for a thaw. Far off in Virginia, Grant, ordinarily a man without nerves, grew worried. He could not, at that distance, see how completely Thomas was in control of the situation; he feared that Hood would get away from him and march all the way north to the Ohio; and after fruitlessly bombarding Thomas with orders to attack at once, Grant prepared orders relieving the general from command and set out himself to go west and take control.

For the only time in his career Grant was suffering from a case of the jitters. The war was on the edge of being won, but if Hood eluded Thomas and kept on to the north the balance might be upset disastrously, and Grant was fretting about it, not realizing that Hood could do nothing whatever but await Thomas' assault. It appears that under everything

Below is a battery of Negro troops, part of the force Sherman sent to Nashville to support Thomas against Hood's anticipated attack.

there was some coolness between Grant and Thomas. Ordinarily a first-rate judge of soldiers, Grant apparently never quite rated Thomas at his true worth, and now he was unable to contain himself. It quickly became evident that Grant was indulging in a lot of quite needless worry.

Before the order relieving Thomas could be transmitted, and before Grant had got any farther on his way than Washington, Thomas struck, the ice at last having melted. On December 15 and 16 the Unionists attacked Hood's army, crushed it, and drove it south in headlong retreat. A rear guard of 5,000 men under Forrest fought a series of delaying actions, and the remnants of Hood's command at last got to safety south of the Tennessee River, but the Confederacy's great Army of Tennessee was no longer an effective fighting force. Hood was relieved from a command which had ceased to mean much, and the bits and pieces of the broken army were assigned to other areas of combat. For the one and only time in all the war, a Confederate army had been totally routed on the field of battle. It goes without saying that Grant never finished his trip west, and his order relieving Thomas was immediately canceled.

Meanwhile, Sherman had kept on moving. As far as the people of the North were concerned, he had disappeared from sight when he left Atlanta. He sent back no progress reports—could not, since all lines of communication with the North were cut—and if he and his whole army had gone underground they could not have been more completely out of touch with the home folks. Lincoln was somewhat worried, at times, but he comforted himself with the grim thought that even if Sherman's army were entirely lost, the North would still have enough soldiers to handle the Confederacy's declining armies; besides which, the President by this time had full confidence in Grant and Sherman, and he was willing to assume that they knew what they were about.

On December 10 Sherman reached the coast just below Savannah, capturing Confederate Fort McAllister, at the mouth of the Ogeechee River, and getting in touch with the U.S. fleet. News of his safe arrival went north promptly, and

Sherman drew his lines to capture Savannah and the force of 10,000 which had been scraped together to defend it.

He succeeded in taking the city—it was bound to fall, once Sherman's army had attained full contact with the navy —but Confederate General William S. Hardee managed to get the garrison out safely. The Confederate troops moved up into South Carolina, and Sherman's men marched proudly into Savannah. On December 24 Sherman sent Lincoln a whimsical telegram, offering him the city of Savannah as a Christmas present.

So 1864 came to an end, and as it did the approaching end of the war was visible for all to see. The Confederacy still had an army west of the Mississippi, where it could have no effect on the outcome of the struggle, and it had isolated forces at Mobile and elsewhere in the deep South, but it had nothing to oppose Thomas' victorious troops in Tennessee, it had no chance to bring together enough men to keep Sherman from coming north from Savannah whenever he elected to try it, and Lee was still pinned in the lines at Petersburg, unable to do more than hold on. To all intents and purposes, the Confederacy at the beginning of 1865 consisted of the Carolinas and of the southern strip of Virginia.

Below, Rebel cotton captured at Savannah is being shipped to New York.

The last gap in the blockade was closed in January, 1865, when an army-navy team took Fort Fisher. This painting shows the Rebel defenses.

One success the South had had, in December. An amphibious expedition under Benjamin Butler had tried to capture Wilmington, North Carolina, the one remaining seaport through which the South could communicate with the outer world. A Union fleet had bombarded Fort Fisher, which commanded the entrance to the Cape Fear River on which Wilmington was situated, Butler had put troops ashore—and then, growing panicky, had concluded that the place was too strong to be taken, had re-embarked his men, and had sailed north in disgraceful panic. But even the savor of this defensive victory did not last long. Butler was removed, and early in January Grant sent down a new expedition, with Admiral Porter commanding for the navy and General A. H. Terry commanding for the army. This time there was no hesitation. The navy pounded the fort hard, then Terry got his troops on the beach and sent them swarming over the defenses. Fort Fisher surrendered, and the Confederacy's last door to the outer world was closed.

Sherman was preparing to march north. In Tennessee a powerful Federal mounted force of 12,000 men armed with repeating carbines was getting ready to cut down into Alabama. Another Federal army was besieging Mobile. Grant was ordering 21,000 Western troops brought east, to move inland from captured Wilmington and join Sherman as he came north. The war was all but finished.

VICTORY

On the first of February, 1865, Sherman and his army started north from Savannah, and the war shuddered toward its conclusion. Sherman had some 60,000 veterans, and when he reached North Carolina he would be reinforced by 21,000 more under Schofield. To oppose him, the Confederacy had the troops that had been pulled out of Savannah, some threadbare levies from the broken Army of Tennessee, and sundry home-guard and cavalry units—upwards of 30,000 men in all, many of them not first-line troops. There was not the slightest possibility that it could increase this number substantially; Joe Johnston, brought back from retirement and put in charge in the hope that he might somehow find a way to halt Sherman, confessed sadly: "I can do no more than annoy him."

Johnston's return was a sign of belated and unavailing effort to put new vigor into the defense of the dwindling Southern nation. Late in January the Congress at Richmond

Still the proud, erect soldier, Robert E. Lee leaves the McLean house at Appomattox after surrendering to Grant on April 9, 1865.

had passed an act providing for a general in chief for the armies of the Confederacy, and Robert E. Lee, inevitably, had been given this position. Lee restored Johnston to command in the Carolinas, but he could do very little to help him, and there was not much Johnston himself could do. His chief immediate reliance would have to be on the weather and geography. Sherman's line of march would carry him through swampy lowland regions, cut by many rivers, and in rainy winter weather roads would be almost impassable and the streams would be swollen; all in all, it seemed improbable that he could make much progress during the winter months.

But Sherman's army had special qualities. Like the Confederate armies, it contained men who had lived close to the frontier, backwoods people who could use the axe and who could improvise their way through almost any obstacle, and these men came up through South Carolina as rapidly as they had gone across Georgia, corduroying roads, building bridges, and fording icy rivers as they came. Johnston, watching from afar, remarked afterward that there had been no such army since the days of Julius Caesar.

Sherman's men laid hard hands on South Carolina. They had been very much on their good behavior in Savannah, but they relapsed into their old habits once they left Georgia, burning and looting and destroying as they marched. There was a personal fury in their behavior now that had been missing in Georgia; to a man, they felt that South Carolina had started the war and that her people deserved rough treatment, and such treatment the unhappy South Carolinians assuredly got. The capital, Columbia, was burned after Sherman's men moved in, and although the Federals insisted that the burning had been accidental—a point which is in dispute to this day—most of the soldiers agreed that if the accident had not taken place they themselves would have burned the place anyway. As they came north their path was marked, Old Testament style, by a pillar of smoke by day and pillars of fire by night. South Carolina paid a fearful price for having led the way in secession.

Above is Barnard's photograph of fire-gutted Columbia, South Carolina.

In Richmond approaching doom was clearly visible, and
the sight stirred men to consider doing what had previously
been unthinkable—to lay hands on the institution of slavery
itself. After much debate the Confederate Congress voted a
bill to make soldiers out of Negro slaves. That this implied
an end to slavery itself was obvious, to turn a slave into a soldier automatically brought freedom, and if part of the race
lost its chains, all of the race must eventually be freed; and
there was bitter opposition when the measure was first suggested. As recently as one year earlier the idea had been
quite unthinkable. One of the best combat soldiers in the
Army of Tennessee, Irish-born General Pat Cleburne, had
proposed such a step at a conclave of generals, and the proposal had been hushed up immediately. But Cleburne was
dead now, one of the generals killed at Franklin, and Lee
himself was supporting the plan; and as spring came the
Confederacy was taking halting steps to arm and train Negro
troops.

At the same time Secretary of State Benjamin played a
card which might have been very effective if it had been
played two or three years earlier. To France and Great Britain he had the Confederacy's emissaries abroad offer the abolition of slavery in return for recognition. Neither London
nor Paris was interested: the Confederacy was beyond recognition now, and nobody could mistake the fact, so the offer
fell flat. If it had been made in 1862 or in the spring of 1863,

it might possibly have bought what Richmond wanted, but like Confederate currency it had depreciated so badly by this time that it would buy nothing of any consequence.

If there was to be a negotiated peace, then, it would have to come from Washington, and in February the government at Richmond tried to find out if Washington cared to talk terms. It was encouraged to take this step by a recent visit paid to the Confederate capital by old Francis P. Blair, Sr., one of whose sons had been Postmaster General in Lincoln's cabinet, while the other was a corps commander in Sherman's army. Old man Blair was believed to be in Lincoln's confidence, and in January he came through the lines and went to the Confederate White House for a talk with Jefferson Davis; to Davis he suggested a reunion of the states and a concerted effort by the restored nation to drive the French out of Mexico. Davis refused to commit himself on this eccentric proposal, and it developed presently that Blair had made the trip on his own hook and definitely had not been speaking for Lincoln; but the mere fact that the feeler had been put out seemed to indicate that the Lincoln government might be willing to talk terms, and a semiformal conference was arranged for February 3 on a Federal steamer in Hampton Roads, Virginia. Representing the Confederacy were Vice-President Alexander Stephens, R. M. T. Hunter of Virginia, president pro tem of the Senate, and Judge John A. Campbell of Alabama, formerly of the United States Supreme Court. Speaking for the Union at this conference were President Lincoln and Secretary Seward.

The conferees seem to have had a pleasant chat, but they got nowhere. Lincoln was leading from strength, and he had no concessions to offer. It was told, later, as a pleasant myth, that he had taken a sheet of paper had written "Reunion" at the top of it, and then had handed it to little Stephens with the remark that Stephens might fill in the rest of the terms to suit himself, but there was no truth in this tale. Lincoln's position was inflexible: there would be peace when the Confederate armies were disbanded and the national authority was recognized throughout the South, and there would be no peace until then. With acceptance of national authority, of course, would go acceptance of the abolition of slavery; the thirteenth amendment to the Constitution, ending slavery forever, had already been submitted to the states for ratification.

What this meant was that the Confederates must simply surrender unconditionally and rely on the liberality of the Federal administration for a reconstruction program that would make the lot of the Southland endurable. Of Lincoln's own liberality there was no question; he was even willing to try to get a Federal appropriation to pay slaveowners for the loss of their human property, and it was clear that he planned no proscription list or other punitive measures. But no Southerner could forget that what would finally happen would depend in large part on the Northern Congress, and such leaders as Thaddeus Stevens, Ben Wade, Zachariah Chandler, and Charles Sumner had ideas very different from Lincoln's. In the end the conference adjourned with nothing accomplished, the Southern delegates went back to Richmond, and Davis told his people that their only hope lay in war to the last ditch.

Sherman kept moving north, inexorably. As he came up through South Carolina his army sliced across the railroad lines that led to Charleston, and that famous city fell at last into Union hands. It had withstood the most violent attacks the Federal army and navy could make, but it had to be abandoned at last because the whole interior of the state was lost. The national flag went up on the rubble-heap that had been Fort Sumter, the Palmetto State was out of the war forever, and Sherman's hard-boiled soldiers tramped on into North Carolina. In this state they went on their good behavior, and the burning and devastation that had marked their path ever since they left Atlanta were held to a minimum. They did not feel the hatred for North Carolina that they had felt for her sister state; and, in point of fact, there was no military need for a policy of destruction now, because the war could not possibly last very much longer.

Well-equipped Union troops await Grant's spring Petersburg offensive.

To the Confederacy there remained just one chance—a very slim chance, with heavy odds against it. In the lines at Petersburg, Lee faced double his own numbers; in North Carolina, Johnston was up against odds that were even longer. The one hope was that Lee might somehow give Grant the slip, get his army into North Carolina, join forces with Johnston, and defeat Sherman in pitched battle. This done, Lee and Johnston might turn back toward Virginia and meet Grant on something like even terms. It was most unlikely that all of this could be done, but it had to be tried because it was the only card that could be played. Lee would try it as soon as the arriving spring made the roads dry enough to permit his army to move.

The Federal army in Lee's front occupied a huge semicircle more than forty miles long, the northern tip of it opposite Richmond itself, the southern tip curling around southwest of Petersburg in an attempt to cut the railroads that led south. Lee proposed to form a striking force with troops pulled out of his attenuated lines and to make a sudden attack on the Federal center. If the striking force could punch a substantial hole and break the military railroad that supplied Grant's amy, the Union left would have to be pulled back to avoid being cut off. That would make possible a Confederate march south and would pave the way for the combined attack on Sherman.

On March 25 the Army of Northern Virginia launched its last great counterpunch. Lee's striking force, led by the fiery young Georgian, General John B. Gordon, made a dawn attack on the Federal Fort Stedman; carried the fort, sent patrols back toward the railroad, seized a portion of the Federal trenches—and then ran out of steam, crumpled under a heavy Union fire, and at last had to confess failure. By noon the survivors of the attack were back in the Confederate lines. Lee's last expedient had misfired; now Grant would take and keep the initiative.

For many months Grant had refused to make frontal attacks on the Confederate fortifications. They were simply too strong to be taken by direct assault, so long as even a skeleton force remained to hold them, and the fearful losses of the first months of 1864 had taught the Federals the folly of trying to drive Lee's men out of prepared positions. Grant's tactics ever since had been to extend his lines to the west, using his superior manpower to compel Lee to stretch his own army past the breaking point. Sooner or later, Grant would be able to put a force out beyond Lee's flank and compel the Confederates to quit their position or fight a battle they could not win. The impassable roads of midwinter had caused a suspension of this movement, but after Fort Stedman it was resumed.

During the final days of March, Federal infantry tried to drive in past Lee's extreme right. The Confederate defenders were alert, and this infantry move was roughly handled; but Phil Sheridan, meanwhile, had brought his cavalry down from the Shenandoah Valley, after cleaning out the last pockets of Confederate resistance there, and with 12,000 mounted men he moved out to Dinwiddie Court House, south and west of the place where Union and Confederate infantry had been fighting for control of the flank. On the last day of the month Sheridan moved north from Dinwiddie Court House, aiming for a road junction known as Five Forks. This was well beyond Lee's lines; if the Federals could seize and hold it they could break Lee's railroad connections with the South, compel the evacuation of Petersburg and Richmond, and interpose themselves between Lee and Johnston. Lee sent a mixed force of cavalry and infantry out to hold Five Forks, and Sheridan called to his aid a veteran infantry corps from Grant's left flank.

On April 1 Sheridan and his powerful column routed the Confederate defenders at Five Forks. The Rebel force there was commanded by George Pickett, who would forever wear the glamour of that magnificent charge at Gettysburg, and Pickett was badly overmatched now. Sheridan had too many men and too much impetus, Pickett appears to have handled his own part of the assignment inexpertly, and as dusk came down on April 1 Pickett's column had been almost wiped out, with about 5,000 men taken prisoner, and most of the survivors fleeing without military formation or control.

Oddly enough, at the very moment that this sweeping victory was being won Sheridan removed Major General G. K. Warren from command of the Federal infantry involved, on the ground that Warren had been slow and inexpert in getting his men into action. Warren had brought the V Corps over from the left end of the Federal entrenched position; he had had a hard march in the darkness over bad roads, the orders he had been given were somewhat confusing, and the delay was not really his fault—and in any case the Union had won the battle and no real harm had been done. But Sheridan was a driver. At the very end of the war the Army of the Potomac was being given a sample of the pitiless insis-

The first Union wagon train enters captured Petersburg after April 2.

As he watched Richmond ablaze and rocked by explosions, a Confederate soldier mused that "the old war-scarred city seemed to prefer annihilation to conquest." Above is a ruined locomotive in the depot.

tence on flawless performance which it had never known before. Warren was treated unjustly, but the army might have been better off if similar treatment had been meted out to some of its generals two years earlier.

The way was clear now for Grant to get in behind the Army of Northern Virginia; to emphasize the extent of the Union victory, Grant ordered a blow at the center of the Petersburg lines for the early morning of April 2. The lines had been stretched so taut that this blow broke them once and for all. That evening the Confederates evacuated Richmond and Petersburg, the government headed for some Carolina haven where it might continue to function, and Lee put his tired army on the road and began a forced march to join forces with Johnston.

He was never able to make it. The Union advance, led by Sheridan, outpaced him, and instead of going south the Army of Northern Virginia was compelled to drift west, with Federals on its flank and following close in its rear. In the confusion that surrounded the evacuation of Richmond the Confederate government got its victualling arrangements into a tangle, and the rations which were supposed to meet Lee's almost exhausted army along the line of march did not appear. The army stumbled on, its march harassed by constant stabs from Yankee cavalry, its men hungry and worn out, staying with the colors only because of their unshakable confidence in Lee himself. At Sayler's Creek, Federal cavalry and infantry struck the Confederate rear, destroying a wagon train and taking thousands of prisoners. Witnessing the rout from high ground in the rear, Lee remarked grimly: "General, that half of our army is destroyed."

The end came on April 9, at a little town named Appomattox Court House. Federal cavalry and infantry had got across Lee's line of march, other powerful forces were on his flank, and a huge mass of infantry was pressing on his rear. He had no chance to get in touch with Johnston, no chance to continue his flight toward the west, no chance to put up a fight that would drive his foes out of the way; Lee had fewer than 30,000 soldiers with him by now, and not half of these were armed and in usable military formation. The rest were worn-out men who were pathetically doing their best to stay with the army, but who could not this day be used in battle.

The break came just as Federal infantry and cavalry were ready to make a final, crushing assault on the thin lines in Lee's front. Out between the lines came a Confederate horseman, a white flag fluttering at the end of a staff, and a sudden quiet descended on the broad field. While the soldiers in both armies stared at one another, unable to believe that the fighting at last was over, the commanding generals made

General Custer receives the flag of truce at Appomattox Court House.

their separate ways into the little town to settle things for good.

So Lee met Grant in the bare parlor of a private home at Appomattox Court House and surrendered his army. For four long years that army had been unconquerable. Twice it had carried the war north of the Potomac. Time and again it had beaten back the strongest forces the North could send against it. It had given to the Confederate nation the only hope of growth and survival which that nation had ever had, and to the American nation of reunited North and South it gave a tradition of undying valor and constancy which would be a vibrant heritage for all generations. Not many armies in the world's history have done more. Now the Army of Northern Virginia had come to the end of the road, and it was time to quit.

One option Lee did have, that day, which—to the lasting good fortune of his countrymen—he did not exercise. Instead of surrendering he might simply have told his troops to disband, to take to the hills, and to carry on guerrilla warfare as long as there was a Yankee south of the Mason and Dixon Line. There were generals in his army who hoped he would do this, and Washington unquestionably would have had immense difficulty stamping out a rebellion of that nature. But the results of such a course would have been tragic beyond comprehension—tragic for Northerners and Southerners of that day and for their descendants forever after. There would have been a sharing in repeated atrocities, a mutual descent into brutality and bitterness and enduring hatred, which would have created a wound beyond healing. Neither as one nation nor as two could the people of America have gone on to any lofty destiny after that. All of this Lee realized, and he set his face against it. He and the men who followed him had been fighting for an accepted place in the family of nations. When the fight was finally lost, they would try to make the best of what remained to them.

In Grant, Lee met a man who was as anxious as himself to see this hardest of wars followed by a good peace. Grant believed that the whole point of the war had been the effort to

Between Federal ranks Lee's army lays down its arms. A Union officer said there was no "roll of drum; not a cheer . . . but an awed stillness"

prove that Northerners and Southerners were and always would be fellow citizens, and the moment the fighting stopped he believed that they ought to begin behaving that way. In effect, he told Lee to have his men lay down their arms and go home; and into the terms of surrender he wrote the binding pledge that if they did this, signing and then living up to the formal articles of parole, they would not at any time be disturbed by Federal authority. This pledge had far-reaching importance, because there were in the North many men who wanted to see leading Confederates hanged; but what Grant had written and signed made it impossible to hang Lee, and if Lee could not be hanged no lesser Confederates could be. If Lee's decision spared the country the horror of continued guerrilla warfare, Grant's decision ruled out the infamy that would have come with proscription lists and hangings. Between them, these rival soldiers served their country fairly well on April 9, 1865.

To all intents and purposes, Lee's surrender ended things. Johnston had fought his last fight—a valiant but unavailing blow at Sherman's army at Bentonville, North Carolina, late in March—and when the news of Lee's surrender reached him he knew better than to try to continue the fight. He would surrender, too, and nowhere in the Southland was

278

there any other army that could hope to carry on. A ponderous Federal cavalry force was sweeping through Alabama, taking the last war-production center at Selma, and going on to occupy the onetime Confederate capital, Montgomery; and this force was so strong that even Bedford Forrest was unable to stop its progress. On the Gulf coast the city of Mobile was forced to surrender; and although there was still an army west of the Mississippi it no longer had any useful function, and it would eventually lay down its arms like all the rest. Lee and his army had been the keystone of the arch, and when the keystone was removed the arch was bound to collapse.

Amid the downfall President Davis and his cabinet moved across the Carolinas and into Georgia, hoping to reach the trans-Mississippi and find some way to continue the struggle. It could not be done, and the cabinet at last dispersed. Davis himself was captured by Federal cavalry, and the government of the Confederate States of America at last went out of existence. The war was over.

Davis went to a prison cell in Fort Monroe, and for two years furious bitter-enders in the North demanded that he be tried and hanged for treason. The demand was never granted; despite the furies that had been turned loose by four years of war, enough sanity and common decency remained to rule out anything like that. Davis' imprisonment, and the harsh treatment visited on him by his jailers, won him new sympathy in the South, where there had been many men who held him chiefly responsible for loss of the war, and he emerged from prison at last to become the embodiment of the Lost Cause, standing in the haunted sunset where the Confederate horizon ended.

He had done the best he could do in an impossible job, and if it is easy to show where he made grievous mistakes, it is difficult to show that any other man, given the materials available, could have done much better. He had great courage, integrity, tenacity, devotion to his cause, and like Old Testament Sisera the stars in their courses marched against him.

END AND
BEGINNING

The war had lasted for four years and it had consumed hundreds of thousands of lives and billions of dollars in treasure. It had destroyed one of the two American ways of life forever, and it had changed the other almost beyond recognition; and it ended as it had begun, in a mystery of darkness and passion. If no one could say exactly why it had come about in the first place, no one could quite say what it meant now that it was finished. (A century of reflection has not wholly answered either riddle.) Things done by men born generations after Appomattox would continue to shed light on the significance of this greatest of all convulsions of the American spirit.

Of all men, Abraham Lincoln came the closest to understanding what had happened; yet even he, in his final backward glance, had to confess that something that went beyond words had been at work in the land. When he tried to sum it up, delivering his second inaugural address on March 4,

On May 23 and 24, 1865, the victorious Union armies paraded up Washington's Pennsylvania Avenue in a final Grand Review.

1865, he could do no more than remind his countrymen that they had somehow done more than they intended to do, as if without knowing it they had served a purpose that lay far beyond their comprehension.

"Neither party," he said, "expected for the war the magnitude or the duration which it has already attained. Neither anticipated that the cause of the conflict might cease with, or even before, the conflict itself should cease." (As he spoke, the Federal Congress had passed the thirteenth amendment and seventeen states had already ratified it; and in Richmond the Congress of the Confederacy was preparing to vote regiments of slaves into the Confederate service. Slavery was dead no matter how the war came out.) "Both read the same Bible and pray to the same God, and each invokes His aid against the other. . . . The prayers of both could not be answered; that of neither has been answered fully. The Almighty has His own purposes."

It was a thing to brood over, this war with its terrible cost and its veiled meanings, and the wisest man could perhaps do little more than ask searching questions about it. As he went on with his speech Lincoln was doing nothing less than remind the people of America that they could not hope to understand what they had done and what had been done to them without examining the central riddle of human existence. As the war storm slowly ebbed he left one of the great questions for all men to ponder: "If we shall suppose that American slavery is one of those offenses which, in the providence of God, must needs come, but which, having continued through His appointed time, He now wills to remove, and that He gives to both North and South, this terrible war, as the woe due to those by whom the offense came, shall we discern therein any departure from those divine attributes which the believers in a living God always ascribe to Him?"

This question was propounded by a man who believed that both sides shared in the blame for the war, just as they had shared in the cost of it. Out of such a belief had to come a determination that both sections must also share in the vic-

From left to right in G. P. A. Healy's painting are Sherman, Grant, Lincoln, and Admiral Porter as they conferred aboard the River Queen.

tory. The peace that would come out of the war must, in Lincoln's view, be broad enough and humane enough to mean some sort of gain for everyone in the land—for the Northerner who had fought to reunite the country and to end slavery, for the Southerner who had fought against that goal, for the Negro who had humbly endured the struggle. In such a peace there could be no question of any punitive measures, any more than there could be any question of seeking to restore what the war had destroyed. If there was a triumph to celebrate, it was not the triumph of one set of men over another set, but of all men together over a common affliction.

To his great lieutenants, Grant and Sherman, Lincoln gave a glimpse of his policy in a meeting on board Lincoln's steamer *River Queen* at City Point, just before the beginning of the last campaign of the war. It was a policy rather than a detailed program, summarized in Lincoln's homely injunction: "Let 'em up easy." He wanted to see the Confederate armies disbanded and the men back at work on their farms and in the shops, and he wanted civil governments reestablished in the secessionist states at the earliest possible moment. Sherman got the impression that Lincoln was perfectly willing to deal with the existing state governments in the South in order to maintain order, until Congress could provide for a more permanent arrangement. When Sherman returned to North Carolina to finish the job against Johnston, he took with him the conviction that Lincoln wanted a peace of reconciliation with no particular concern about formalities.

So when Johnston surrendered, Sherman was guided by what he thought Lincoln wanted. Two things, however, were wrong: Sherman appears to have gone beyond anything Lincoln was prepared to offer—and when he and Johnston met to discuss surrender terms Lincoln was dead, and the atmosphere in which Northern politicians could be magnanimous and farsighted had been fatally poisoned.

Johnston was brought to bay a few days after Lee surrendered. The Union army, more than 80,000 strong, was in camp around Raleigh, North Carolina. Johnston had fewer than half that many men, and not all of them were fully armed and organized. He and Sherman met near a place called Durham's Station, aware that Lee had given up and that the only task remaining was to get the Confederacy out of existence as smoothly as possible, and on April 18 they agreed on a document. Considering the fact that Sherman was looked upon as the South's most pitiless enemy, the hard man of war who struck without compassion and laid waste whole states without remorse, it was an amazing agreement.

To begin with, it covered not simply Johnston's army, but all of the remaining armed forces of the Confederacy. (Johnston had no authority over these, but he had with him the Confederate Secretary of War, General John C. Breckinridge, and Breckinridge's word would be binding.) It went far beyond the terms Grant had given Lee. Confederate regiments were to march to their respective state capitals, deposit their weapons there, and then disband, each man signing a pledge not to take up arms again. Each state government would be recognized as lawful once its officers had taken oath to support the Constitution of the United States. No one was to be punished for the part he had taken in bringing on or supporting secession, all political rights were to be guaranteed, and the rights of person and property as defined in the Federal Constitution were to be fully respected—which might, conceivably, give slavery a new lease on life. All in all, this treaty—for it was a treaty of peace, rather than a simple surrender document—gave all that any Southerner in this spring of 1865 could hope to ask; and by this time there was not a chance in the world that the government in Washington would ratify it.

Lincoln himself would almost certainly have modified it. From the moment when Confederate surrender became an imminent probability, he had insisted that generals in the field were not to concern themselves with political questions; they should give liberal terms to the surrendering armies, but all issues involving the readmission of the states to the Union, the restoration of civil and political rights, and the abolition of slavery, they were to leave in the President's hands. (Sherman apparently had missed this particular point.) To bring the seceded states back into full relationship with the rest of the Union would take the most delicate kind of political finesse, and Lincoln proposed to handle all of this himself. Congress would not be in session until late in the fall, and it was just possible that Lincoln could have his moderate reconstruction program well enough established by that time so that the bitter-enders in House and Senate could not upset it, but he never would have let any general set the pattern for him.

But an actor named John Wilkes Booth had chosen this moment to upset everything. On Good Friday evening, April 14—driven by an insane compulsion of hatred and perverted loyalty to a cause which he had never felt obliged to fight for as a soldier—Booth strode into the President's box at Ford's Theatre in Washington, fired a bullet into Lincoln's brain, vaulted from the box to the stage, and rode off desperately through the night, fancying that if he could just reach Confederate territory he would be hailed as a hero and a savior. His twisted, inadequate mind was never able to see that his trigger finger had done the South more harm than all the lawless bummers in Sherman's army.

In all American history there is no stranger story than the story of the plot that took Lincoln's life. Booth had been

At 7:22 A.M., the moment when Lincoln died, Secretary of War Stanton, standing at right, reportedly said, "Now he belongs to the ages."

conspiring for months, doing it flamboyantly, dramatically, in a way that fairly invited detection. He had first nourished a crackbrained plan to kidnap Lincoln alive and take him down to Richmond, shifting to a scheme for wholesale murder after Lee surrendered and Richmond was captured. He planned to kill Lincoln, Grant, Vice-President Johnson, and Secretary of State Seward, and he conspired with a weird set of dimwitted incompetents who could hardly have carried out a plan to rob a corner newsstand. The odds that the whole scheme would fall of its own weight were fantastically long. And yet, somehow—the luck of the American people just then being out—the thing worked. Lincoln was assassinated; Seward barely escaped death when one of Booth's minions forced a way into his sickroom and slashed him with a knife. The plot to kill Grant and Johnson misfired, but the central, disastrous feature of the plan worked. Lincoln died.

Lincoln died early on the morning of April 15, and his death left the Republican radicals—the men who hated the South and hoped to see stern punishment inflicted on it—in full control of the Federal government. Vice-President Andrew Johnson had demanded that treason be made odious: now he was President, with full power to make the peace as stern as anyone could wish, and although he would finally come to see that Lincoln's policy was the better one, and would wreck his career trying to put it into effect, he was surrounded by men of great force and determination who would put Lincoln's ideas into the grave along with Lincoln's lifeless body.

For the immediate present the Federal government would be effectively operated by Secretary of War Stanton, who made himself something very like a dictator during the first week or two of Johnson's regime.

Booth (top, right) hatched his plot while boarding with Mrs. Mary Surratt (top, left). In the bottom row are David Herold, Booth's aide; Lewis Paine, whom Herold sent to murder Seward; George Atzerodt, who backed out of his assignment of killing Andrew Johnson; and Edward Spangler, a stage carpenter, who apparently helped Booth to escape.

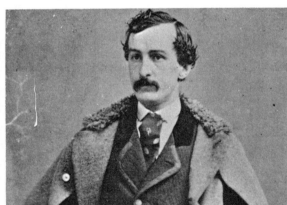

Above is Lincoln's funeral train on a Lake Michigan pier in Chicago.

Stanton was a man of immense drive; ruthless, often arrogant, of an incurably suspicious nature. The task of unraveling Booth's mad plot was in his hands, and as the details of the scheme came to light Stanton was convinced that Booth was no lone-wolf operator, but was in fact an agent for the Confederate government itself. In part this deduction came simply because Stanton was always ready to believe the worst, especially where his enemies were concerned; and in part it rested on the fact that the Confederate government had been operating that fifth-column business in the North, with agents trying to burn Northern cities, wreck railroads, seize military prison camps, and raid Yankee banks. The War Department had collected a great deal of information about this operation, some of it false, some of it true. It knew, among other things, that these operations had been directed by Confederate agents established in Canada, and it also knew that Booth himself had recently been in Canada. Under the circumstances it is hardly surprising that a man like Stanton should suspect that Booth might be a part of the Southern conspiracy which had been keeping Federal counterespionage operatives so busy.

Stanton did more than suspect: he informed the nation, without any qualifications, that Lincoln had been murdered by Jefferson Davis' agents, and that the whole tragedy was a direct part of the dying Confederate war effort. That he was never able to prove a word of this—it soon became clear that no one in Richmond had had anything at all to do with the murder, and that Booth had been as much an irresponsible fanatic as John Brown had been when he descended on

The journey virtually retraced his route to his first inauguration.

Harpers Ferry—made no difference whatever. The damage was done; in the terrible revulsion of feeling that swept across the North few people would bother to speak out for the sort of peace Lincoln himself had wanted.

Stanton and the other bitter-enders saw to it that no one in the North was allowed to get over his grief quickly. Lincoln's body lay in state beneath the Capitol dome, and there was a state funeral in the White House. Then, in a special train, the body was taken back to Springfield, Illinois, for burial—taken there in the most roundabout way imaginable, put on display in New York and Chicago and in many other cities, made the occasion for the most elaborately contrived funeral procession in American history. Millions of Americans saw it. Those who could not file past the open casket, in places where it was on display, at least could gather by the railroad tracks and watch the train as it moved slowly past. Millions of people took part in this parade of sorrow. It lasted for two weeks, and although the grief which was expressed was undoubtedly sincere, the whole affair amounted to turning a knife in a wound—turning it again and again, so that the shock of sorrow and outraged indignation which had gone all across the North might continue to be felt.

In trying to capitalize on the nation's tragedy the radicals had something real and deep to work with. The millions who stood in silence to watch the funeral car, with its black bunting, drift past on its way to Illinois were the people who had supported Lincoln through thick and thin. They had provided the armies that he had called into being. They had sustained him at the polls when the issue was in doubt. He had spoken to their hearts, in a way no one else had ever done, when he explained the ultimate meaning of the war in his address at Gettysburg and groped for the unattainable truth in his second inaugural. He had expressed the best that was in them, speaking not so much to them as for them, and he had gone with them through four years of trial by doubt and fire. As the war ended they had come to understand his greatness: and now, when he was struck down at the very moment of his triumph, they felt an anger so black that Lincoln's own vision was blotted out.

The first step was to undo what Sherman had tried to do. His treaty with Johnston went first to Grant, who could see that Sherman had done much more than any general was authorized to do. Grant sent the papers on to Stanton and suggested that the whole cabinet might want to consider them. The cabinet did want to consider them, and it disapproved them in short order; Grant was ordered to go to Sherman at once, to cancel the armistice which was a part of the Sherman-Johnston agreement, and to resume hostilities. Grant obeyed and Johnston was notified that the deal was off. There was no more fighting, as he promptly surrendered on terms identical with those Grant had given Lee.

None of this disturbed Sherman greatly. He could see that he had tried to exercise powers which belonged to the civil government, and when he was overruled he was ready to accept the fact quietly. What infuriated him was the way Stanton used the whole espisode to inflame public opinion.

For Stanton made a public announcement concerning the Sherman-Johnston agreement in a way which strongly suggested that Sherman was disloyal or crazy. This agreement, Stanton declared, practically recognized the Confederacy, reestablished the secessionist state governments, put arms and ammunition in the hands of Rebels, permitted the re-establishment of slavery, possibly made the Northern taxpayer responsible for debts run up by the Confederate government, and left the defeated Rebels in position to renew the rebellion whenever they saw fit.

The mark of war: at left is Lincoln on August 13, 1860, and at right as he appeared five years later in Washington on April 10, 1865.

An announcement of this kind, coming at the moment when the electorate was still in a state of shock because of Lincoln's assassination, and coming also at a time when the complicity of the Confederate government in Booth's murder plot was being proclaimed as an established fact, was a stunner. It raised Sherman to a high pitch of rage, and made him one of Stanton's most devout and enduring enemies; but this did no particular damage, since Sherman was a good hater and Stanton already had many enemies, and the public outcry that was raised against the general eventually subsided. In a few years no one in the North or the South would remember that Sherman had nearly wrecked his career in his attempt to befriend the South, and he would be enshrined as an unstained hero in the North and as an unmitigated villain in Southern memories. The real harm that was done was the mortal injury that was inflicted on the Lincolnian policy which Sherman, however clumsily, had tried to put into effect.

For the basis of Lincoln's whole approach to reconstruction was the belief that the broken halves of the Union could be fitted together without bitterness and in a spirit of mutual understanding and good will. The war was over, and there was no undoing of anything that had happened. No one had really intended that things should go as they had gone; the responsibility for it all was strangely divided, just as the almost unendurable suffering and heartache had been divided . . . the Almighty did indeed have His own purposes, and now it was up to the people of both sections to try to adjust themselves to those purposes and to work together in the adjustment. But by the time Lincoln's body had finished its long journey and lay in the tomb at Springfield, an atmosphere had been created in the North which put such an effort out of reach. President Johnson would try to make the effort, but he had not a fraction of Lincoln's political skill, and the job was too much for him. He was never able to use what might have been his greatest asset—the whole-hearted support which the two most famous Northern generals, Grant and Sherman, would have given to an attempt to put Lincoln's policy into effect.

No one in the North, after Lincoln's death, had anything approaching the prestige which these two soldiers had, and Johnson could have used them if he had known how. But Sherman's experience following the rejection of his "treaty" left him embittered, deeply disgusted with anything smacking of politics; thereafter he would be nothing but the soldier, letting the people at Washington commit any folly they chose to commit, and President Johnson never understood how to soften him. And Grant before long became estranged, not because he opposed what Johnson wanted to do, but simply because Johnson could not handle him. In the end he would be counted among Johnson's enemies because the radicals were able to take advantage of Johnson's clumsiness and Grant's own political innocence.

So things happened in the familiar and imperfect way that every American knows about. The Union was reconstructed, at last, at the price of bitterness and injustice, with much work left for later generations to do. A measure of the amount of work bequeathed to those later generations is the fact that nearly a century after Appomattox the attempt to work out a solution for the race problem—that great untouchable which, many layers down, lay at the abyssal depth of the entire conflict—would still be looked upon as a sectional matter and would still be productive of sectional discord. In the anger and suspicion of the reconstruction era the chance that the thing might be approached rationally, so that it could perhaps be solved rather than simply shoved aside and ignored, flickered out like a candle's flame in a gale of wind.

Nothing could be done rationally at that time because wars do not leave men in a rational mood. Bone-weary of fighting in 1865, the American people greatly desired magnanimity and understanding and a reasonable handling of vexing problems; but those virtues had gone out of fashion, and they could not immediately be re-established. What happened after the war ended grew out of the hot barren years when anger and suspicion went baying down the trail of violence: the years in which bitter appeals to unleashed emotion had made the fury of a few the common affliction of all . . . years of desperate battles, of guerrilla snipings and hangings, with a swinging torch for town and home place and the back of a hard hand to silence dissent. These had created the atmosphere in which men tried to put the Union back together, to turn enmity into friendship, and to open the door of freedom for a race that had lain in bondage. The wonder is not that the job was done so imperfectly, but that it was done at all.

For it was done, finally; if not finished, at least set on the road to completion. It may be many years before the job is really completed; generations before the real meaning and the ultimate consequences of the Civil War are fully comprehended. We understand today a little more than could be understood in 1865, but the whole truth remains dim.

Here was the greatest and most moving chapter in American history, a blending of meanness and greatness, an ending and a beginning. It came out of what men were, but it did not go as men had planned it. The Almighty had His own purposes.

A SOUND
OF DISTANT
DRUMS

The Civil War left America with a legend and a haunting memory. These had to do less with things that remained than with the things that had been lost. What had been won would not be entirely visible for many years to come, and most people were too war-weary to look at it anyway, but what had been lost could not be forgotten. The men who had marched gaily off in new uniforms and who had not come back; the dreams that had brought fire and a great wind down on a land that meant to be happy and easygoing; the buildings the war had wrecked, the countryside it had scarred, the whole network of habits and hopes and attitudes of mind it had ground to fragments—these were remembered with proud devotion by a nation which had paid an unimaginable price for an experience compounded of suffering and loss and ending in stunned bewilderment.

North and South together shared in this, for if the consciousness of defeat afflicted only one of the two sections,

The ruins of Richmond's Gallego flour mills stand stark and grim. A Northern newspaperman found in the city "the stillness of a catacomb."

The statue of a Union officer stands on Cemetery Hill at Gettysburg.

both knew that something greatly cherished was gone forever, whether that something was only a remembered smile on the face of a boy who had died or was the great shadow of a way of life that had been destroyed. People clung to the memory of what was gone. Knowing the cruelty and insane destructiveness of war as well as any people who ever lived, they nevertheless kept looking backward, and they put a strange gloss of romance on what they saw, cherishing the haunted overtones it had left.

As the postwar years passed the remembrances became formalized. In cities and in small towns the Decoration Day parade became a ritual; rank after rank of men who unaccountably kept on growing older and less military-looking would tramp down dusty streets, bands playing, flags flying, ranks growing thinner year by year until finally nobody remained to march at all. In the South the same ceremonial was performed, although the date on the calendar was different; and in both sections orators spoke at vast length, reciting deeds of bravery and devotion which somehow, considered from the increasing distance, had the power to knit the country together again. Their stereotyped speeches were oddly made significant by the deeds which they commemorated.

The South had the bitterer memories, and it wrapped them in a heavier trapping of nostalgia. Decaying plantation buildings, with empty verandas slowly falling apart under porticoes upheld by insecure wooden pillars, became shrines simply because they somehow spoke for the dream that had died, the vitality of the dream gaining in strength as the physical embodiment of it drifted off into ruin. There were cemeteries for both sections—quiet, peaceful fields where soldiers who had never cared about military formality lay in the last sleep, precisely ranked in rows of white headstones which bespoke personal tragedies blunted at last by time. There were statues, too, with great men frozen in cold marble, presiding over drowsy battlefields which would never again know violence or bloodshed.

And, finally, there was the simple memory of personal valor—the enduring realization that when the great challenge comes, the most ordinary people can show that they value something more than they value their own lives. When the last of the veterans had gone, and the sorrows and bitternesses which the war created had at last worn away, this memory remained. The men who fought in the Civil War, speaking for all Americans, had said something the country could never forget.

THE LEADING
PARTICIPANTS

The selection of military figures is limited chiefly to those who achieved corps command in the major armies or to those who gained fame through some particular exploit. Among the civilians included are Union and Confederate cabinet officers, principal war governors, and Congressional leaders. Prewar experience of most civilian figures and of certain "political generals" is included, but the emphasis is on war service. The rank listed is the highest achieved during the Civil War, and only participation in major battles or campaigns is cited.

The designation in parentheses following the name of an army indicates what command was held by the man; for example, Army of Northern Virginia (division)—Peninsula *shows that the officer was a division commander of the Army of Northern Virginia during the Peninsula Campaign. The name of the army is repeated only when the individual assumed command of that army.*

A ADAMS, CHARLES FRANCIS (1807–86)
U.S. Minister to Great Britain, 1861–68

ALEXANDER, EDWARD P. (1835–1910), Brig. Gen. CSA
1st Bull Run; Army of Northern Virginia (artillerist)—Peninsula to Appomattox; Longstreet's Corps (chief of artillery), 1864–65

ANDERSON, JOSEPH REID (1813–92), Brig. Gen. CSA
Army of Northern Virginia (brigade)—Peninsula; resigned, July '62; civilian director of Tredegar Iron Works, July '62–Apr '65

Joseph R. Anderson

299

Richard Anderson

B

P. G. T. Beauregard

ANDERSON, RICHARD (1821–79), Lt. Gen. CSA
Army of Northern Virginia (brigade and division)—
Peninsula to Appomattox; (corps)—Spotsylvania, Cold
Harbor

ANDERSON, ROBERT (1805–71), Maj. Gen. USA
Surrendered Fort Sumter; Departments of Kentucky and
the Cumberland commander, May–Oct '61; retired, Oct
'63

ANDREW, JOHN A. (1818–67)
Governor of Massachusetts, 1861–66; abolitionist leader
and vigorous supporter of the Union cause

BAKER, LAFAYETTE C. (1826–68)
Union spy and chief of the War Department's detective
bureau after 1862

BANKS, NATHANIEL P. (1816–94), Maj. Gen. USA
Governor of Massachusetts, 1858–61; Army of the Potomac (corps)—Shenandoah Valley (1862); Army of Virginia
(corps)—Cedar Mountain; Department of the Gulf commander, Nov '62–Sept '64—Port Hudson, Red River

BARTON, CLARA (1821–1912)
Clerk in the U.S. Patent Office, 1854–61; during the war
solicited and distributed medical supplies for the
wounded, and in 1881 became the first president of the
American Red Cross.

BATES, EDWARD (1793–1869)
U.S. Attorney General, Mar '61–Nov '64

BEAUREGARD, P. G. T. (1818–93), General CSA
Received surrender of Fort Sumter; field command—1st
Bull Run; Army of Mississippi commander—Shiloh; Department of South Carolina, Georgia, and Florida commander, Aug '62–Apr '64; Department of North Carolina
and Southern Virginia commander, Apr '64–Mar '65—
Petersburg, Carolinas

BENJAMIN, JUDAH P. (1811–84)
U.S. senator (La.), 1853–61; Confederate Attorney Gen-
eral, Feb–Sept '61; Secretary of War, Sept '61–Feb '62;
Secretary of State, Mar '62–Apr '65

BLAIR, AUSTIN (1813–83)
Governor of Michigan, 1861–65

BLAIR, FRANCIS PRESTON (1791–1876)
A founder of the Republican Party; exerted influence on
Lincoln through his two sons, Montgomery and Francis
Preston, Jr.; undertook an unauthorized peace mission to
Richmond, Jan '65

BLAIR, FRANCIS PRESTON, JR. (1821–75), Maj. Gen. USA
U.S. congressman (Mo.), 1857–59 and 1861–63; Army of
the Tennessee (division)—Vicksburg; (corps)—Chattanooga, Atlanta, March to the Sea, Carolinas

BLAIR, MONTGOMERY (1813–83)
U.S. Postmaster General, Mar '61–Sept '64

Braxton Bragg

BOOTH, JOHN WILKES (1838–65)
Assassinated Lincoln, Apr 14 '65; killed, Apr 26 '65

BRAGG, BRAXTON (1817–76), General CSA
Army of Mississippi (corps)—Shiloh; Army of Mississippi commander—Perryville; Army of Tennessee commander—Murfreesboro, Chickamauga, Chattanooga; military adviser to Jefferson Davis, Feb '64–Jan '65

BRAGG, THOMAS (1810–72)
U.S. senator (N.C.), 1859–61; Confederate Attorney General, Nov '61–Mar '62

BRECKINRIDGE, JOHN C. (1821–75), Maj. Gen. CSA
U.S. Vice-President, 1857–61; Army of Mississippi (corps)—Shiloh; Army of Tennessee (division)—Murfreesboro, Chickamauga, (corps)—Chattanooga; Army of Northern Virginia (division)—Cold Harbor; Confederate Secretary of War, Feb '64–Apr '65

BROWN, JOSEPH E. (1821–95)
Governor of Georgia, 1857–65; opponent of Davis administration

BUCHANAN, FRANKLIN (1800–74), Admiral CSN
First superintendent of U.S. Naval Academy (Annapolis), 1845–47; commanded ironclads *Merrimac* at Hampton Roads, Mar 8 '62, and *Tennessee* at Mobile Bay, Aug 5 '64

BUCHANAN, JAMES (1791–1868)
U.S. President, 1857–61

BUCKNER, SIMON BOLIVAR (1823–1914), Lt. Gen. CSA
Surrendered Fort Donelson; exchanged, Aug '62; Army of Mississippi (division)—Perryville; Army of Tennessee (corps)—Chickamauga

Don Carlos Buell

BUELL, DON CARLOS (1818–98), Maj. Gen. USA
Department of the Ohio commander, Nov '61–Mar '62; Army of the Ohio commander—Shiloh, Perryville; relieved, Oct '62; resigned, June '64

BUFORD, JOHN (1826–63), Maj. Gen. USA
Army of Virginia (cavalry brigade)—2nd Bull Run; Army of the Potomac (chief of cavalry)—Antietam, Fredericksburg; (cavalry division)—Gettysburg; died, Dec 16 '63

BURNSIDE, AMBROSE E. (1824–81), Maj. Gen. USA
(Brigade)—1st Bull Run; Roanoke Island; Army of the Potomac (corps)—Antietam; Army of the Potomac commander—Fredericksburg; Army of the Ohio commander, Mar–Dec '63—Knoxville; Army of the Potomac (corps)—the Wilderness, Spotsylvania, Cold Harbor, Petersburg; relieved, Aug '64

BUTLER, BENJAMIN F. (1818–93), Maj. Gen. USA
Occupation of Baltimore; Hatteras Inlet; occupation of

New Orleans, May–Dec '62; Army of the James commander, Nov '63–Jan '65—Bermuda Hundred, Fort Fisher; relieved, Jan '65

BUTTERFIELD, DANIEL (1831–1901), Maj. Gen. USA
Army of the Potomac (brigade)—Peninsula, 2nd Bull Run; (corps)—Fredericksburg; (chief of staff)—Chancellorsville, Gettysburg; Army of the Cumberland (corps chief of staff)—Chattanooga; (division)—Atlanta

C

CAMERON, SIMON (1799–1889)
U.S. Secretary of War, Mar '61–Jan '62; Minister to Russia, 1862

CANBY, EDWARD R. S. (1817–73), Maj. Gen. USA
Military Division of West Mississippi commander, May '64–May '65—capture of Mobile, received surrender of last Confederate armies

CHANDLER, ZACHARIAH (1813–79)
U.S. senator (Mich.), 1857–75; leader of Radical Republicans; member of Joint Committee on the Conduct of the War

Salmon P. Chase

CHASE, SALMON P. (1808–73)
Governor of Ohio, 1855–59; U.S. Secretary of the Treasury, Mar '61–June '64; Chief Justice of the United States, 1864–73

CHEATHAM, BENJAMIN F. (1820–86), Maj. Gen. CSA
Army of Mississippi (division)—Shiloh; (right wing)—Perryville; Army of Tennessee (division)—Murfreesboro, Chickamauga, Chattanooga, Atlanta; (corps)—Franklin-Nashville; (division)—Carolinas

CLEBURNE, PATRICK (1828–64), Maj. Gen. CSA
Army of Mississippi (brigade)—Shiloh, Perryville; Army of Tennessee (division)—Murfreesboro, Chickamauga, Chattanooga, Atlanta, Franklin-Nashville; killed at Franklin, Nov 30 '64

COBB, HOWELL (1815–68), Maj. Gen. CSA
U.S. Secretary of the Treasury, 1857–60; Army of Northern Virginia (brigade)—Antietam; District of Georgia commander, Sept '63–Apr '65

COBB, THOMAS R. R. (1823–62), Brig. Gen. CSA
Georgia secessionist and brother of Howell; Army of Northern Virginia—Peninsula, 2nd Bull Run, Antietam; (brigade)—Fredericksburg; killed at Fredericksburg, Dec 13 '62

COOKE, JAY (1821–1905)
Philadelphia banker; served as a U.S. Treasury Department fiscal agent, 1862–64, 1865, to sell government war bonds on commission

COOPER, SAMUEL (1798–1876), General CSA
Highest-ranking Confederate officer (by date of rank); Adjutant and Inspector General, CSA

COUCH, DARIUS (1822–97), Maj. Gen. USA
Army of the Potomac (division)—Peninsula, Antietam; (corps)—Fredericksburg, Chancellorsville; Army of the Cumberland (division)—Nashville

CRITTENDEN, GEORGE B. (1812–80), Maj. Gen. CSA
Son of John J.; defeated at Mill Springs; arrested, censured, and resigned, Oct '62

CRITTENDEN, JOHN J. (1787–1863)
U.S. senator (Ky.), 1854–61; offered compromise to avert war, Dec '60; U.S. congressman, 1861–63; author of Crittenden Resolution, July 25 '61, declaring preservation of the Union to be sole war aim

CRITTENDEN, THOMAS L. (1819–93), Maj. Gen. USA
Son of John J.; Army of the Ohio (division)—Shiloh; Army of the Cumberland (left wing)—Murfreesboro; (corps)—Chickamauga; resigned, Dec '64

CURTIN, ANDREW (1815–94)
Governor of Pennsylvania, 1861–67

Samuel R. Curtis

CURTIS, SAMUEL R. (1817–66), Maj. Gen. USA
Army of the Southwest commander, Feb–Aug '62—Pea Ridge; Department of the Missouri commander, Sept '62–May '63; Department of Kansas commander, May '63–Feb '65—Westport

CUSTER, GEORGE A. (1839–76), Maj. Gen. USA
1st Bull Run; Army of the Potomac (cavalry brigade)— Peninsula to Petersburg; Army of the Shenandoah (cavalry division)—Shenandoah Valley (1864), Appomattox

D DAHLGREN, JOHN A. (1809–70), Rear Adm. USN
Inventor of Dahlgren gun; Washington Navy Yard commander, Apr '61–July '62; Chief of the Ordnance Bureau, July '62–July '63; South Atlantic Blockading Squadron commander, July '63–July '65

DAHLGREN, ULRIC (1842–64), Col. USA
Son of John A.; Army of the Potomac (artillerist and aide-de-camp), 1862–63; killed on Kilpatrick-Dahlgren Richmond Raid, Mar 3 '64

DAVIS, GEORGE (1820–96)
Confederate senator (N.C.), 1862–64; Confederate Attorney General, Jan '64–Apr '65

DAVIS, JEFFERSON (1808–89)
U.S. senator (Miss.), 1847–51 and 1857–61; U.S. Secretary of War, 1853–57; elected temporary Confederate President, Feb 9 '61, and permanent President, Nov 6 '61; inaugurated, Feb 22 '62; fled Richmond, Apr 2 '65; captured, May 10 '65

DAVIS, JEFFERSON C. (1828–79), Brig. Gen. USA
Ft. Sumter; Wilson's Creek; Pea Ridge; murdered his
commanding officer, Maj. Gen. William Nelson, Sept 29
'62; Army of the Cumberland (division)—Murfreesboro,
Chickamauga, Chattanooga; (corps)—Atlanta; Army of
Georgia (corps)—March to the Sea, Carolinas

DENNISON, WILLIAM (1815–82)
Governor of Ohio, 1860–62; U.S. Postmaster General,
Sept '64–July '66

DODGE, GRENVILLE (1831–1916), Maj. Gen. USA
(Brigade)—Pea Ridge; Army of the Tennessee (division
and corps), Sept '62–Aug '64—Atlanta; Department of
Missouri commander, Dec '64–June '65

DOUBLEDAY, ABNER (1819–93), Maj. Gen. USA
Defense of Fort Sumter; Army of Virginia (brigade)—2nd
Bull Run; Army of the Potomac (division) Antietam,
Fredericksburg, Chancellorsville; (corps)—Gettysburg

DOUGLAS, STEPHEN A. (1813–61)
U.S. senator (Ill.), 1847–61; debated with Lincoln in 1858
Illinois senatorial campaign; nominated for President by
Democrats, June 23 '60; died, June 3 '61

DU PONT, SAMUEL F. (1803–65), Rear Adm. USN
Port Royal; commanded naval attacks on Charleston,
Apr–July '63; relieved, July '63

John Ericsson

E EARLY, JUBAL A. (1816–94), Lt. Gen. CSA
(Brigade)—1st Bull Run; Army of Northern Virginia
(brigade)—Peninsula, 2nd Bull Run; (division)—
Antietam, Fredericksburg, Chancellorsville, Gettysburg,
the Wilderness, Spotsylvania; (corps)—Cold Harbor,
Shenandoah Valley (1864)

ERICSSON, JOHN (1803–89)
Inventor, a naturalized Swedish immigrant whose ironclad
Monitor revolutionized naval warfare

EWELL, RICHARD S. (1817–72), Lt. Gen. CSA
(Division)—Shenandoah Valley (1862); Army of North-
ern Virginia (division)—Peninsula, 2nd Bull Run; (corps)
—Gettysburg, the Wilderness, Spotsylvania; Richmond
defenses, June '64–Apr '65; captured at Sayler's Creek,
Apr 6 '65

David G. Farragut

F FARRAGUT, DAVID G. (1801–70), Vice-Adm. USN
West Gulf Blockading Squadron commander—capture of
New Orleans, bombardment of Vicksburg, Port Hudson,
Mobile Bay

FESSENDEN, WILLIAM (1806–69)
U.S. senator (N.H.), 1854–64; U.S. Secretary of the Treasury, July '64–Mar '65

FLOYD, JOHN B. (1806–63), Brig. Gen. CSA
U.S. Secretary of War, 1857–60; turned command of Fort

Donelson over to Simon Buckner and fled; relieved, Mar '62

FOOTE, ANDREW (1806–63), Rear Adm. USN
Command of upper Mississippi River fleet, Aug '61–May '62—Forts Henry and Donelson, Island No. 10; Bureau of Equipment and Recruiting, June '62–June '63; died en route to command of South Atlantic Blockading Squadron, June 26 '63

Nathan B. Forrest

FORREST, NATHAN BEDFORD (1821–77), Lieut. Gen. CSA
Fort Donelson (cavalry command), Feb '62; Shiloh (regiment), Apr '62; capture of entire cavalry brigade, Rome, Apr '63; Fort Pillow, Apr '64; Brice's Crossroads, June '64; cavalry raids in Mississippi, Tennessee, Alabama, '64; surrendered Selma, May '65

FOX, GUSTAVUS (1821–83)
US First Assistant Secretary of the Navy, Aug '61–May '66; planned New Orleans Expedition and opening of the Mississippi River

FRANKLIN, WILLIAM B. (1823–1903), Maj. Gen. USA
(Brigade)—1st Bull Run; Army of the Potomac (corps)—Peninsula, Antietam; (Left Grand Division)—Fredericksburg; relieved, Jan '63; Department of the Gulf (corps)—Red River

FRÉMONT, JOHN C. (1813–90), Maj. Gen. USA
Western Department commander, July–Nov '61; relieved, Nov '61; Mountain Department commander, Mar–June '62—Shenandoah Valley (1862); relieved, June '62; nominated for President, May 31 '64, but withdrew, Sept 22 '64

G

GIBBON, JOHN (1827–96), Maj. Gen. USA
Army of Virginia (brigade)—2nd Bull Run; Army of the Potomac (brigade)—Antietam; (division)—Fredericksburg; (corps)—Gettysburg; (division)—the Wilderness, Spotsylvania, Petersburg, Cold Harbor; Army of the James (corps)—Appomattox

GORDON, JOHN B. (1832–1904), Maj. Gen. CSA
Army of Northern Virginia—Peninsula, Antietam; (brigade)—Chancellorsville, Gettysburg, the Wilderness, Spotsylvania; (division)—Shenandoah Valley (1864); (corps)—Petersburg, Appomattox

GORGAS, JOSIAH (1818–83), Brig. Gen. CSA
Confederate Chief of Ordnance, 1861–65

GRANGER, GORDON (1822–76), Maj. Gen. USA
Cavalry command—New Madrid, Island No. 10; Army of the Cumberland (corps)—Chickamauga, Chattanooga, Knoxville; Department of the Gulf (corps)—capture of Mobile

GRANT, ULYSSES S. (1822–85), Lt. Gen. USA
Commander—Belmont, Forts Henry and Donelson; Army

Ulysses S. Grant

Wade Hampton

of the Tennessee commander—Shiloh, Vicksburg; Military Division of the Mississippi commander, Oct '63–Mar '64—Chattanooga; named general in chief, March 12 '64; directed 1864–65 campaigns of Army of the Potomac; received Lee's surrender at Appomattox, Apr 9 '65

GREELEY, HORACE (1811–72)
Editor of the New York *Tribune,* 1841–72; radical anti-slavery leader who urged emancipation and condemned Lincoln's conciliatory policies in a famous editorial ("The Prayer of Twenty Millions," Aug 20 '62); conducted futile peace negotiations in Canada, July '64

GRIERSON, BENJAMIN H. (1826–1911), Maj. Gen. USA
Army of the Tennessee (cavalry brigade), Dec '62–May '63—Grierson's Raid, Apr 17–May 2 '63; cavalry commands, Tennessee and Mississippi, to Mar '65—Brice's Crossroads

GRIFFIN, CHARLES (1825–67), Maj. Gen. USA
1st Bull Run; Army of the Potomac (brigade)—Peninsula, Antietam; (division)—Fredericksburg, Chancellorsville, the Wilderness, Spotsylvania, Petersburg; (corps)—Appomattox

H HALLECK, HENRY WAGER (1815–72), Maj. Gen. USA
Department of the Missouri commander, Nov '61–Mar '62; Department of the Mississippi commander, Mar–July '62; general in chief of Union armies, July '62–Mar '64; chief of staff, Mar '64–Apr '65

HAMLIN, HANNIBAL (1809–91)
U.S. senator (Me.), 1848–57 and 1857–61; U.S. Vice-President, 1861–65

HAMPTON, WADE (1818–1902), Lt. Gen. CSA
1st Bull Run; Army of Northern Virginia (brigade)—Peninsula; (cavalry brigade)—Antietam, Gettysburg; (cavalry division)—the Wilderness, Spotsylvania, Cold Harbor; (cavalry corps)—Petersburg; Army of Tennessee (cavalry corps)—Carolinas

HANCOCK, WINFIELD SCOTT (1824–86), Maj. Gen. USA
Army of the Potomac (brigade)—Peninsula; (division)—Antietam, Fredericksburg, Chancellorsville; (corps)—Gettysburg, the Wilderness, Spotsylvania, Cold Harbor, Petersburg

HARDEE, WILLIAM J. (1815–73), Lt. Gen. CSA
Army of Mississippi (corps)—Shiloh; (left wing)—Perryville; Army of Tennessee (corps)—Murfreesboro, Chattanooga, Atlanta, Carolinas; Department of South Carolina, Georgia, and Florida commander, Sept '64–Apr '65

HARRIS, ISHAM G. (1818–97)
Governor of Tennessee, 1857–62; led Tennessee into the

Confederacy, May 7 '61; fled the state when Federal troops completed occupation

HAUPT, HERMAN (1817–1905), Brig. Gen. USA
In charge of transportation and construction of U.S. military railroads, Apr '62–Sept '63

HEINTZELMAN, SAMUEL P. (1805–80), Maj. Gen. USA
(Division)—1st Bull Run; Army of the Potomac (corps)—Peninsula, 2nd Bull Run; Washington defenses, Oct '62–Oct '63

HETH, HARRY (1825–99), Maj. Gen. CSA
Army of Mississippi (division)—Perryville; Army of Northern Virginia (division)—Chancellorsville, Gettysburg, the Wilderness, Spotsylvania, Petersburg, Appomattox

HICKS, THOMAS H. (1798–1865)
Governor of Maryland, 1858–62; refused to convene pro-Southern legislature, thus preventing secession; U.S. senator, 1862–65

HILL, AMBROSE POWELL (1825–65), Lt. Gen. CSA
Army of Northern Virginia (division)—Peninsula, 2nd Bull Run, Antietam, Fredericksburg, Chancellorsville; (corps)—Gettysburg, the Wilderness, Cold Harbor, Petersburg; killed at Petersburg, Apr 2 '65

HILL, DANIEL HARVEY (1821–89), Lt. Gen. CSA
Big Bethel; Army of Northern Virginia (division)—Peninsula, Antietam; Army of Tennessee (corps)—Chickamauga; relieved Oct '63; (division)—Carolinas

HOKE, ROBERT F. (1837–1912), Maj. Gen. CSA
Peninsula; 2nd Bull Run; Antietam; Army of Northern Virginia (brigade)—Fredericksburg, Chancellorsville; (division)—Cold Harbor, Petersburg; Army of Tennessee (division)—Carolinas

HOOD, JOHN BELL (1831–79), General CSA
Army of Northern Virginia (brigade)—Peninsula; (division)—2nd Bull Run, Antietam, Fredericksburg, Gettysburg; Longstreet's Corps commander—Chickamauga; Army of Tennessee (corps)—Atlanta; Army of Tennessee commander—Atlanta, Franklin-Nashville; relieved at his own request, Jan '65

HOOKER, JOSEPH (1814–79), Maj. Gen. USA
Army of the Potomac (division)—Peninsula, 2nd Bull Run; (corps)—Antietam; (Center Grand Division)—Fredericksburg; Army of the Potomac commander—Chancellorsville; Army of the Cumberland (corps)—Chattanooga, Atlanta; relieved at his own request, July '64

HOWARD, OLIVER O. (1830–1909), Maj. Gen. USA
(Brigade)—1st Bull Run; Army of the Potomac (brigade)—Peninsula; (division)—Antietam, Fredericksburg;

(corps)—Chancellorsville, Gettysburg; Army of the Cumberland (corps)—Chattanooga, Atlanta; Army of the Tennessee commander—Atlanta, March to the Sea, Carolinas

HUMPHREYS, ANDREW A. (1810–83), Maj. Gen. USA
Army of the Potomac (chief topographical engineer)—Peninsula; (division)—Fredericksburg, Chancellorsville, Gettysburg; (chief of staff), July '63–Nov '64; (corps)—Petersburg, Appomattox

HUNT, HENRY JACKSON (1819–89), Maj. Gen. USA
1st Bull Run; Army of the Potomac (artillerist)—Peninsula, Antietam; (chief of artillery)—Fredericksburg, Chancellorsville, Gettysburg, the Wilderness; in charge of Petersburg siege operations

HUNTER, DAVID (1802–86), Maj. Gen. USA
(Division)—1st Bull Run; Department of Kansas commander, Nov '61–Mar '62; Department of the South commander, Mar–Aug '62—Fort Pulaski; sanctioned first Negro regiment; West Virginia commander, May–Aug '64—Shenandoah Valley Campaign (1864)

HUNTER, R. M. T. (1809–87)
U.S. senator (Va.), 1847–61; Confederate Secretary of State, July '61–Feb '62; Confederate senator, 1862–65; Confederate representative at Hampton Roads peace conference, Feb 3 '65

J

JACKSON, CLAIBORNE (1806–62)
Governor of Missouri, 1860–62; rejected Lincoln's call for volunteers and organized state militia to defend Missouri against Federal troops

JACKSON, THOMAS J. "STONEWALL" (1824–63), Lt. Gen. CSA
(Brigade)—1st Bull Run; commander—Shenandoah Valley (1862); Army of Northern Virginia (division)—Peninsula; (left wing)—2nd Bull Run; (Jackson's command)—Antietam; (corps)—Fredericksburg, Chancellorsville; shot by his own men at Chancellorsville, May 2 '63, and died, May 10 '63

Joseph E. Johnston

JOHNSON, ANDREW (1808–75)
Governor of Tennessee, 1853–57; U.S. senator, 1857–62; member of Joint Committee on the Conduct of the War; military governor of Tennessee, 1862–65; elected U.S. Vice-President, Nov 8 '64; succeeded to the Presidency, Apr 15 '65

JOHNSTON, ALBERT SIDNEY (1803–62), General CSA
Western Department commander, Sept '61–Apr '62; Army of Mississippi commander—Shiloh; killed at Shiloh, Apr 6 '62

JOHNSTON, JOSEPH E. (1807–91), General CSA
Commander—1st Bull Run, Fair Oaks; Division of the West commander, Nov '62–Dec '63; Army of Tennessee

commander, Dec '63–July '64—Atlanta, and Feb–Apr '65—Carolinas

K KEARNY, PHILIP (1814–62), Maj. Gen. USA
Army of the Potomac (division)—Peninsula, 2nd Bull Run; killed at Chantilly, Sept 1 '62

KERSHAW, JOSEPH B. (1822–94), Maj. Gen. CSA
1st Bull Run; Army of Northern Virginia (brigade)— Peninsula, Antietam, Fredericksburg, Chancellorsville, Gettysburg; Longstreet's Corps (brigade)—Chickamauga, Knoxville; Army of Northern Virginia (division)—the Wilderness, Spotsylvania, Cold Harbor, Petersburg, Appomattox

KILPATRICK, HUGH JUDSON (1836–81), Maj. Gen. USA
Big Bethel; 2nd Bull Run; Army of the Potomac (cavalry division)—Gettysburg; Kilpatrick-Dahlgren Richmond Raid; Army of the Cumberland (cavalry division)— Atlanta; (cavalry commander)—March to the Sea, Carolinas

KIRKWOOD, SAMUEL J. (1813–94)
Governor of Iowa, 1860–64

L LANE, JAMES H. (1814–66)
Kansas Free State leader, 1855–60; U.S. senator 1861–66; strong supporter of Lincoln and Union recruiting commissioner for Kansas

Robert E. Lee

LEE, FITZHUGH (1835–1905), Maj. Gen. CSA
Army of Northern Virginia (cavalry)—Peninsula; (cavalry brigade)—Antietam, Chancellorsville, Gettysburg; (cavalry division)—Spotsylvania, Shenandoah Valley (1864); (cavalry corps)—Appomattox

LEE, ROBERT E. (1807–70), General CSA
Offered command of Union armies, Apr 18 '61, but resigned from U.S. Army, Apr 20 '61, to take command of Virginia troops, Apr–Nov '61; Department of South Carolina, Georgia, and Florida commander, Nov '61–Mar '62; military adviser to Jefferson Davis, Mar–June '62; Army of Northern Virginia commander, June 1 '62–Apr 9 '65— Peninsula to Appomattox; named Confederate general in chief, Feb 6 '65; surrendered to Grant, Apr 9 '65

LEE, STEPHEN D. (1833–1908), Lt. Gen. CSA
Army of Northern Virginia (artillery)—Peninsula, 2nd Bull Run, Antietam; Vicksburg defenses (division)— Chickasaw Bluffs, Champion's Hill; captured at Vicksburg and exchanged; cavalry command in Mississippi— Tupelo; Army of Tennessee (corps)—Atlanta, Franklin-Nashville, Carolinas

LETCHER, JOHN (1813–84)
Governor of Virginia, 1860–64

LINCOLN, ABRAHAM (1809–65)
Nominated for Presidency, May 18 '60, and elected, Nov 6 '60; inaugurated, Mar 4 '61; ordered reinforcements to Fort Sumter, Apr 4 '61; called for volunteers, Apr 15 '61; proclaimed blockade, Apr 19 '61; Emancipation Proclamation, Jan 1 '63; Gettysburg Address, Nov 19 '63; renominated, June 8 '64, and re-elected, Nov 8 '64; inaugurated, Mar 4 '65; visited Richmond, Apr 4 '65; shot, Apr 14 '65, and died, Apr 15 '65

James Longstreet

LOGAN, JOHN A. (1826–86), Maj. Gen. USA
Fort Donelson; Army of the Tennessee (division)— Vicksburg; (corps)—Atlanta; Army of the Tennessee commander—July 22–27 '64; (corps)—Carolinas

LONGSTREET, JAMES (1821–1904), Lt. Gen. CSA
(Brigade)—1st Bull Run; Army of Northern Virginia (division)—Peninsula; (right wing)—2nd Bull Run; (Longstreet's command)—Antietam; (corps)—Fredericksburg, Gettysburg; Army of Tennessee (left wing) —Chickamauga; Confederate commander—Knoxville; Army of Northern Virginia (corps)—the Wilderness, Petersburg, Appomattox

LYON, NATHANIEL (1818–61), Brig. Gen. USA
Department of the West commander, May–July '61; killed at Wilson's Creek, Aug 10 '61

LYONS, RICHARD, 1ST EARL LYONS (1817–87)
British Minister to the United States, 1858–65

M

McCLELLAN, GEORGE B. (1826–85), Maj. Gen. USA
Department of the Ohio commander, May–July '61— Philippi, Rich Mountain; District of the Potomac commander, July–Aug '61; Army of the Potomac commander, Aug '61–Nov '62—Peninsula, Antietam; general in chief, Nov '61–July '62; relieved, Nov '62; Democratic candidate for Presidency, 1864

George B. McClellan

McCLERNAND, JOHN A. (1812–1900), Maj. Gen. USA
U.S. congressman (Ill.), 1859–61; Forts Henry and Donelson; Army of the Tennessee (division)—Shiloh; commander—Fort Hindman; Army of the Tennessee (corps)—Vicksburg; relieved, June '63

McCOOK, ALEXANDER McD. (1831–1903), Maj. Gen. USA
(Brigade)—1st Bull Run; Army of the Ohio (division)— Shiloh; (corps)—Perryville; Army of the Cumberland (right wing)—Murfreesboro; (corps)—Chickamauga; relieved, Oct '63

McCOOK, DANIEL (1798–1863)
U.S. Army paymaster; father of Alexander McD., Daniel, Jr., and five other sons in the Union army; wounded attempting to trap Morgan's raiders at Buffington, Ohio, July 19 '63, and died, July 21 '63

McCook, Daniel, Jr. (1834–64), Brig. Gen. USA
Wilson's Creek; Shiloh; Army of the Ohio (brigade)—Perryville; Army of the Cumberland (brigade)—Chickamauga, Atlanta; wounded at Kennesaw Mountain, June 27 '64, and died, July 17 '64

McCook, Edward M. (1833–1909), Maj. Gen. USA
Shiloh; Army of the Ohio (cavalry brigade)—Perryville; Army of the Cumberland (cavalry division)—Chickamauga, Atlanta

McCook, John (1806–65)
U.S. Army surgeon; father of Edward M. and four other sons in the Union army; brother of Daniel

McCulloch, Hugh (1808–95)
U.S. Secretary of the Treasury, Mar '65–Mar '69

McDowell, Irvin (1818–85), Maj. Gen. USA
Commander—1st Bull Run; Army of the Potomac (division and corps), Oct '61–Apr '62; Army of the Rappahannock commander, Apr–June '62; Army of Virginia (corps)—2nd Bull Run; relieved, Sept '62

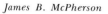

James B. McPherson

McLaws, Lafayette (1821–97), Maj. Gen. CSA
Army of Northern Virginia (division)—Peninsula, Antietam, Fredericksburg, Chancellorsville, Gettysburg; Longstreet's Corps (division)—Chickamauga, Knoxville; relieved, Dec '63; District of Georgia commander, May '64–Apr '65; Army of Tennessee (division)—Carolinas

McPherson, James B. (1828–64), Maj. Gen. USA
Chief engineer—Forts Henry and Donelson, Shiloh; Army of the Tennessee (brigade)—Iuka; (division) Oct '62–Jan '63; (corps)—Vicksburg; Army of the Tennessee commander—Atlanta; killed at Atlanta, July 22 '64

Magoffin, Beriah (1815–85)
Governor of Kentucky, 1860–62, whose efforts to call secession conventions in May and June '61 were blocked by Unionist legislature; resigned under pressure, Aug '62

Magruder, John B. (1810–71), Maj. Gen. CSA
Confederate commander—Big Bethel; Army of Northern Virginia (Magruder's command)—Peninsula; district command in Texas and Arkansas, Oct '62–May '65

Mahone, William (1826–95), Maj. Gen. CSA
Norfolk District commander, Nov '61–May '62; Army of Northern Virginia (brigade)—Peninsula, 2nd Bull Run, Fredericksburg, Chancellorsville, Gettysburg, the Wilderness, Spotsylvania, Petersburg (Crater); (division)—Petersburg, Appomattox

Mallory, Stephen R. (1813–73)
U.S. senator (Fla.), 1851–61; Confederate Secretary of the Navy, Mar '61–Apr '65

Mansfield, Joseph K. F. (1803–62), Maj. Gen. USA
Department of Washington commander, Apr '61–May '62;

Army of the Potomac (corps)—Antietam; killed at Antietam, Sept 17 '62

MASON, JAMES M. (1798–1871)
U.S. senator (Va.), 1847–61; named Confederate commissioner to Great Britain, Aug '61; captured on board *Trent*, Nov 8 '61; imprisoned in Boston; released, Jan 1 '62; in England from Jan '62

Montgomery Meigs

MEADE GEORGE GORDON (1815–72), Maj. Gen. USA
Army of the Potomac (brigade)—Peninsula, 2nd Bull Run; (division)—Antietam, Fredericksburg; (corps)—Chancellorsville; Army of the Potomac commander, June '63–Apr '65—Gettysburg to Appomattox

MEIGS, MONTGOMERY (1816–92), Maj. Gen. USA
Quartermaster General, USA, 1861–65

MEMMINGER, CHRISTOPHER G. (1803–88)
Confederate Secretary of the Treasury, Mar '61–June '64

MILROY, ROBERT H. (1816–90), Maj. Gen. USA
West Virginia district command, Oct '61–Apr '62; Army of Virginia (brigade)—2nd Bull Run; district commands, West Virginia, Nov '62–June '63; Nashville and Chattanooga R.R. defenses, July '64–Apr '65

John S. Mosby

MORGAN, JOHN HUNT (1825–64), Brig. Gen. CSA
Shiloh; Kentucky raids, July, Oct, Dec '62; Ohio Raid, July '63; captured at New Lisbon, Ohio, July 26 '63; escaped from Ohio State Penitentiary, Nov 26 '63; killed at Greeneville, Tenn., Sept 4 '64

MORTON, OLIVER P. (1823–77)
Governor of Indiana, 1861–67; governed his state as a virtual pro-Union dictator, 1863–65

MOSBY, JOHN S. (1833–1916), Col. CSA
1st Bull Run; Stuart's first ride around McClellan; commander of Partisan Rangers in Virginia, Jan '63–Apr '65

N NEWTON, JOHN (1823–95), Maj. Gen. USA
Washington defenses, Aug '61–Mar '62; Army of the Potomac (brigade)—Peninsula, Antietam; (division)—Fredericksburg, Chancellorsville; (corps)—Gettysburg; Army of the Cumberland (division)—Atlanta

O ORD, EWARD O. C. (1818–83), Maj. Gen. USA
Washington defenses, Oct '61–Mar '62; Army of the Tennessee (division and district), June–Oct '62; (corps)—Vicksburg; Department of the Gulf (corps), Sept '63–Feb '64; Army of the James (corps)—Petersburg; Army of the James commander—Appomattox

OSTERHAUS, PETER J. (1823–1917), Maj. Gen. USA
Wilson's Creek; (division)—Pea Ridge; Army of the Tennessee (division)—Vicksburg, Chattanooga, Atlanta; (corps)—March to the Sea

P

PAINE, LEWIS (1845–65)
Attempted assassination of Secretary of State Seward, Apr 14 '65; tried and convicted; hanged, July 7 '65

PEGRAM, JOHN (1832–65), Brig. Gen. CSA
West Virginia (1861); Army of Mississippi (chief engineer), Apr–Oct '62; Army of Tennessee (cavalry brigade) —Murfreesboro; (cavalry division)—Chickamauga; Army of Northern Virginia (brigade)—the Wilderness; (division)—Shenandoah Valley (1864), Petersburg; killed at Hatcher's Run, Feb 6 '65

John C. Pemberton

PELHAM, JOHN (1838–63), Maj. CSA
1st Bull Run; Peninsula; 2nd Bull Run; Antietam; Stuart's second ride around McClellan; Fredericksburg; led Stuart's Horse Artillery; killed at Kelly's Ford, Mar 17 '63

PEMBERTON, JOHN C. (1814–81), Lt. Gen. CSA
Department of South Carolina, Georgia, and Florida commander, Mar–Sept '62; Department of Mississippi, Tennessee, and East Louisiana commander, Oct '62–July '63—Vicksburg defenses; surrendered at Vicksburg, July 4 '63; exchanged, and resigned, May '64

PENDER, WILLIAM D. (1834–63), Maj. Gen. CSA
Army of Northern Virginia (brigade)—Peninsula, 2nd Bull Run, Antietam, Fredericksburg, Chancellorsville; (division)—Gettysburg; wounded at Gettysburg, July 2 '63, and died, July 18 '63

PENDLETON, WILLIAM N. (1809–83), Brig. Gen. CSA
Army of Northern Virginia (chief of artillery), Mar '62–Apr '65

PICKETT, GEORGE E. (1825–75), Maj. Gen. CSA
Army of Northern Virginia (brigade)—Peninsula; (division)—Fredericksburg, Gettysburg; Department of Virginia and North Carolina commander, Sept '63–May '64—Drewry's Bluff; Army of Northern Virginia (division)—Cold Harbor, Petersburg, Appomattox

PINKERTON, ALLAN (1819–84)
Department of the Ohio chief detective, May–July '61; organized the Secret Service in 1861; Army of the Potomac chief detective, Aug '61–Nov '62

PLEASONTON, ALFRED (1824–97), Maj. Gen. USA
Peninsula; Army of the Potomac (cavalry division)—Antietam, Fredericksburg, Chancellorsville; (cavalry corps)—Gettysburg

POLK, LEONIDAS (1806–64), Lt. Gen. CSA
Western Department commander, July–Sept '61—Belmont; Army of Mississippi (corps)—Shiloh; Army of Mississippi commander—Perryville; Army of Tennessee (corps)—Murfreesboro; (right wing)—Chickamauga;

(corps)—Atlanta; killed at Pine Mountain, Ga., June 14 '64

Pope, John (1822–92), Maj. Gen. USA
Army of the Mississippi commander, Feb–June '62—New Madrid, Island No. 10; Army of Virginia commander—2nd Bull Run; Department of the Northwest commander, Sept–Nov '62 and Feb '63–Feb '65

Porter, David Dixon (1813–91), Rear Adm. USN
Capture of New Orleans; Mississippi Squadron commander, Oct '62–July '63—Fort Hindman, Vicksburg; command of lower Mississippi River fleet, Aug '63–Oct '64—Red River; North Atlantic Blockading Squadron commander, Oct '64–Apr '65—Fort Fisher

David D. Porter

Porter, Fitz-John (1822–1901), Maj. Gen. USA
Army of the Potomac (division)—Yorktown siege; (corps)—Peninsula, 2nd Bull Run, Antietam; relieved, Nov '62, and cashiered, Jan '63, for conduct at 2nd Bull Run; exonerated, May '82

Price, Sterling (1809–67), Maj. Gen. CSA
Missouri State Guard commander—Wilson's Creek, Lexington, Pea Ridge; Army of the West commander—Iuka; Army of West Tennessee (corps)—Corinth; Price's Missouri Raid—Westport

Q **Quantrill, William C.** (1837–65), Col. CSA
Wilson's Creek; guerrilla raids on Independence, Mo., Aug 11 '62, Lawrence, Kan., Aug 21 '63, and Baxter Springs, Kan., Oct 6 '63; killed in Kentucky, May 10 '65

R **Randolph, George W.** (1818–67)
Confederate Secretary of War, Mar–Nov '62

Reagan, John H. (1818—1905)
Confederate Postmaster General, Mar '61–Apr '65

Reynolds, John F. (1820–63), Maj. Gen. USA
Army of the Potomac (brigade)—Peninsula; (division)—2nd Bull Run; (corps)—Fredericksburg, Chancellorsville, Gettysburg; killed at Gettysburg, July 1 '63

Rhett, Robert Barnwell (1800–1876)
U.S. senator (S.C.), 1851–55; advocated secession in the Charleston *Mercury*

Ricketts, James B. (1817–87), Maj. Gen. USA
1st Bull Run; Army of Virginia (division)—2nd Bull Run; Army of the Potomac (division)—Antietam, the Wilderness, Spotsylvania, Cold Harbor, Petersburg, Monocacy; Army of the Shenandoah (corps)—Shenandoah Valley (1864)

Rodes, Robert E. (1829–64), Maj. Gen. CSA
1st Bull Run; Army of Northern Virginia (brigade)—Peninsula, Antietam, Fredericksburg; (division)—Chancellorsville (temporary corps command), Gettysburg, the

Wilderness, Spotsylvania, Shenandoah Valley (1864); killed at Winchester, Sept 19 '64

ROSECRANS, WILLIAM S. (1819–98), Maj. Gen. USA
Rich Mountain; Army of Occupation and Department of West Virginia, July '61–Mar '62; Army of the Mississippi commander—Iuka, Corinth; Army of the Cumberland commander—Murfreesboro, Chickamauga; relieved, Oct '63

RUFFIN, EDMUND (1794–1865)
Virginia agriculturist and secessionist; credited with firing first shot at Fort Sumter; fought at 1st Bull Run; committed suicide, June 18 '65

S SCHOFIELD, JOHN McA. (1831–1906), Maj. Gen. USA

John McA. Schofield

Wilson's Creek; district and department commander in Missouri, Nov '61–Jan '64; Army of the Ohio (or XXIII Corps) commander—Atlanta, Franklin-Nashville, Carolinas

SCHURZ, CARL (1829–1906), Brig. Gen. USA
U.S. Minister to Spain, 1861–62; Army of Virginia (division)—2nd Bull Run; Army of the Potomac (division)—Chancellorsville; Army of the Cumberland (division)—Chattanooga; relieved at his own request and campaigned for Lincoln in 1864

SCOTT, WINFIELD (1786–1866), Lt. Gen. USA
General in chief, USA, 1841–61; proposed so-called Anaconda Plan strategy for Civil War; succeeded by McClellan, Nov '61

SEDDON, JAMES A. (1815–80)
Confederate Secretary of War, Nov '62–Feb '65

SEDGWICK, JOHN (1813–64), Maj. Gen. USA
Army of the Potomac (brigade and division), Oct '61–Mar '62—Washington defenses; (division)—Peninsula, Antietam; (corps)—Chancellorsville, Gettysburg, the Wilderness, Spotsylvania; killed at Spotsylvania, May 9 '64

SEMMES, RAPHAEL (1809–77), Rear Adm. CSN
Commander of Confederate commerce raiders *Sumter*, June '61–Jan '62, and *Alabama*, Aug '62–June '64; lost naval battle with *Kearsarge* off French coast, June 19 '64; returned to Confederacy to assume command of James River squadron until Apr '65

SEWARD, WILLIAM H. (1801–72)
U.S. senator (N.Y.), 1849–61; U.S. Secretary of State, Mar '61–Mar '69; participated in Hampton Roads peace conference, Feb 3 '65; victim of unsuccessful assassination attempt, Apr 14 '65

SEYMOUR, HORATIO (1810–86)
Governor of New York, 1853–55 and 1863–65; prominent Democratic opposition leader

SEYMOUR, TRUMAN (1824–91), Maj. Gen. USA
Fort Sumter; Army of the Potomac (brigade and division) —Peninsula; (brigade)—2nd Bull Run; (brigade and division)—Antietam; Department of the South, Dec '62–Mar '64—Charleston siege, Olustee; Army of the Potomac (brigade)—the Wilderness; (division)—Petersburg, Appomattox

SHELBY, JOSEPH O. (1830–97), Brig. Gen. CSA
Wilson's Creek; Lexington; Pea Ridge; Arkansas and Missouri cavalry raids, June '62–Oct '64

SHERIDAN, PHILIP H. (1831–88), Maj. Gen. USA
Army of the Ohio (division)—Perryville; Army of the Cumberland (division)—Murfreesboro, Chickamauga, Chattanooga; Army of the Potomac (cavalry corps)—the Wilderness, Spotsylvania, Richmond Raid, Cold Harbor, Appomattox; Army of the Shenandoah commander, Aug '64–Mar '65

William T. Sherman

SHERMAN, WILLIAM TECUMSEH (1820–91), Maj. Gen. USA
(Brigade)—1st Bull Run; Department of the Cumberland commander, Oct–Nov '61; Army of the Tennessee (division)—Shiloh; (corps)—Chickasaw Bluffs, Fort Hindman, Vicksburg; Army of the Tennessee commander, Oct '63–Mar '64—Chattanooga, Meridian; Military Division of the Mississippi commander, Mar '64–Apr '65—Atlanta, March to the Sea, Carolinas

SHIELDS, JAMES (1806–79), Maj. Gen. USA
Army of the Potomac (division and corps)—Shenandoah Valley (1862); resigned, Mar '63

SICKLES, DANIEL E. (1825–1914), Maj. Gen. USA
U.S. congressman (N.Y.), 1857–61; Army of the Potomac (brigade)—Peninsula; (division)—Fredericksburg; (corps) —Chancellorsville, Gettysburg

Franz Sigel

SIGEL, FRANZ (1824–1902), Maj. Gen. USA
Union leader of German-Americans; Wilson's Creek; (division)—Pea Ridge; Army of Virginia (corps)—2nd Bull Run; Army of the Potomac (corps), Sept '62–Feb '63; Department of West Virginia commander, Mar–May '64—New Market; relieved, July '64

SLIDELL, JOHN (1793–1871)
U.S. senator (La.), 1853–61; named Confederate commissioner to France, Aug '61; captured on board *Trent*, Nov 8 '61; imprisoned in Boston; released, Jan 1 '62; in France from Feb '62

SLOCUM, HENRY W. (1827–94), Maj. Gen. USA
1st Bull Run; Army of the Potomac (division)—Peninsula, Antietam; (corps)—Chancellorsville, Gettysburg; Army of the Cumberland (corps)—Atlanta; Army of Georgia commander—March to the Sea, Carolinas

SMITH, ANDREW J. (1815–97), Maj. Gen. USA
Department of the Mississippi (cavalry), Feb–July '62;
(division)—Chickasaw Bluffs, Fort Hindman; Army of the
Tennessee (division)—Vicksburg, Tupelo; (corps)—Red
River, Nashville

SMITH, CALEB BLOOD (1808–64)
U.S. Secretary of the Interior, Mar '61–Dec '62

SMITH, CHARLES F. (1807–62), Maj. Gen. USA
(Division)—Forts Henry and Donelson; advised Grant to
ask for unconditional surrender at Donelson; temporary
command of Grant's army in the Shiloh campaign, Mar
4–13 '62; died, Apr 25 '62

SMITH, EDMUND KIRBY (1824–93), General CSA
(Brigade)—1st Bull Run; Department of East Tennessee
commander—Invasion of Kentucky; Trans-Mississippi Department commander, Mar '63–May '65— Red River; surrendered last Confederate army, May 26 '65

Gustavus W. Smith

SMITH, GUSTAVUS W. (1822–96), Maj. Gen. CSA
Army of Northern Virginia (left wing)—Fair Oaks; Confederate Secretary of War (interim), Nov '62; resigned,
Feb '63; Georgia militia commander—Atlanta, March to
the Sea

SMITH, WILLIAM (1796–1887), Maj. Gen. CSA
U.S. congressman (Va.), 1853–61; 1st Bull Run; Army of
Northern Virginia—Peninsula; (brigade)—Antietam,
Chancellorsville, Gettysburg; served in Confederate Con-
gress between campaigns; Governor of Virginia, Jan
'64–Apr '65

SMITH, WILLIAM F. (1824–1903), Maj. Gen. USA
Army of the Potomac (division)—Peninsula, Antietam;
(corps)—Fredericksburg; "cracker line" operations at
Chattanooga; Army of the Potomac (corps)—Cold Harbor, Petersburg; relieved, July '64

SMITH, WILLIAM SOOY (1830–1916), Brig. Gen. USA
Army of the Ohio (brigade)—Shiloh; (division)—
Perryville; Army of the Tennessee (division)—Vicksburg;
(chief of cavalry), July '63–July '64—Okolona; resigned,
July '64

SPEED, JAMES (1812–87)
U.S. Attorney General, Dec '64–July '66

SPRAGUE, WILLIAM (1830–1915)
Governor of Rhode Island, 1859–63; led a militia regiment at 1st Bull Run, Yorktown, Williamsburg; U.S. senator (R.I.), 1864–75

STANTON, EDWIN MCMASTERS (1814–69)
U.S. Attorney General, Dec '60–Mar '61; U.S. Secretary of
War, Jan '62–May '68; assumed near-dictatorial powers
after Lincoln's assassination

317

STEELE, FREDERICK (1819–68), Maj. Gen. USA
Wilson's Creek; (division)—Chickasaw Bluffs, Fort Hindman; Army of the Tennessee (division)—Vicksburg; Arkansas expeditions, 1863, 1864—Little Rock, Jenkins Ferry; Department of the Gulf (corps)—capture of Mobile

STEPHENS, ALEXANDER H. (1812–83)
U.S. congressman (Ga.), 1843–59; Confederate Vice-President, Feb '61–Apr '65; Confederate representative at Hampton Roads peace conference, Feb 3 '65

STEVENS, THADDEUS (1792–1868)
U.S. congressman (Pa.), 1859–68; leader of Radical Republicans and chairman of Ways and Means Committee

STEWART, ALEXANDER P. (1821–1908), Lt. Gen. CSA
Belmont; Army of Mississippi (brigade)—Shiloh, Perryville; Army of Tennessee (brigade)—Murfreesboro; (division)—Chickamauga, Chattanooga; (corps)—Atlanta, Franklin-Nashville, Carolinas

STONEMAN, GEORGE (1822–94), Maj. Gen. USA

J. E. B. Stuart

Army of the Potomac (cavalry division)—Peninsula; (corps)—Fredericksburg; (cavalry corps)—Chancellorsville; Cavalry Bureau chief, July '63–Jan '64; Army of the Ohio (cavalry division)—Atlanta; captured near Macon, Ga., July 30 '64, and exchanged; Department of the Ohio commander, Nov '64–Jan '65; District of East Tennessee commander, Mar–Apr '65

STUART, J. E. B. (1833–64), Maj. Gen. CSA
1st Bull Run; Army of Northern Virginia (cavalry command)—Peninsula, first ride around McClellan, 2nd Bull Run, Antietam, second ride around McClellan, Fredericksburg, Chancellorsville (temporarily in command of Jackson's corps), Brandy Station, Gettysburg Raid, the Wilderness, Spotsylvania; wounded at Yellow Tavern, May 11 '64; died, May 12 '64

STURGIS, SAMUEL D. (1822–89), Maj. Gen. USA

Edwin V. Sumner

Wilson's Creek; Army of Virginia (brigade)—2nd Bull Run; Army of the Potomac (division)—Antietam, Fredericksburg; Department of the Ohio (chief of cavalry), July '63–April '64; defeated at Brice's Crossroads

SUMNER, CHARLES (1811–74)
U.S. senator (Mass.), 1851–74; abolitionist and prominent leader of the Radical Republicans

SUMNER, EDWIN V. (1797–1863), Maj. Gen. USA
Army of the Potomac (corps)—Peninsula, Antietam; (Right Grand Division)—Fredericksburg; relieved at his own request, Jan '63; died, Mar 21 '63

SYKES, GEORGE (1822–80), Maj. Gen. USA
1st Bull Run; Army of the Potomac (division)—Peninsula, 2nd Bull Run, Antietam, Fredericksburg,

Chancellorsville; (corps)—Gettysburg, Mine Run; relieved, Mar '64

George H. Thomas

Emory Upton

T Taylor, Richard (1826–79), Lt. Gen. CSA
(Brigade)—Shenandoah Valley (1862); Army of Northern Virginia (brigade)—Peninsula; District of Western Louisiana commander—Red River; Department of East Louisiana, Mississippi, and Alabama commander, Aug '64–May '65; surrendered, May 4 '65

Terry, Alfred H. (1827–90), Maj. Gen. USA
1st Bull Run; Port Royal; Fort Pulaski; Department of the South and Department of Virginia and North Carolina (division and corps), Oct '62–Jan '65—siege of Charleston, Petersburg; Terry's Provisional Corps—Fort Fisher; Army of the Ohio (corps)—Carolinas

Thomas, George H. (1816–70), Maj. Gen. USA
Army of the Ohio (division)—Mill Springs; (second in command)—Perryville; Army of the Cumberland (center)—Murfreesboro; (corps)—Chickamauga; Army of the Cumberland commander—Chattanooga, Atlanta, Franklin-Nashville

Tod, David, 1805–68
Governor of Ohio, 1862–64

Tompkins, Sally L. (1833–1916)
Operated, at her own expense, a hospital for Confederate wounded at Richmond, 1861–65; only woman to receive a commission in the Confederate army (Captain, Sept 9 '61)

Toombs, Robert (1810–85), Brig. Gen. CSA
U.S. senator (Ga.), 1853–61; Confederate Secretary of State, Mar–July '61; Army of Northern Virginia (brigade)—Peninsula, 2nd Bull Run, Antietam; resigned, Mar '63.

Trenholm, George A. (1806–76)
Confederate Secretary of the Treasury, July '64–Apr '65

U Upton, Emory (1839–81), Maj. Gen. USA
1st Bull Run; Peninsula; Antietam; Fredericksburg; Chancellorsville; Gettysburg; Army of the Potomac (brigade)—the Wilderness, Spotsylvania, Cold Harbor, Petersburg; Army of the Shenandoah (brigade)—Shenandoah Valley (1864)

Usher, John P. (1816–89)
U.S. Secretary of the Interior, Jan '63–May '65

V Vallandigham, Clement L. (1820–71)
U.S. congressman (Ohio), 1858–63; leader of Copperhead Democrats; exiled to South, May '63; defeated for Ohio governorship, Oct '63; returned to the North to write peace platform at Democratic convention, Aug '64

Vance, Zebulon B. (1830–94)
Governor of North Carolina, 1863–65

Van Dorn, Earl (1820–63), Maj. Gen. CSA
Army of the West commander—Pea Ridge; Army of West Tennessee commander—Corinth, Holly Springs; murdered by a civilian, May 8 '63

W

Wade, Benjamin F. (1800–78)
U.S. senator (Ohio), 1851–69; Radical Republican and chairman of Joint Committee on the Conduct of the War; co-author of Wade-Davis Reconstruction Bill, July 4 '64, which received a "pocket veto" from Lincoln, and Wade-Davis Manifesto, Aug 5 '64, which denounced Lincoln for the veto

Walker, Leroy P. (1817–84)
Confederate Secretary of War, Mar–Sept '61

Lew Wallace

Wallace, Lew (1827–1905), Maj. Gen. USA
(Division)—Fort Donelson; Army of the Tennessee (division)—Shiloh; commander—Monocacy; served on court-martial of Lincoln's assassins; president of court-martial which convicted Henry Wirz, commandant of Andersonville

Wallace, William H. L. (1821–62), Brig. Gen. USA
Forts Henry and Donelson; Army of the Tennessee (division)—Shiloh; wounded at Shiloh, Apr 6 '62, and died, Apr 10 '62

Warren, Gouverneur K. (1830–82), Maj. Gen. USA
Big Bethel; Army of the Potomac (brigade)—Peninsula, 2nd Bull Run, Antietam, Fredericksburg; (chief engineer) —Gettysburg; (corps)—the Wilderness, Spotsylvania, Cold Harbor, Petersburg; relieved by Sheridan at Five Forks, Apr '65; exonerated of charges of incompetence, Nov '81

Watts, Thomas H. (1819–92)
Confederate Attorney General, Mar '62–Dec '63; Governor of Alabama, 1863–65

Welles, Gideon (1802–78)
U.S. Secretary of the Navy, Mar '61–Mar '69

Wheeler, Joseph (1836–1906), Lt. Gen. CSA
Shiloh; Army of Mississippi (cavalry brigade)—Perryville; Army of Tennessee (cavalry brigade)—Murfreesboro; (cavalry corps)—Chickamauga, Knoxville, Atlanta, March to the Sea, Carolinas

Wilkes, Charles (1798–1877), Commodore USN
Captain of U.S.S. *San Jacinto;* removed Confederate commissioners James M. Mason and John Slidell from British mail steamer *Trent,* Nov 8 '61

Wilson, James H. (1837–1925), Maj. Gen. USA
Port Royal; Fort Pulaski; Antietam; Army of the Tennessee (engineer and Inspector General)—Vicksburg, Chattanooga, Knoxville; Cavalry Bureau chief, Feb–Apr '64;

Army of the Potomac (cavalry division)—Spotsylvania to Petersburg; Military Division of the Mississippi (cavalry corps)—Franklin-Nashville, capture of Selma, Ala.

WIRZ, HENRY (1822–65), Maj. CSA
Swiss immigrant; commandant of Andersonville Prison, Jan '64–Apr '65; tried and convicted of responsibility for prison conditions; executed, Nov 10 '65

WOOD, THOMAS J. (1823–1906), Maj. Gen. USA
Army of the Ohio (division)—Shiloh, Perryville; Army of the Cumberland (division)—Murfreesboro, Chickamauga, Chattanooga, Atlanta; (corps)—Franklin-Nashville

WRIGHT, HORATIO G. (1820–99), Maj. Gen. USA
1st Bull Run; Port Royal; Department of the Ohio commander, Aug '62–Mar '63; Army of the Potomac (division)—Gettysburg, the Wilderness; (corps)—Spotsylvania, Cold Harbor, Petersburg, Shenandoah Valley (1864), Appomattox

Y YANCEY, WILLIAM L. (1814–63)
Leading secessionist orator; Confederate commissioner to Great Britain and France, 1861–62; Confederate senator, 1862–63

YATES, RICHARD (1815–73)   Governor of Illinois, 1861–64

INDEX

Fort Munroe, 40, 62, 206, 279
Fort Pemberton, 129
Fort Pulaski, 75
Fort St. Philip, 75
Fort Stedman, 273
Fort Sumter, *18*, 20, *21*, 22, 26, 32, 70, 202, 271
Fort Walker, 74, *76*
Fort Warren, 103
Fortifications, 158, 161, 189, 273
Fox, Gustavus, 305
France, 36–37; and the Confederacy, 36–37, 102, 111, 269–70; relations with United States, 102, 111–12
Frankfort, Ky., 98
Franklin, Maj. Gen. William B., 305
Franklin, Tenn., 260–61, 269; map, *255*
Frayser's Farm, Va., 67
Frederick, Md., 91–92, 143, 244
Fredericksburg, Va., 63, 88, 132–33, 135, 209; Battle of, *115*, 116–19, *122*, 127, 141; pontoon bridges, *162*
Free-soilers, 12
Frémont, Maj. Gen. John Charles, 26, 54, 56, 64–65, 226, 228, 305
Frémont's Dragoons, *166*
Fugitive Slave Act, 7–8, 16

Gaines' Mill, Va., 67
Gardner, Alexander, *145*
Garrison, William Lloyd, 5
General Bragg (Confederate gunboat), *72*
Georgia, 199; campaigns in, 191, 214–15, 257, 268; secession of, 15; Sumter Light Guards, *24*
Georgia Railroad, 238, *242*
Gettysburg: Battle of, 143–47, *145*, *148*, 149, 178, 191, 228, 238; battlefield dedication, *146–47*, 169–70, 290; captured war material, 156; casualties, 169; cemeteries, *296*; Devil's Den, 145; map, *143*; Pickett's charge, 144, 260, 274
Gettysburg Address, *146–47*, 169–70, 290
Gibbon, Maj. Gen. John, 205
Giroux, C., painting by, *2*

Gladstone, William E., 106–7
Goldsborough, Louis M., 74
Gordon, Gen. John B., 273, 305
Gorgas, Brig. Gen. Josiah, 305
Grand Gulf, Miss., 137, 138
Granger, Maj. Gen. Gordon, 305
Grant, Gen. Ulysses S., 92–93, 98–99, 116, 123, 193, 201–17, 242, 244–45, 256, 262–63, 265, *283*, 286, 292, 305, *306*; Appomattox campaign, 112, 205, 276–78, 284; Army of the Potomac under, 206; Chattanooga campaign, 196–99; at Fort Henry, 57; general in chief, 199, 204, 206; Jackson, Miss., occupied by, 139; Kentucky campaign, 54, 57–58; Lee's surrender to, 277–78, 284; military ability, 202–4, 209, 233, 251, 253, 256–57, 273; at Petersburg, 201, 206, *207*, 211–12, *213*, 215–16, 243, 249, *272*, 273, 275; pictures of, *200*, *212*; Shiloh, Battle of, 58–60; Sherman-Johnston treaty, 283–84, 292; at Spotsylvania, 209–11; Vicksburg campaigns, 99, 122–29, 131, 136–41, *139*, *140*, 146, 191–92, 207–9
Great Britain, 36–37, 82; Confederacy and, 94, 102, 105–8, 110, 111, 113, 269; commerce raiders, 82, *83*, 113; relations with Federal government, 82, 102–13, 175; ships outfitted for the South, 82, 107–8, 111; Trent affair, 103–5; troops sent to Canada, 103, 105
Great Lakes, 234
Greeley, Horace, 39, 306
"Greenbacks," 177
Greenhow, Rose, *234*
Grenada, Miss., 122
Grierson, Col. Benjamin H., 138, 306
Griffin, Maj. Gen. Charles, 306
Guerrilla warfare, 246–47, 277–78, 293
Gunboats, 54, *56*, 57, 60, *70*, *72*, 73, 76, 81, 125, 129, 136, *137*, 202, 211

Hagerstown, Md., 92, 94, 244
Halleck, Maj. Gen. Henry Wager,

56–58, 60, 85–88, 92–93, 123, 124, 147, 197, 306; chief of staff, 204; general in chief of Union armies, 86–87, 204; Western Theater commander, 56, 57, 85–88

Hamlin, Hannibal, 306
Hampton, Lt. Gen. Wade, *306*
Hampton Roads, Va., 62, 78, 270
Hancock, Maj. Gen. Winfield Scott, 306
Hardee, Gen. William S., 239, 264, 306
Harney, Brig. Gen. William A., 26, 31–32
Harpers Ferry, 13–14, 40, 94, *95*, 96, 288
Harris, Isham G., 306–7
Harrison's Landing, 67
Hatteras Inlet, N.C., 73, 74
Haupt, Brig. Gen. Herman, *176*, 307
Havana, Cuba, 103
Hayes, Rutherford B., 97
Hazen, William, *197*
Healy, G. P. A., paintings by, *283*
Heintzelman, Maj. Gen. Samuel P., 307
Henry House Hill, 44–45
Herold, David, *287*
Heth, Maj. Gen. Harry, 307
Hicks, Thomas H., 307
Hill, Lt. Gen. Ambrose Powell, 141–42, *307*
Hill, Lt. Gen. D. H., 94, 307
Hoke, Maj. Gen. Robert F., 307
Holly Springs, Miss., 122, 124
Homestead Act (1862), 12, 13, 173
Hood, Gen. John Bell, 253–63, 307; Army of Tennessee under, 255–56, 261; Atlanta campaign, 238–42, 254; at Chickamauga, *194;* Franklin-Nashville campaign, 255–63; relieved of command, 263
Hooker, Maj. Gen. Joseph, 127, 131–32, 141–42, 209, *307;* at Chancellorsville, 132–34, *135*, 239; at Chattanooga, 196–98; in pursuit of Lee, 141–43; relieved of command, 143–44
Hospitals, 127; field, *67, 122;* medical treatment, *164*

Howard, Maj. Gen. Oliver O., 307
Humphreys, Maj. Gen. Andrew, *114*, 308
Hunchbeick (U.S. gunboat), *70*
Hunley (Confederate submarine), *76*
Hunt, Maj. Gen. Henry Jackson, 308
Hunter, Maj. Gen. David, 308
Hunter, R. M. T., 270, 308

Illinois, 187, 228; Lincoln-Douglas debates, 12; support for Lincoln, 288–89; volunteer soldiers, 123–24
Immigration, 5, *174*
Indian warfare, 91
Indiana, 187
Industrial development, 171–72; factory system, 5, 171, 176, 186; in the North, 5, 28, 81, 171–72, 175–77; in the South, 81, 179–82, *180*
Infantry, 156–57, 159, 161
Inflation, 170, 177, 182
Intelligence service, 43, 53, *234*, *235*
International law, 103, 104
Intrepid (observation balloon), *66*
Iowa, 8
Iron and coal, 28, 175, 181, 189
Island No. Ten, 60, *61*, 86–87
Iuka, Miss., 98

Jackson, Claiborne, 308
Jackson, Lt. Gen. Thomas J. ("Stonewall"), 33, 46, 48, 51, 64–66, 86–87, *88*, 89, 94, 118, *130*, 146, 260, *308;* at Bull Run, 181; at Cedar Mountain, *88–90;* Chancellorsville, 133–34, 135, 239; at Harpers Ferry, 94, *95*, 96; Shenandoah Valley campaign, 51, 243
Jackson, Miss., 117, 137–39
James River, 67, 70, 80, 86, 132, 206, *211*, 212
Johnson, Andrew, 228, 286–87, 292, 308
Johnston, Gen. Albert Sidney, 27, 54–59, 308
Johnston, Gen. Joseph E., 27, 41, 43–44, 46, 48, 51, 64, 66, 138–41, 192, 204, 214–15,

Johnston, Gen. Jos. E. (*cont.*)
230, 275–76, *308;* Army of
Tennessee commanded by, 203,
267; Atlanta campaign, 237–
42; Carolinas campaign, 267–
68, 272, 275–76; removal of,
238; surrender of, 278, 284–
85; treaty with Sherman, 284–
85, 290–92
Joint Committee on the Conduct
of the War, 53, 227, 302
Jones, John Paul, 70
Julio, E. B. F., painting by, *131*

Kansas, admission to the Union,
8–10, 12, 13
Kansas-Nebraska Act, 8–9, 12
Kearny, Philip, 309
Kennesaw Mountain, 214, *215,*
255
Kentucky, 116, 240, 256, 261;
border state, 27, 30; campaigns in, 54–55, 86, 93–94,
98, 203; neutrality proclaimed,
30, 54
Kershaw, Maj. Gen. Joseph B.,
309
Kilpatrick, Maj. Gen. Hugh Judson, 309
Kirkwood, Samuel J., 309
Knoxville, Tenn., *23,* 93, 192,
194, 198, 199

Labor, 177–78; manpower shortage, 174
La Fayette, Ga., 194
Lake Providence, 128
Lamb, A. A., painting by, *110*
Lane, James H., 309
Lawrence, Kansas, 10, *247*
Lee, Maj. Gen. Fitzhugh, 309
Lee, Gen. Robert E., 14, 86–88,
127, *130,* 132, 191, 194, 204,
230, 238, 244, 256, 259, *309;*
Antietam, Battle of, 96–97;
at Appomattox, *266,* 276–77;
Army of Northern Virginia
commanded by, 66, 90, 203,
206; at Chancellorsville, 132–
34; at Fredericksburg, 116,
117–19; at Gettysburg, 143–
47; general in chief, 268; invasion of Pennsylvania, 134–
37, 141–47; invasion of the
North, 91, 94–97, 106, 131–

47; military ability, 26–27,
88–90, 94, 134, 136–37, 141,
162, 272–73; Petersburg
seige, 211–13, 249–51, 264,
272–73, 275–76; return to
Virginia, 144; Richmond, defense of, 206–17; at Spotsylvania, 209–11; surrender of,
266, 277, *278,* 279, 284, 286; at
The Wilderness, 207, *208,* 209
Lee, Gen. Stephen D., 241, 309
Leslie's magazine, 40, 128
Letcher, John, 309
Lincoln, Abraham, *17,* 20–21,
76, 78, *98,* 117, 132, 192, 264,
283, 291, 310; administration,
221; assassination, 284–86,
286, 291; attempt to hold border states, 27, 30; blockade of
Southern ports, 71–72; cabinet, 221–22, 226, 270; call
for volunteers, *29,* 91; *cartoons,*
104, 110, 250; commander in
chief, 49, 62–64, 85–86, 91,
98, 123, 201, 214, 226–27, 233,
248–49, 263, 282; Congress
and, 226; criticism of, 222,
248–49; debates with Douglas, 12; Emancipation Proclamation, 108–9, *110,* 111, 186–
88; fear for safety of Washington, 62–63, 67; foreign policy, 105; Fort Sumter, 20–21;
funeral procession, *288, 289,*
292; Gettysburg Address, *146–*
47, 169–70, 290; inauguration,
1, 20–22; McClellan ap-
pointed general in chief, 49,
53; peace proposals, 270–71,
283, 287–88, 291; pictures,
17, 98, 283, 291; political ex-
periences, 27, 117, 221–22,
226, 227; as President, 219–
20; Presidential elections, 1860,
12, 14–16; 1864, 217, 227–
30, 235, 248, *249,* 251, 287; reconstruction plans, 281–85,
291–92; removal of McClellan, 116; second inaugural address, 281–84, 290; state governors and, 226
Logan, Gen. John A., *240,* 310
London *Times,* 107
Longstreet, Maj. Gen. James,
89–90, 94, 118, 132, 135, 141,

142, 144, 146, 162, 194, 198, 206, *310;* at Chattanooga, 198
Lookout Mountain, *185,* 193, 196, 197, *198–99*
Louisiana, 126, 128, 136, 137, 192, 202, 220; secession of, 15
Louisiana (Confederate ironclad), 81
Louisiana Purchase, 6
Lyon, Brig. Gen. Nathaniel S., 32–33, 310
Lyons, Lord Richard, 105, 310

McClellan, Maj. Gen. George B., 26, 33, 39–40, 56, 92, *98,* 205–6, 235, *310;* Antietam, Battle of, 96–97; Army of the Potomac commanded by, 40, 91, 98; criticism of, 60, 62, 67; general in chief, 53–54, 62, 116; military ability, 52, 53, 56; at Philippi, 39, *40;* Presidential candidate, *229,* 230, 251; pursuit of Lee, 94, 96; removed from command, 62, *98,* 116; Richmond, campaign against, *50,* 52–67, 80, 85, 86–87, 132; Second Battle of Bull Run, 88–90; Virginia, campaign in, 60–*67;* withdrawal to Washington, 87–88, 109
McClernand, Maj. Gen. John A., 123–24, 125–26, 127, 310
McCook, Maj. Gen. Alexander M., 310
McCook, Daniel, 310
McCook, Daniel, Jr., 311
McCook, Maj. Gen. Edward M., 311
McCook, John, 311
McCulloch, Hugh, 311
McDowell, Maj. Gen. Irwin, 26, 39–40, 41–44, 47–48, 53, 63, 65, 311
McLaws, Lafayette, 311
Macon and Western Railroad, 239
McPherson, Maj. Gen. James B., 28, 204, 214, *311;* Atlanta campaign, 238–39
Magoffin, Beriah, 311
Magruder, Maj. Gen. John Bankhead, 64, 311

Mahone, Maj. Gen. William, 311
Maine, 105
Mallory, Stephen R., 220–21, 311
Malvern Hill, 67
Manassas, 51, 64, 91; artillery, *42–43*
Manassas (Confederate ship), *68*
Manassas Junction, 40, 41–44, 89
Mansfield, Maj. Gen. Joseph K. F., 311
Mansfield, La., 202
Manufacturing, 5, 171, 176, 186; in the North, 175–77; in the South, 181–82
Maps: Allatoona and Franklin, *255;* Atlanta-Peachtree Creek, *239;* blockade effectiveness, *74;* Federal offensives, *205;* Franklin-Nashville campaign, *255;* Gettysburg campaign, *143;* Mississippi Valley campaigns, *55*
March to the Sea, 256–59, *259,* 263–65, 268, 271–72
Marye's Heights, Fredericksburg, 119
Maryland, 91–92, 94, 214; border state, 27, 30, 33; campaigns in, 91–92
Mason, James M., 103, 105–6, 312
Mason and Dixon Line, 277
Massachusetts, abolitionists in, 10
Maximilian, Emperor of Mexico, 112
Meade, Maj. Gen. George Gordon, 144–45, 191, 196, 204–5, 207, 312; Army of the Potomac commanded by, 155–56; at Gettysburg, 144–45
Mechanicsville, Va., 67
Medical care, *67,* 127, 163, *164,* 165, *183;* field hospitals, *67,* *122, 164;* prison camps, 233
Meigs, Maj. Gen. Montgomery, *312*
Memminger, Christopher G., 312
Memphis, Tenn., 58, 60, *61,* 76, 81, 86, 92, 116, 124, 126, 181, 196, 197, 240
Memphis and Charleston Railroad, 197
Merrimac (Confederate iron-

Merrimac (cont.)
clad), 77–80, *79*, 81; vs.
Monitor, 78, *79*, 80
Merritt, Wesley, 187
Mexico, 112, 202; French in, 112,
202, 270; war with, 6, 26, 35
Militia, state, 23–24, *29*, 30, 223–
24
Mill Springs, Ky., 57
Milliken's Bend, 125, 129
Milroy, Maj. Gen. Robert H.,
312
Mine fields, 243
Mines and minerals, 177
Minnesota, Indian warfare in, 91
Minnesota (Union warship), 78
Missionary Ridge, 196, 198
Mississippi, 55, 138, 194, 240–41,
254; campaigns in, 98–99, 117,
189, 191–92, 202; 9th Missis-
sippi Infantry, *125;* secession
of, 15
Mississippi (U.S. frigate), *68*
Mississippi Central Railroad, 138
Mississippi River, 30, 54, 56, 60,
93, 125, 147, 203; attempts to
divert, 126, 127, *128*, 129; cam-
paigns, 54–60, *55*, 85, 86, 99,
115, 117, 123–24; crossing by
Grant's army, 137–38; map, *55;*
naval warfare, *68*, 71; Vicks-
burg campaign, 122–24, 136–
41
Missouri, 192; admission to the
Union, 6, 9; "Border Ruffians,"
9; border state, 27, 30, 31–33;
campaigns in, 85, 86; guerrilla
warfare, 247; partisan warfare,
30–33
Missouri Compromise, 6, 8, 16
Missouri River, 8
Mobile, Ala., 192, 264, 265, 279
Mobile and Ohio Railroad, 54,
58, 138
Mobile Bay, 81; Battle of, 242–
43, 248
Monitor (Union ironclad), 78–
79, 80; vs. *Merrimac*, 78, *79*, 80
Monocacy River, 214
Monroe Doctrine, 112
Montgomery, Ala., 15, 279
Morgan, Brig. Gen. John Hunt,
160, 312
Morrill Land Grant Act, 173
Morris Island, *21*

Morton, Oliver P., 312
Mosby, Col. John S., 246, *312*
"Mud March," *119*
Murfreesboro, Tenn., 116, 119,
120; Battle of, *120, 121*, 127,
203, 261
Muscle Shoals,Tenn., 260

Napoleon III, 111–12, 202
Nashville, Tenn., 55, 58, 98, 116,
181, 240, 254, 256, 257, 261;
Battle of, 259–60, 263; campaigns, *262;* capitol of Tenn.,
252; Union occupation, 253,
261, *262*
Nashville (blockade-runner), *83*
Nassau, Bahamas, 82–83, 103
National Bank Act (1863), 177
National Road, 92
Naval power, 29, 69–83, 201–2,
263–64, 265, 271; blockade
duty, 71–73; blockade-runners, 82–83; commerce raiders, 81–82; Confederate navy,
72–73; frigates and sloops,
71; gunboats, 54, *56*, 57, 60,
70, 72–73, 76, 81, 125, 129,
136, *137*, 202, 211; ironclad
ships, 77–81; *Merrimac vs.
Monitor*, 78, *79*, 80; Mississippi River, *68*, 71, 137; Mobile Bay, 242–43; mortar vessels, 75; Port Royal, *76;* revolution in, 69–70, 80; side-
wheelers, 71; South vs. North,
70–71; submarines, *76;* torpedoes, 80, 81; *Trent* affair, 103–
5; Union navy, 70–71, 137,
263–64, 271
Nebraska territory, 8
Negroes, 282; citizenship, 190;
escaping, 90; guard detachments, 189; at Nashville, *262;*
problems of emancipated, 189–
90; regiments, 189, 190–91,
202
Nelson, Lord, 70
Nevada, 177
New Bern, N.C., 75
New England, 186; abolitionists, 5, 10; Kansas settlement,
9–10
New Madrid, Mo., 60, 87
New Market, Va., 211
New Mexico, 7, 8

New Orleans, 117, 128, 181, 196, *231;* capture of, 75–76, 81, 85, 86, 129, 218, 219

New York City, 234, 288; draft riots, *228–229;* Presidential election (1864), 251; visit of Russian fleet, 112; waterfront, *173*

New York Highlanders, 42

New York State, 117; Excelsior Brigade, *154*

New York *Tribune,* 39

Newton, Maj. Gen. John, 312

Norfolk, Va., 77, 80

North, the, 217; advantages, 28, 233; armies. *See* Union armies; conservatives, 185; destruction wrought by, 186, *187,* 188–89, 244–45, *246,* 257–59, 268, 271, 296; economy, 169–78; effect of war on, 213; exports to Great Britain, 175; fifth column in, 288; financing the war, 177; industrial development, 5, 28, 81, 171–72, 175–77; Lee's invasion of, 91–92, 94–97, 131–47; political and economic program, 15; population, 28, 175; prisoners of war, 230, *231, 232,* 233; railway networks, 175–76; sea power, 29; resources for war, 170; society, 3–5; unrest and discontent with war, 127, 216–17, 228–30, 234, 237; war aims, 27; *See also* United States

North Anna River, 211, *212*

North Carolina, 73–75, 271–72; naval bombardment, 73–74, 81; secession of, 22–23

North-South differences, 19; advantages of the North, 28, 233; in Congress, 5–6; secession, 19–20; slavery, 6–7; society, 3–5; tariff rates, 6, 13

Northern armies. *See* Union armies

Northwest, 117, 123

Ogeechee River, 263

Ohio, 228; regiments, 97

Ohio River, 33, 39, 54, 55, 93, 98

Olustee, Fla., 202

Orange and Alexandria Railroad, 41, 87, 116, 181, 191

Ord, Maj. Gen. Edward O. C., 312

Order of American Knights, 234

Osliaba (Russian ship), *113*

Osterhaus, Maj. Gen. Peter J., 312

O'Sullivan, Timothy, 207

Paducah, Ky., 54

Paine, Lewis, *287,* 313

Palmerston, Lord, 106, *107,* 108, 111

Pamlico Sound, 74

Pamunkey River, 65

Panic of 1857, 12–13, 171–72

Parkersburg, W. Va., 39

"Pathfinder, The," 26

Patterson, Maj. Gen. Robert, 40–41, 43–44

Pea Ridge, Arkansas, 60, *61*

Peace organizations, 234

Peace proposals, 186, 270–71, 277–78, 283, 284–85

Peachtree Creek, Ga., 239; map, *239*

Pegram, Brig. Gen. John, 313

Pelham, Maj. John, 313

Pemberton, Lt. Gen. John C., 117, 124–26, 136–37, 138–40, 146–47, *313*

Pender, Maj. Gen. William D., 313

Pendleton, George H., 230

Pendleton, Brig. Gen. William N., 313

Peninsula campaigns, 40, *62–64,* 80, 87, 109, *211*

Pennsylvania, *151, 161,* 177, 216; campaigns in, 94, 134–37, 141–47

Pennsylvania Academy of Fine Arts, *29*

Perryville, Ky., Battle of, 98, *99*

Petersburg, Va., 211–13, 215–16; entrenchments, *213, 216, 217;* siege of, *178,* 211–13, 216, 249, 264, 272–73, *272, 274,* 275

Philadelphia, 243

Philippi, W. Va., 39, *40*

Slaves and slavery (*cont.*)
ery, 269, 282; extremists, 9–
11; fugitive slaves, 7–8, 187,
257; insurrection of slaves, 14;
Kansas-Nebraska Act, 8–9;
Lincoln-Douglas debates, 12;
Missouri Compromise, 6, 8,
16; refugee camps, 189; Supreme Court decisions, 11–
12; in the South, 28, 170–
71, 188, 282–83; underground
railroad, 8; as war issue,
102–3, 106, 111
Slidell, John, 103, 111, 316
Slocum, Maj. Gen. Henry W.,
316
Smith, Maj. Gen. Andrew J.,
241, 317
Smith, Caleb Blood, 317
Smith, Maj. Gen. Charles F.,
317
Smith, Maj. Gen. Edmund Kirby, 93, 98, 203, 317
Smith, Maj. Gen. Gustavus W.,
317
Smith, Maj. Gen. William, 317
Smith, Gen. William F., 212–
13, 317
Smith, Brig. Gen. William Sooy,
202, 317
Smuggling, *183.* See also Blockade-running
Soldiers, 149–55, 268; camp
life, *49, 65, 153, 165, 166,
167;* conscription, 222–24; deserters, 257–58; discipline,
149, 151–52; foraging parties, *165,* 257; medical treatment, *67,* 163–65; recruiting,
22, 91, 150–51, *223, 227;*
training, 149–55; uniforms,
175, 178; voting in election of
1864, *249,* 251; See also Armies
Songs and music, 167, 248, 255
Sons of Liberty, 234
South, the, 217; aftermath of
war, 295–97; conservatives,
185; defense of slavery, 188;
destruction by Union forces,
186, *187,* 188–89, 244–45,
246, 257–59, 268, 271, 296;
disadvantages, 233; economy,
13, 178–83; food and tex-
tiles, 171; imports, 5; indus-

trial facilities, 38, 81, 171;
number of slaves, 28; popu-
lation, 28; slavery, 28, 170–
71, 282–83; society, 3, 5,
185–86; states' rights, 6;
See also Confederate States of
America
South Carolina, 264; naval bom-
bardment, 74; secession of,
15; Sherman's march across,
268, 271
South Mountain, 92, 94, 96,
97
Spangler, Edward, *287*
Speed, James, 317
Spies, 43, 53, *234, 235*
"Spirit of '61," 29
Spotsylvania Court House, Va.,
209–11
Sprague, William, 317
Spring Hill, Tenn., 260
Springfield, Ill., 14, 289, 292
Stanton, Edwin McMasters, Sec-
retary of War, 60, 62–65, 78,
85–86, 91, 123, 221–22, 226,
286, 287–89, 290–91, 317
State governments: postwar treat-
ment, 284; readmission to the
Union, 284–85; relations with
Davis, 223, 226; relations with
Lincoln, 226
State militia regiments, 23–24,
29, 30, 223–24
States' rights, 6, 52, 101, 220,
222
Staunton, Va., 39, 65, 207
Steele, Maj. Gen. Frederick,
318
Stephens, Alexander H., 16,
221, 270, 318
Stevens, Thaddeus, 271, 318
Stevenson, Ala., *193*
Stewart, Alexander P., 239, 318
Stone Bridge, 44
Stoneman, Maj. Gen. George,
318
Stones River, 116, 127; battle
at, 178
Stowe, Harriet Beecher, 8
Streeter, William, painting by,
32
Stringham, Flag Officer Silas,
73–74
Strother, David Hunter, draw-
ing by, *25*

Union armies (*cont.*)
regiments, 35, 52, 150, 223–24; war aims, 101–2, 201–4, 206
II Corps, 134
V Corps, 274
IX Corps, 206
XI Corps, *134*
107th Colored Infantry, *191*
6th Massachusetts Regiment, 30, *31*
Army of the Cumberland, *22*, 115, 116, 127, *161, 178*, 188, 192–95, 204, 214; at Chattanooga, 196; at Chickamauga, 194–95; commanded by Gen. Rosecrans, 192–95; commanded by Gen. Thomas, 198–99
Army of the James, 206
Army of the Ohio, 204
Army of the Potomac, 26, 52, 54, 65, 87, 98, 115, 131, 135, 143, 204–5, 207–9, 211, 213–14, 274–75; cavalry corps, 160, 204–5; at Chancellorsville, 141; commanded by Gen. Burnside, 116, 119; commanded by Gen. Grant, 206; commanded by Gen. Hooker, 127, 198–99; commanded by Gen. McClellan, 49, 62, 91, 98; commanded by Gen. Meade, 155–56; Fredericksburg, Battle of, 117–19; at Gettysburg, 143–47; officer corps, 205–6; Petersburg siege, 249–50; reconstitution of, 91; riots suppressed by, 229
Army of the Tennessee, 115, 198–99, 204; commanded by Gen. McPherson, 204; commanded by Gen. Sherman, 196, 198–99
Union Navy, 70–71, 137, 263–64, 271; offensive operations, *68*, 73–79; size of, 70–71
Union Party, 228
United States: Congress, 167, 271, 282–85; foreign relations, 101–13; France and, 102, 111–12; Great Britain and, 82, 102–13, 175; North-South antagonisms, 11–13, 15; peace pro-

posals, 270–71; Sanitary Commission, 178; secession and, 19–20; war aims, 101–2, 109–10, 201–2, 206; War Department, 206
Upton Emory, *319*
Usher, John P., 319
Utah, 7

Vallandigham, Clement L., 230, 319
Vance, Zebulon B., 319
Van Dorn, Maj. Gen. Earl, 60, 93, 98–99, 116, 122, 124, 320
Van Dorn (Confederate gunboat), *61*
"Veteran volunteers," 226
Vicksburg, 81, 99, 126; campaigns and siege of, 117, 122–29, *128*, 136–41, *139, 140, 146*, 147, 189, 191–92, 202–3; McClernand's proposals, 123–24
Violence resulting from war, 293
Virginia, 58, 115, 132, 135, 141, 144; campaigns in, 53–54, 60–67, 86–87, 90, 94, 97, 191, 192, 207, 250; Lee's return to, 144, *145;* Peninsula campaigns. *See* Peninsula campaigns; secession of, 22–23; slaves and slavery, 188–89; western counties, 33, 39, 64, 66
Virginia (Confederate ironclad), 77
Virginia Armory, Richmond, *180*
Virginia Military Institute, 33, 211
Volck, Adalbert, drawings by, *110, 183, 224, 225, 232*
Volunteer regiments, 23, 35, 52, 150, 223–24, 226

Wade, Benjamin F., 91, 271, 320
Wages and prices, 177
Wagon trains, *274*
Walker, Leroy P., 320
Wallace, Lew, *320*
Wallace, Brig. Gen. William H. L., 320
War aims, 27–28, 101–2, 109–10, 201–2, 206
War loans, 177
War of 1812, 104
War relief organizations, 178

Warren, Maj. Gen. G. K., 274–75, 320
Warrenton, Va., 116
Washington, D.C., 52–53, 167, 204, 207; Capitol, *1;* Confederate threats to, 51, 62–67, 90–92, 214, 230, 243–45; defense of, 142; Federal troops in, 30, 31, *38,* 39; McClellan withdrawn to, 87–88; military strategy, 192; parade of Union armies, *280;* spies in, 43
Watts, Thomas H., 320
Waud, Alfred R., drawings by, *119, 134, 154, 163, 194*
Waud, William, drawings by, *21, 45*
Webster, Daniel, 109
Weir, John Ferguson, paintings by, *168*
Weld, Theodore, 5
Welles, Gideon, 103, 320
West, the: campaigns in, 54–60, 86, 92–93, 97–99, 105, 115, 136–41, 204; stalemate in, 115–29
West Point foundry, *168*
West Pointers, 26–27, 35, 54, 117; in Confederate Army, 26–27
West Virginia, 33
Western and Atlantic Railroad, 193, 204

Westward expansion, 8, 15
Wheeler, Lt. Gen. Joseph, 160, 256, 320
Whig Party, 12
Whitney, Eli, 3
Wilderness, The, *155,* 207, *208,* 209
Wilkes, Capt. Charles, 103–4, 320
Williamsburg, Va., 64
Wilmington, N.C., 83, 265
Wilmot, David, 6
Wilmot Proviso, 7
Wilson, Hunt, *61*
Wilson, James H., 320–21
Wilson's Creek, Battle of, 33
Winchester, Va., 245; Battle of, *245*
Wirz, Henry, 321
Wood, Thomas J., 321
Wright, Horatio G., 321

Yalobusha River, 129
Yancey, William Lowndes, 11, 321
Yates, Richard, 321
Yazoo River, 126, 128–29, 139
Yellow Tavern, Va., 210
York, Pa., 143
Yorktown, Va., *51, 63,* 64
Young's Point, 125

PICTURE CREDITS

200, 207, 208, 210, 211, 212, 213 Library of Congress. 215 New-York Historical Society; Library of Congress. 216, 217 Both: Library of Congress. 218 Maryland Historical Society. 223 Library of Congress. 224 Levi Berman Collection. 225 Prints Division, N. Y. Public Library. 227 National Archives. 228 Museum of the City of New York. 229 Prints Division, N. Y. Public Library. 231 New-York Historical Society; Library of Congress; Iowa State Department of History and Archives. 232 Both: Maryland Historical Society. 234 Library of Congress; Collection of Mrs. Lorraine Dexter. 235, 236 Library of Congress. 240, 242 Courtesy of the City of Atlanta. 244 Library of Congress. 245, 246 Western Reserve Historical Society. 247 Kansas State Historical Society, Topeka. 248, 249, 252 Library of Congress. 258 Illinois State Historical Library, Springfield. 259 Courtesy Kenneth M. Newman, Old Print Shop, New York. 261, 262 Library of Congress. 264 New-York Historical Society. 265 Houghton Library, Harvard University. 266 Library of Congress. 269 Kean Archives. 272 National Archives. 274, 275, 276, 278, 280 Library of Congress. 283 White House Historical Association. 286 Armed Forces Institute of Pathology. 287 Meserve Collection; Meserve Collection; Meserve Collection; Library of Congress; Library of Congress. 289 Courtesy Illinois Central Railroad. 291 Library of Congress; Meserve Collection. 295 Library of Congress. 296 Kosti Ruohomaa, Black Star. 299 Library of Congress. 300 Both: National Archives. 301 Cook Collection, Valentine Museum. 301 Library of Congress. 302 National Archives. 303 Library of Congress. 304 Library of Congress; National Archives. 305 Library of Congress. 306 Library of Congress; Cook Collection, Valentine Museum. 307 Both: Library of Congress. 308 Cook Collection, Valentine Museum. 309 Library of Congress. 310 Cook Collection, Valentine Museum; Library of Congress. 311 Library of Congress. 312 National Archives; Cook Collection, Valentine Museum. 313 Confederate Museum. 314, 315 Library of Congress. 316 National Archives; Collection of Lloyd Ostendorf. 317 Cook Collection, Valentine Museum. 318 Cook Collection, Valentine Museum; Library of Congress. 319, 320 Library of Congress. **Back endpaper** Library of Congress